Alastair Sawday's

Special
places to stay

French Hotels, Inns and Other Places

Edited by Susan Luraschi

Typesetting, Conversion & Repro:	Avonset, Bath
Design:	Caroline King & Springboard Design, Bristol
Mapping:	Springboard Design, Bristol
Maps:	Bartholomew Mapping Services, a division of HarperCollins Publishers, Glasgow
Printing:	Butler & Tanner, Frome
UK Distribution:	Portfolio, Greenford, Middlesex
US Distribution:	The Globe Pequot Press, Guilford, Connecticut

Published in November 2001

Alastair Sawday Publishing Co. Ltd
The Home Farm Stables, Barrow Gurney, Bristol BS48 3RW
Tel: +44 (0)1275 464891 Fax: +44 (0)1275 464887
E-mail: info@specialplacestostay.com Web: www.specialplacestostay.com

The Globe Pequot Press
P. O. Box 480, Guilford, Connecticut 06437, USA
Tel: +1 203 458 4500 Fax: +1 203 458 4601
E-mail: info@globe-pequot.com Web: www.globe-pequot.com

Second edition

ISBN 1-901970-21-3 in the UK

ISBN 0-7627-1248-1 in the US

Printed in England

The publishers have made every effort to ensure the accuracy of the information in this book at the time of going to press. However, they cannot accept any responsibility for any loss, injury or inconvenience resulting from the use of information contained therein.

ALASTAIR SAWDAY'S

Special
places to stay

Hôtel Relais Sainte Anne, no. 205

FRENCH HOTELS, INNS AND OTHER PLACES

I never travel without my diary. One should always have something
sensational to read on the train.

Oscar Wilde 1854-1900

The
Globe
Pequot
press

Guilford
Connecticut, USA

Alastair Sawday Publishing
Bristol, UK

Contents

Contents

Contents

Contents

Acknowledgements

Susan Luraschi has been something of a star to have produced the second edition of this wonderful book largely on her own. She is unique among our editors in having started life as an American and we all appreciate the slightly different light she throws on things though, having lived in Europe for many years and taken French nationality, she also sees them through European eyes. Her intelligence, passion and sense of humour have worked to turn her into an expert and the book is the product of that real expertise and professionalism. For it is eclectic, finely judged and full of good taste, the tastes that will appeal to all discerning travellers, including the 'Sawday' readers. So, I applaud Susan's hard work and very considerable skill.

In support has been Ann Cooke-Yarborough, as usual, with all good sense, charm and good humour. A small army of inspectors have checked all over France to Susan's command and we owe them much.

Back in Bristol, Susan's efforts have been ably backed by Annie Shillito, Julia Richardson, our brilliant accounts team under Sheila Clifton, and many others listed below.

Alastair Sawday

Series Editor:	Alastair Sawday
Editor:	Susan Luraschi
Managing Editor:	Annie Shillito
Production Manager:	Julia Richardson
Administration:	Rachel Brook, Mathias Fournier, Marie Hodges, Laura Kinch
Web editor:	Russell Wilkinson
Accounts:	Jenny Purdy
Inspections:	Douglas Arestegui, Richard & Linda Armspach, John Edwards, Robin Fleet, Georgina Gabriel, Susan Gill, Michèle Goëmon, Ana Halama, Hugh Mitford-Raymond, Caroline Portway, Ann Cooke-Yarborough, Elizabeth Yates
Additional writing:	Lindsay Butler, Ann Cooke-Yarborough
Additional photos:	Betrand Limbour (11), Studio Véronique (77), Denis Paillard (78), Jacques-Bertrand Cauvin (88), Denis Darrault-Harris (145), Jean-Christophe Sannicolas (218), M. Captim (282), Jean-François Lepage (283).

Special thanks, too, to those people not mentioned here who visited - often at short notice - just one or two houses for us.

A word from Alastair Sawday

The hotels of France are as varied as her cheeses, which probably makes them as oblivious to regulations as the country itself. Somehow you know, when travelling in France, that wherever you go you will find interesting and regional differences, peculiarly personal ways of doing things. The bureaucrats of Brussels will have been politely fobbed off with reassuring noises. Individuality will have survived in small, defiant pockets of France.

Anyone who travelled in France during the '50s and '60s will still remember with vivid fondness the 'shambolic' but engaging hotels of the period. Well, the good news is that there is still a very French quality to its most 'special' hotels even if the 'shambols' have metamorphosed into a modern, and very encouraging, individuality.

Let me describe the sort of hotel that I like, so that you can work out if this book is for you. An early favourite was one run by an opera singer in a perfect village overlooking a river. Each year he would build a new bedroom out of local stone, with quarry-tiled floors and locally-made pine furniture. It was uncluttered, simple, and allowed us to focus on the views and on his wife's cooking. He'd never run a hotel before and it showed; he was fun, easy going, kind and interested in his guests.

We're not excited by inappropriate luxury, overpriced 'facilities', primly cool owners, executive suites and conference facilities. There's little point in paying through the nose for jacuzzis, pools, gyms, butlers and assorted paraphernalia when all you're interested in is sleeping, eating, talking and feeling good in a lovely building. That is why our 'special places' are almost invariably run by individuals and families; apart from anything else they are such good value.

Open the pages and you'll see what we enjoy, and admire.

Alastair Sawday

Introduction

Who is this book for?

This book is for people who would rather have claw-foot bathtubs than
minibars or fabulous views rather than a shoe-shine kit. Hotels are going
through a mini revolution in France: small independents are waking up to
a changing market and properties are polarising into mass-market hotels
that can cater to both business and holiday travellers or small niche hotels
that serve a very specific kind of customer: one that values character and
individuality. Some hotels aim to appeal to guests who would rather have
modem phone sockets than a friendly welcome; which leads to mundane
makeovers and stultifying standardisation. We ignore those. If you think
that hospitality is an art best practised by those with flair and passion for
bringing people and places together, then this book is for you.

How we choose our Special Places

We search for the best of everything and write a book without fixed
boundaries. If we discover a place run with inspired professionalism, good
humour and commitment, we want to include it. We visit every property;
atmosphere, welcome and value for money are key considerations. We like
people who do their own thing, though eccentricity is no excuse for poor
standards. Friendly staff are more important than de luxe toiletries, good
walks more important than jacuzzis.

We include a range of very different places. It was Charles de Gaulle who
once complained about governing a country that has 365 kinds of cheese.
Thomas Moore mentioned 685 ways to dress eggs. There's a similar choice
when it comes to finding somewhere to sleep in France. We have a convent
in Cannes and hanging gardens in Lyon, an alchemist's garden in Provence
and farms galore. France is blessed with great food and a richness of scenery
and rural life that is hard to beat. Our owners have originality, energy and
independence and give more than a passing nod to tradition and regional
differences. They know their territories and their *terroirs*, so let them show
you a thing or two.

What to Expect

Hotels

You may have noticed that we have ignored the 'star' system. That is
because it works in strange ways, using criteria very different from ours.
A hotel that we think the world of can be kept near the bottom of the
official 'star' list simply because it has no lift. Some owners, unwilling to
be swept into a bureaucratic system they despise, refuse to apply for a star
rating. The system is technical and incapable of accounting for character,

style or warmth of welcome - things that we rate very highly, along with authenticity. Value for money is another.

Auberges (or Inns)

The food always takes top priority here. Rooms, however, will be good value, clean and comfortable. Be sure to book as the typical *auberge* can feed more people that it can sleep. Remember, too, that dinner is not served before 7.30pm and outside the larger towns, last orders may be taken no later than 9pm.

Other Places

Our Other Places are diverse and individual and range from manor houses to châteaux, from farmhouses to entire villages. Some of them are private homes. Many of their owners were reticent at first about joining us because they are not set up to provide the same services as a fully-fledged hotel, and fear the arrival of guests with grand hotel expectations. We told them that our readers know the difference. So please read the descriptions carefully and pick out the places where you will be comfortable. Do not expect someone to take your bags to your room. Do not expect room service. But do plan to stay more than one night as these Other Places offer a real insight into things French. We also welcome an emerging new category of owners: corporate drop-outs, some having taken early retirement, who have lovingly restored farmhouses, coaching inns, and castles - not to mention some magnificent gardens - and who thoroughly enjoy their new lives and the contact with their guests.

How to use this book

The General Map of France is divided into the same regions as the Contents and marked with the page numbers of the Detailed Maps. The Detailed Maps are not designed to be used as road maps; they show roughly where the Special Places are and should be used with a large-scale road atlas or map such as Michelin or Collins.

The entry number, at the bottom of each page, is the number to use when looking for places on the map pages (NB Paris flags are not positioned geographically).

Directions

Apart from motorway exits, our directions take you to each place from one direction only. They have been checked by the owners but you may occasionally find that '3 kilometres' turns out to be '5 kilometres'. It's worth going the extra distance before turning around. We give cardinal

Introduction

indications - N S E W - where appropriate and name the French roads with the letters they carry on French maps and road signs:

A = Autoroute. Toll motorways with junctions that usually have the same name/number on both sides.

N = Route Nationale. The old trunk roads that are still fast, don't charge tolls, but often go through towns.

D = Route Départementale. Smaller country roads with relatively little traffic.

1 mile = 1.6 km (Tip for the mathematically challenged: take the kms, divide by 8 and multiply by 5. Hey presto, you've got miles.)

Ask for a brochure when booking ahead - they usually include maps. Even better, ask them to send you their map *(plan d'accès)*. Or, have it faxed to the place you're staying before your visit. If our directions are poor, please tell us; you may save others a row over map-reading!

Our directions are as succinct as possible. Here is an example of how to read them:

From A7 exit Valence Sud A49 for Grenoble; exit 33; right D538a for Beaumont 2.5km; right at sign for 800m; house on right.

Interpretation: Take A7 motorway from north or south; leave at junction named 'Valence Sud' and get onto motorway A49 going towards Grenoble; leave this road at junction No. 33 and turn right onto road No. D538a (the 'a' means there are liable to be other roads numbered 538 in the vicinity...) towards Beaumont for 2.5km until you meet a meaningful sign; turn as indicated by this sign; the house is 800 metres down this road on the right.

Bedrooms and bathrooms

In this book a 'double' means one double bed, a 'twin' means two single beds. When we indicate 'double/twin' this means that there is a selection of both. If you ask for a 'double' when booking there is scope for confusion as it may be taken to mean simply a room for two people. If this is important to you, make sure your specific request is very clear and that you receive confirmation. If you are used to a lot of space when you sleep, you may want to check on the size of the double beds. There are still quite a few around measuring 1.40m which is the smallest (honeymoon) standard size.

Most rooms have their own bathrooms and many have separate toilets. We indicate those with rooms sharing baths or showers, but this is becoming more of a rarity. A 'triple' or 'family' room may have any mix of beds (sometimes sofabeds) for three, four or more people. A 'suite' may be one large room with a sitting area or, like an 'apartment', it will have two or more interconnecting rooms and one or more bathrooms. A 'duplex' is on two floors; one of them will be a sitting room. Extra beds and cots for children, at an extra cost, can often be provided; ask when booking.

Prices

The Euro becomes legal tender on 1 January 2002; the French Franc is to be phased out by 17 February 2002. From this edition onwards, our prices will be listed exclusively in Euros. We have rounded them off to the nearest 50 cents so you may find that in practice some prices differ by a few cents from those printed. There will be a period of adaption so that you might have an e-mail confirming your price in Euros, but Francs may still be used by the receptionist on the telephone. There is a Euro/Franc/£/$ conversion table at the back of the book.

The price range is for two people sharing a room: the lower price indicates the least expensive room in low season; the highest price, the most expensive room in high season. Prices are presumed to be for 2002 but are not guaranteed so please always check. If there are no single rooms, there will often be a reduction for single occupancy of a double room. Do look into attractive half-board terms and special prices for children. Half-board *demi-pension* includes breakfast and dinner. Full-board *pension complète* includes all three meals. Prices given are generally per person (the abbreviation 'p.p.') and include the room. Ask about reduced rates when booking longer stays and off-season visits.

Practical Matters

Telephoning. All telephone numbers in France have ten digits, e.g. (0)5 15 25 35 45. You should know that:

- the initial zero (bracketed here) is for use when telephoning from inside France only, i.e. dial 05 15 25 35 45 from any private or public telephone;

- when dialling from outside France use the international access code then the country code for France - 33 - followed by the last 9 digits of the number you want, e.g. 00 33 5 15 25 35 45;

- numbers beginning (0)6 are mobile phone numbers;
- to telephone from France -

- to Great Britain: 00 44 then the number without the initial zero,

- to the USA, dial 00 1 then the number without the initial zero.

Introduction

Télécartes phone cards are widely available in France and there are plenty of telephone boxes, even in the countryside (they often take only cards).

Types of houses

For a definition of château, *bastide, mas* see French words & expressions at the back (where most of the French words we've used are explained).

Booking

It is essential to book well ahead for July and August and wise for other months. More and more places now have web sites and e-mail addresses. We have a helpful booking form at the back of this book and on our web site at www.specialplacestostay.com. However, please remember that technology may be put aside in the summer months and a small place may just not have the time nor the personnel to respond to e-mail requests.

Deposits

Most places require a deposit to confirm a booking. If you cancel you are likely to lose part, or all, of it. Check the exact terms when you book. A credit card number is the standard manner in which to place a deposit but not all places accept credit cards and some readers may prefer to:

- Have a number of Euro banknotes at home and send the appropriate amount with your confirmation by registered mail.

- Send an ordinary cheque, which the owner will destroy when you arrive.

If your arrival is likely to be later than 5pm, do make this clear as you may otherwise be considered a 'no show' and lose your room.

Payment

Visa and MasterCard are usually welcome. American Express and Diners Card are generally only accepted in the more expensive places Those places requiring payment by cash or cheque are indicated. Drawing cash is easy as virtually all ATMs in France take Visa and MasterCard.

Tipping

All restaurants include tax and a 15% percent service charge; the words *service compris* indicate this on this bill. If a meal or service has been particularly good, leaving another €2-€4 is customary as is leaving the small change from your bill if you paid in cash.

Pets

Even though a place may be listed as accepting animals, some will only take small animals, some only dogs, some will limit the number of animals

Introduction

staying at the same time. Some allow them in the rooms, some don't. Do check ahead. There is always a supplement to pay.

Taxe de séjour

This is a small tax that local councils (mostly those near the sea) are allowed to levy on all visitors to be used for the upkeep of the beaches. Some councils do, some don't. So you may find your bill increased by a Euro or two per person per day.

Electricity

You need an adaptor plug for the 220-volt 50-cycle AC current. Americans also need a voltage transformer (heavy and expensive) for appliances that are not bi-voltage.

Meals

The number and type of courses you will be offered for lunch and dinner varies, although price may be an indicator. The new expression *menu du marché* means that the chef has picked up whatever was fresh and interesting at the market that morning and that the price and number of items on the menus will be reduced to a minimum.

Many places offer a *table d'hôtes* dinner to overnight guests. Sometimes this means separate tables, but often you eat with other guests at a long table. These meals are sometimes hosted by Monsieur or Madame (or both). In some regions of France, such as Burgundy, the *table d'hôtes* may only be offered to overnight guests. In other regions, such as Alsace, a small number of *table d'hôtes* places offer dinners to anyone. Note that advance notice is required for these and they may not be available every night. So make sure your place is reserved on the first night, especially if you are staying deep in the countryside.

Many of our places serve an early children's menu to give the adults peace.

Closed

When given in months, this means the whole of both months named, so Closed: November-March means closed from 1 November to 31 March.

Quick reference indices - activities, courses & special facilities

At the back of the books we direct you to places where you can hunt for truffles, rent or borrow a bike, get a seaweed wrap, catch up on your cookery lessons, test your wine tasting abilities, or practise a craft. We also direct you to those places that have wheelchair or limited mobility access.

Introduction

Subscriptions

Owners pay to appear in this guide; their fee goes towards the high production costs of an all-colour book. We really do only include places and owners that we find special. It is not possible for anyone to bribe their way in!

Environment

We reduce our impact on the environment where possible by:

* planting trees to compensate for our carbon emissions (as calculated by Edinburgh University): we are officially a Carbon Neutral® publishing company. The emissions directly related with the paper production, printing and distribution of this book have been made Carbon Neutral® through the planting of indigenous woodlands with Future Forests.

* re-using paper, recycling stationery, tins, bottles, etc.

* encouraging staff use of bicycles (they're loaned free) and encouraging car sharing.

* celebrating the use of organic, home- and locally-produced food.

* publishing books that support, in however small a way, the rural economy and small-scale businesses.

www.specialplacestostay.com

Our web site has online entries for many of the places in this book and in our other books, with up-to-date information and with direct links to their own email addresses and web sites. With this book in one hand, your mouse and a pen in the other and a cup of tea balanced precariously on top of your computer monitor, you'll be perfectly equipped to plan and book your trip. You'll find more about the site at the back of this book.

Disclaimer

We make no claims to pure objectivity in judging our *Special Places to Stay*. They are here because we like them. Our opinions and tastes are ours alone and this book is a statement of them; we hope you will share them.

We have done our utmost to get our facts right but apologise for any mistakes that may have crept in. Sometimes, too, prices shift, usually upwards and 'things' change. We will be grateful to be told of any errors and changes that you encounter on your travels, however small.

Introduction

And finally

If you find anything we say misleading (things do change in the lifetime of a guide), or you think we miss the point - if for example you were led to expect a very child-friendly, relaxed country house/hotel and were surprised by elegant white carpets and delicate ornaments at toddler height - please let us know. And do discuss any problem with the owners or member of staff at the time - they are the only ones who can do something about it immediately. They would be mortified to discover afterwards that you were, for example, cold in bed, when extra blankets could have been provided.

- Poor reports are followed up with the owners in question: we need to hear both sides of the story. Really bad reports lead to incognito visits after which we may exclude a place. It is very helpful to us if you can let us know the date of your visit.

- Recommendations are followed up with inspection visits where appropriate.

We are hugely grateful to those of you who write to us about your experiences - good and bad - or to recommend new places. We love your letters and your comments make a real contribution to this book, be they on our report form, by letter or by email to frenchhotels@sawdays.co.uk.

Bon Voyage!

Susan Luraschi

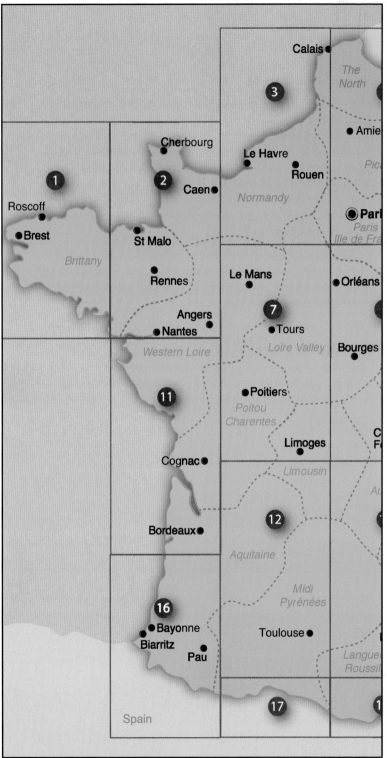

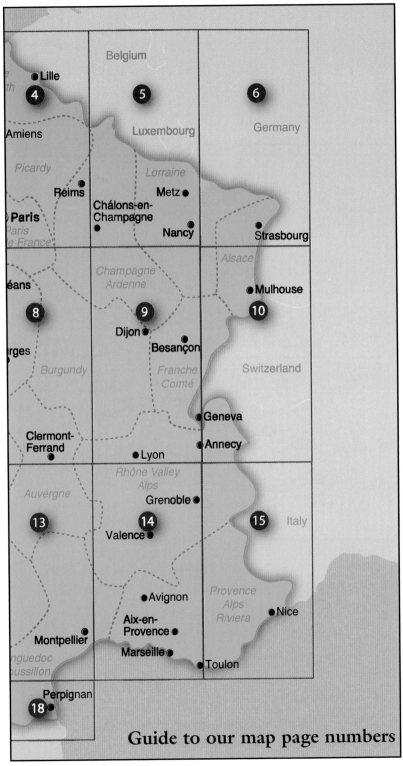

Guide to our map page numbers

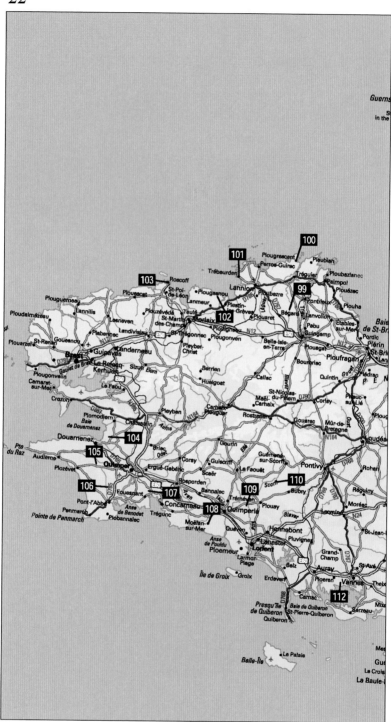

Scale for colour maps 1:1 600 000
(1cm:16km or 1 inch:25.25 miles)

Map 1

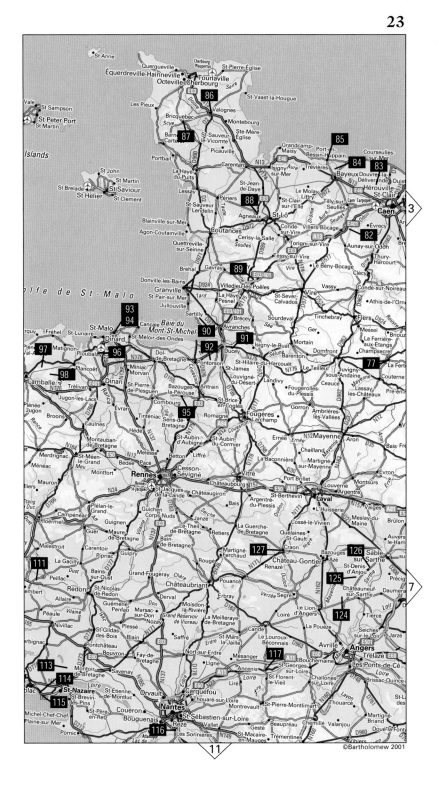

©Bartholomew 2001

Map 2

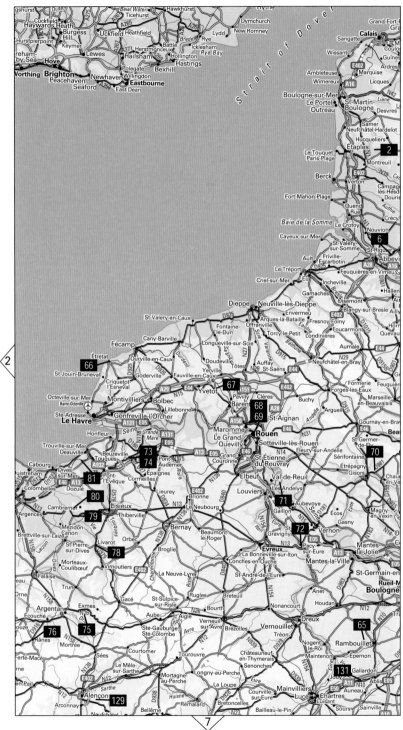

Map 3

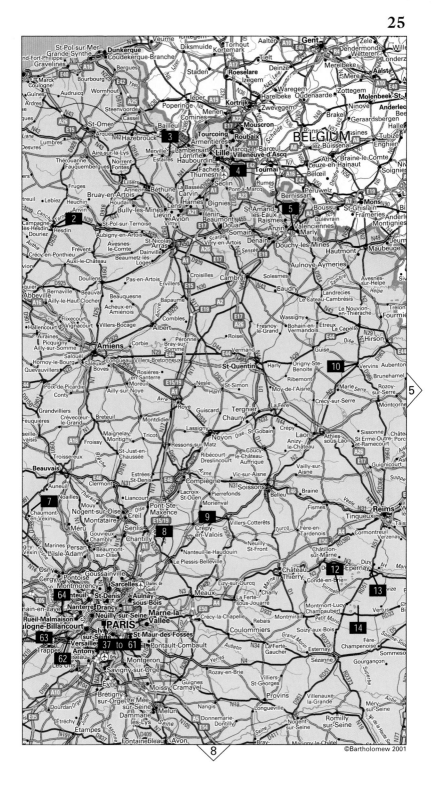

©Bartholomew 2001

Map 4

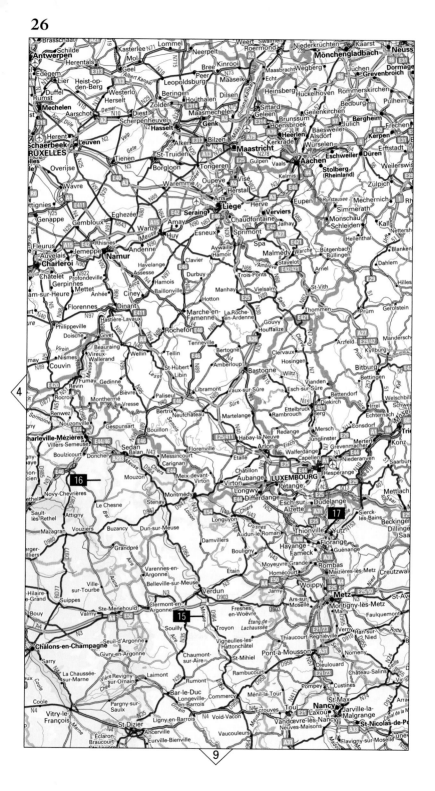

Map 5

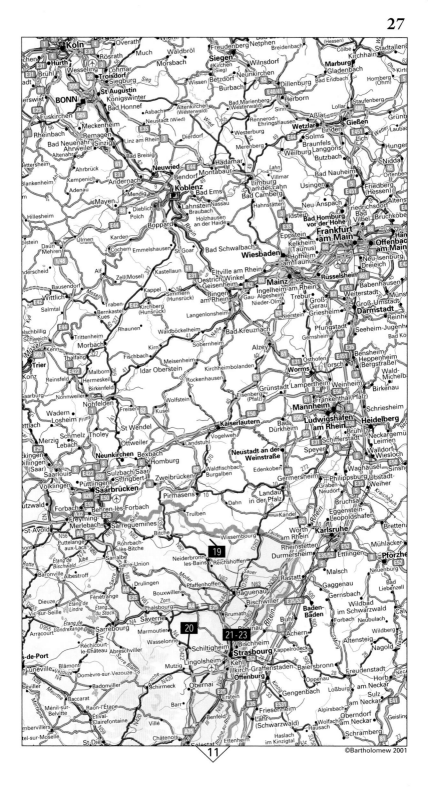

©Bartholomew 2001

Map 6

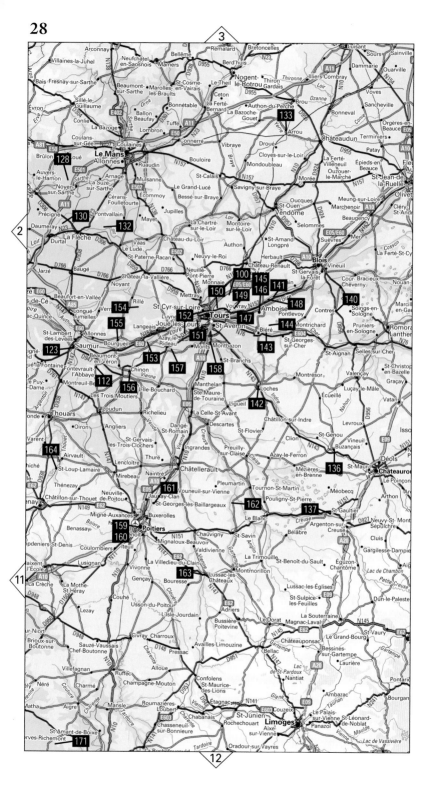

Map 7

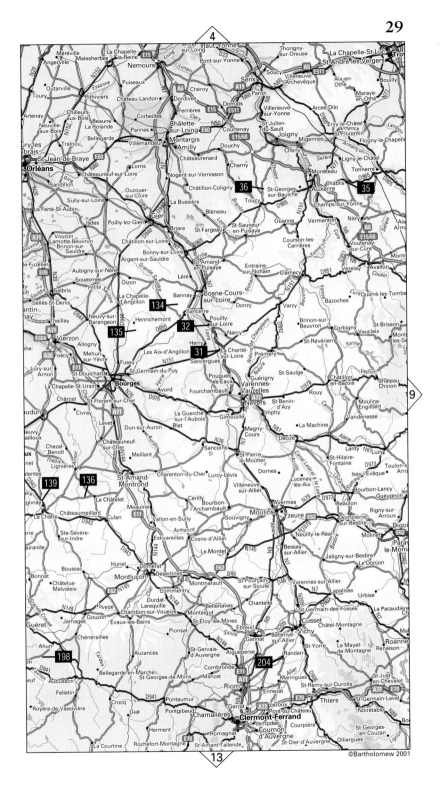

Map 8

©Bartholomew 2001

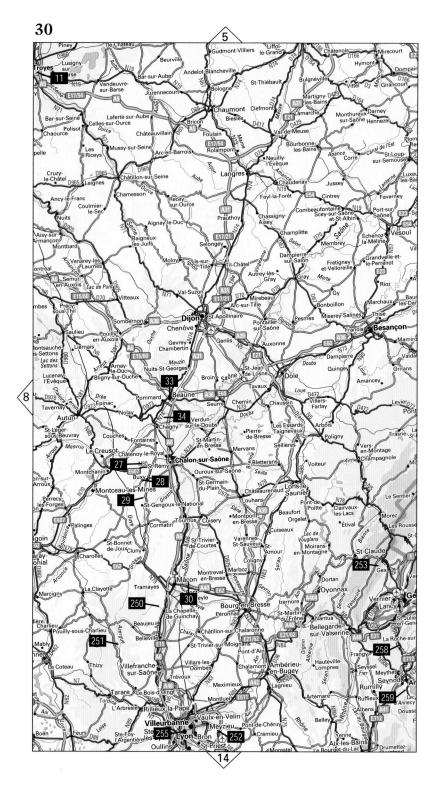

Map 9

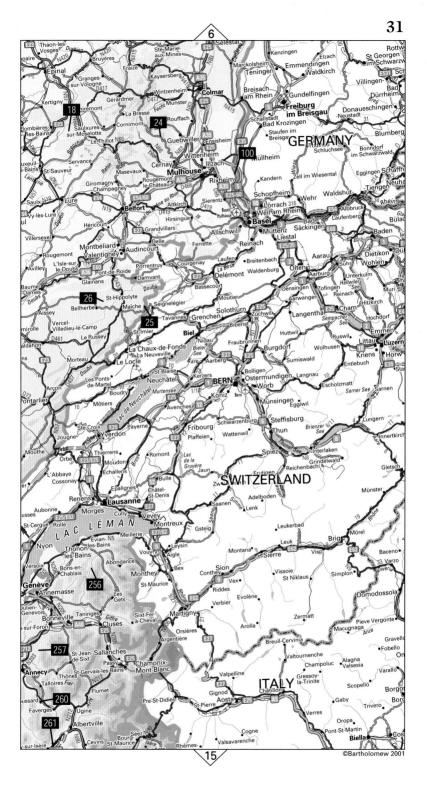

Map 10

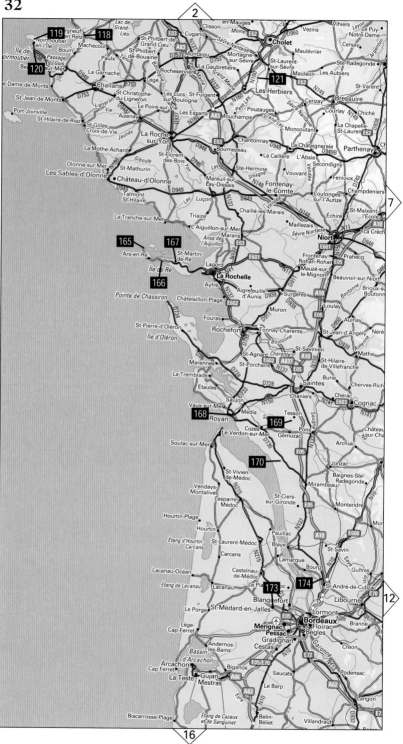

Map 11

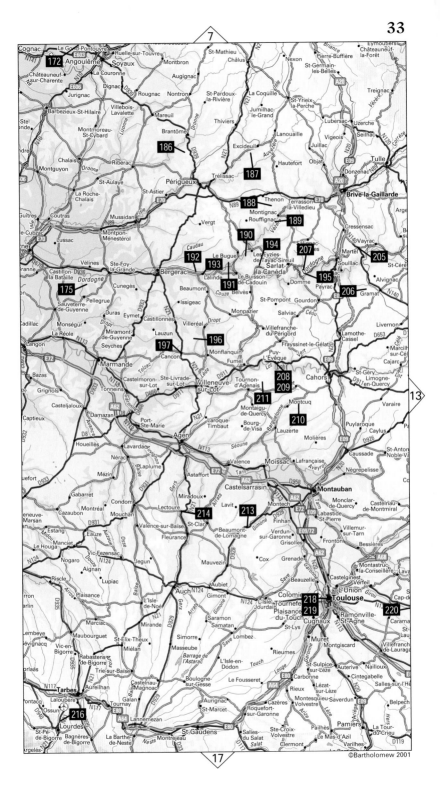

Map 12

©Bartholomew 2001

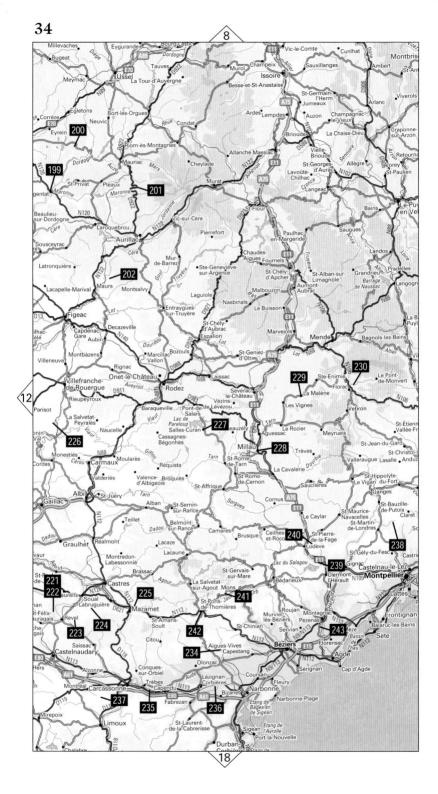

Map 13

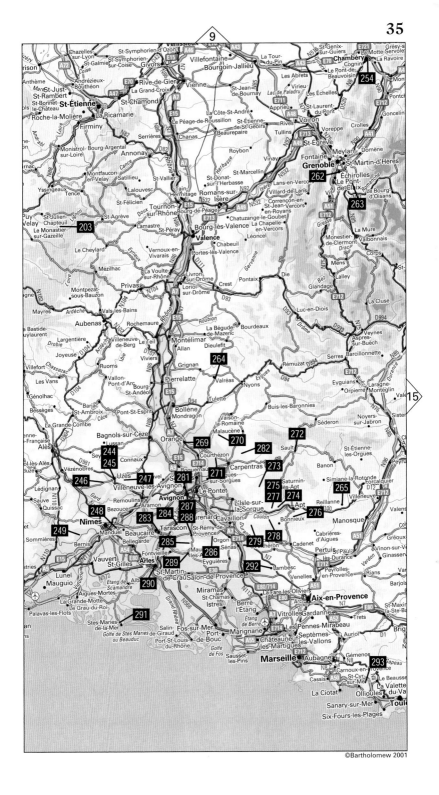

Map 14

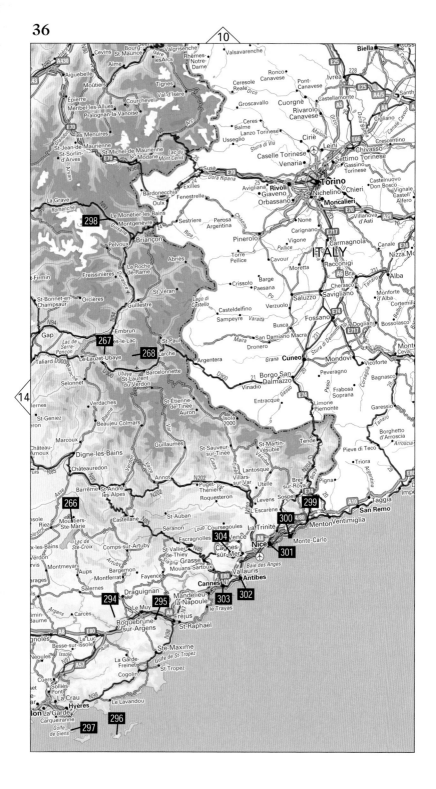

Map 15

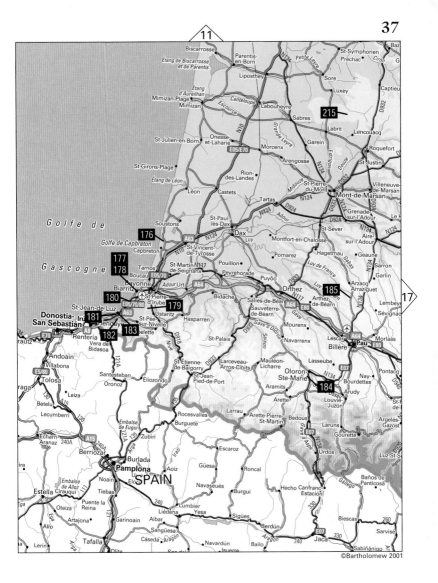

Map 16

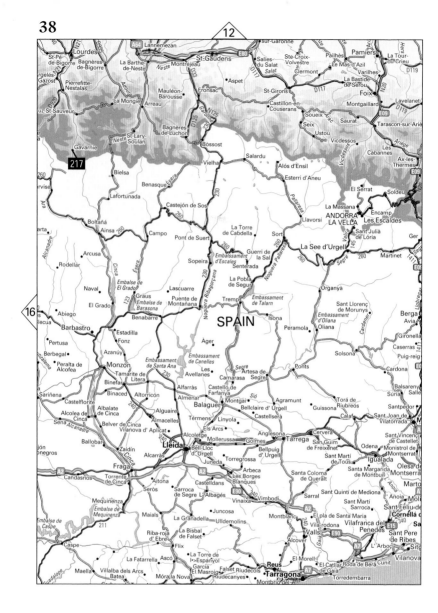

Map 17

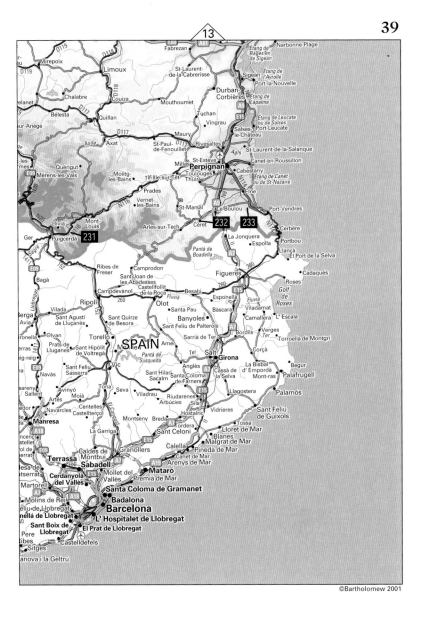

Map 18

The North
Picardy
Champagne-Ardenne

There is no such thing as a little garlic.

Arthur Baer (b.1886)

Ph. Praliaud, CDT Aube

Auberge d'Inxent

La Vallée de la Course
62170 Inxent
Pas-de-Calais

Tel: (0)3 21 90 71 19
Fax: (0)3 21 86 31 67

Laurence & Jean-Marc Six

And, the lucky winner is... Believe it or not, some people who collect bottle caps do win prizes. As *sommelier* in a large restaurant in Lille, Jean-Marc won the Perrier contest on the luck of a draw. Off he tripped with his young wife and two children to a most emerald green valley and claimed a whitewashed, geranium-boxed dream of an 18th-century country inn. Order a trout on their vine-covered terrace and back comes a live one in a bucket from their superb trout farm across the road on the banks of the river Course. Needless to say Jean-Marc's exceptional, reasonably priced wine list and creative use of local produce should lead to a prolonged stay. Inside all is wonky wood beams, low ceilings, a battery of copper pans behind the original zinc countertop, red-checked tablecloths and the warmth and cosiness of a country kitchen with burning fireplaces on chilly days. The beamed-ceiling bedrooms have been recently furnished with cherry-wood copies of antiques and the walls papered to look ragged. Some of the best people win the best prizes.

Rooms: 6 doubles.
Price: €46-€57.
Meals: Breakfast €6.50; lunch & dinner €13-€35. Restaurant closed Tuesdays and Wednesdays during low season.
Closed: 20 December-20 January.

From Montreuil sur Mer N1 towards Boulogne for about 4km; right on D127 to Inxent/Vallée de la Course. Signposted.

Map No: 3

Les Trois Fontaines

16 rue d'Abbeville
62140 Marconne Hesdin
Pas-de-Calais

Tel: (0)3 21 86 81 65
Fax: (0)3 21 86 33 34

Arnaud Descamps

Here is a long, low, plain modern building dressed up to look like a typical French inn - and succeeding. With its half-length nets and flower boxes, it fits into the little market town (wonderful market on Thursday mornings) as if it had always been there and the pavement tables are well used by locals. So, of course, is the restaurant. Arnaud Descamps is friendly and anxious to please. He took over in 1999 and is concentrating on the quality of the food he serves in his panelled, chequer-floored dining room: menus change every day and there's a special one for children. Bedrooms are in a separate building overlooking the fine garden. This building has its own, very pleasant lobby and a long terrace that runs in front of the French windows: each room has its own table and chairs for summer breakfasts. The rooms are in traditional French style with quiet wallpapers and candlewick bedcovers. It is, indeed, a very typical small French hotel; it's quiet, good value and well placed for cross-Channel visitors and the great beaches of Le Touquet and Berck.

Rooms: 16 doubles.
Price: €46-€53.
Meals: Breakfast €6; picnic available; lunch & dinner €14-€27. Restaurant closed December 20-31.
Closed: Never.

From Calais for Arras. After Montreuil N39 for Hesdin. Follow signs to Marconne centre. Hotel opposite Mairie.

Map No: 4

Station Bac Saint-Maur

La Gare des Années Folies
77 rue de la Gare
62840 Sailly sur la Lys
Pas-de-Calais

Tel: (0)3 21 02 68 20
Fax: (0)3 21 02 74 37
E-mail: chefdegare@wanadoo.fr
Web: perso.wanadoo.fr/station-bac-saint-maur/

Vincent & Valérie Laruelle

Vincent, *Chef de Gare*, and his young crew of conductors man this 1921 bistro-converted, red-bricked train station filled with vintage suitcases and trunks spewing ancient tourist brochures. There are miniature tin trains, a wind-up wooden telephone, hand-held lanterns, sepia etchings on the walls, antique wall clocks and a paraphernalia of reminders of the golden era of train travel. You may dine in the station and then retire to your rooms in the carriage of an authentic 'PLM' that travelled the Paris, Lyon, Mediterranean lines. Let Valérie know in advance and you will be served in the elegant restaurant compartment with its warm mahogany walls inlaid with mother-of-pearl. Retire to your first class *couchettes* to dreams of the Orient Express. As if on cue, a real train passes by every now and again adding its clanking to the authenticity. A full playground just outside, a children's menu, antique highchairs and Socrates the parrot - this is a super place for kids. The next day take a tour along the La Lys aboard a barge; the lock is only 400m from the station.

Rooms: 6 Pullman compartments with 2 singles each.
Price: €30-€60.
Meals: Breakfast €6; lunch & dinner in train station €8-€24; served on board €28-€50. Children's meals €6.50.
Closed: 2-16 January.

From A25 exit 9 for Erquinghem to Sailly. At Bac St Maur 2nd left immed. after Havet factory.

Hôtel Brueghel
5 Parvis Saint Maurice
59000 Lille
Nord

Tel: (0)3 20 06 06 69
Fax: (0)3 20 63 25 27

Danièle Lhermie

A quick stroll from the train station along lively pedestrian streets, keeping your eye out for the spires of the Saint Maurice church, will get you there in no time. How Danièle Lhermie achieves such a homely feel in such a big city hotel is a bit of a mystery, but you feel it as soon as you walk in the door. Could it be the restored 19th-century elevator with its clanking wrought-iron doors, the warm wooden panelling of the reception desk or the cheery young staff? The Flemish grandmother in one painting is no relation but all the other objects in the lobby and breakfast rooms belong to Danièle; she confesses her obsession with, and joy in, haunting the many local antique markets. There is even an annual three-day antique orgy when all of Lille empty their attics and survive on chips, mussels and beer. The rooms are small and stylishly decorated; antique rattan chairs, 'distressed' desks, splashes of sea blue in the bathrooms. Try 204 with a pale yellow wall and a view of the church. If you come by car, public parking is no problem but call ahead to avoid getting lost in the one-way streets.

Rooms: 66: 53 doubles, 12 twins, 1 family room for 4.
Price: Doubles/twins €59-€87, family room €76-€91.
Meals: Breakfast €7. Many fine restaurants in town.
Closed: Never.

In centre of town on pedestrian street. Best to call for directions for nearest car park.

Map No: 4

Auberge du Bon Fermier

64 rue de Famars
59300 Valenciennes
Nord

Tel: (0)3 27 46 68 25
Fax: (0)3 27 33 75 01
E-mail: contact@home-gastronomie.com
Web: www.home-gastronomie.com

M Beine

Forget your high heels, for the cobblestones in the flowered courtyard penetrate into the bar, reception and restaurant of this 16th-century auberge. It is a maze of passageways, burnished beams and tiny staircases. A bright copper-bellied *lavabo* greets you at the top of the stairs leading to the rooms. Looking down from a glassed-in corridor, you can almost hear the clatter of hooves arriving in the courtyard, now a quiet terrace for afternoon tea and snacks. The rooms are delightful, one with tapestried curtains and walls, another with red bricks and wooden struts, all with baths and bathrobes. There are also two larger, lighter ground-floor rooms with post-modern lamps and tables. Downstairs a suit of armour guards a wooden reception dais and comes to life in the evenings when the main restaurant is lit only by candles. The passengers jostling between Paris and Brussels were probably delighted to have been delayed in this cosy staging inn. Monsieur Beine, who also runs the wine shop up the street, takes enormous trouble to create new menus with his chef.

Rooms: 16 doubles.
Price: €80-€120.
Meals: Breakfast €8; lunch & dinner €20-€45.
Closed: Never.

From Cambrai A2 for Brussels, exit Valenciennes Centre. Do not get off the autoroute before. Continue for Valenciennes Centre. Signposted.

Map No: 4

Hôtel Jean de Bruges

18 place de l'Eglise
80135 Saint Riquier
Somme

Tel: (0)3 22 28 30 30
Fax: (0)3 22 28 00 69
E-mail: jeandebruges@wanadoo.fr
Web: perso.wanadoo.fr/saint.riquier/

Bernadette Stubbe

Starting from scratch can be a blessing. Being bang next to a flamboyant gothic 15th-century abbey can be another. Both these and a popular classical music festival in July led Bernadette Stubbe and her husband to take a deep breath and re-design the magnificent white-stone 17th-century mansion on the main square. An astute architect brought in light from above to diffuse a soft glow on beige rattan chairs and white linen curtains. A cluster of decanters sparkle on a perfect honey-coloured country-style table top. There's is a minimum of decoration but each piece is exquisite, like the tall glass-door bookcase in the breakfast room. Continuing the theme into the bedrooms it becomes simple luxury with textured wallpaper, white piqué bedspreads, beige in the thick muslin drapes and carpeting. A desk and an antique *armoire* complete the picture. Soft robes and white-tiled bathrooms follow suit. Snacks and drinks are served on the terrace overlooking the square with its rural museum and the town hall. Five minutes off the Calais autoroute and you are in the centre of Medieval France.

Rooms: 11: 9 doubles, 2 suites.
Price: €84-€175.
Meals: Breakfast €9; sandwiches & snacks on terrace available, not Sunday nights.
Closed: January.

From Calais A16 towards Paris, exit 22 St Riquier, then 8km on D925. Right on main square next to Cathedral.

Map No: 3

Château de Reilly

60240 Reilly
Oise

Tel: (0)3 44 49 03 05
Fax: (0)3 44 49 23 39
E-mail: reilly@terre-net.fr

Hilary & David Gauthier

They are young, enthusiastic and bright... and they love their old family house. David, who's French, has converted the mill house into a French country 'pub': Toby jugs and a pianist on Saturdays. You breakfast there or in your room. Hilary, who's English, has unleashed her decorating flair on the big château bedrooms, using just enough fabric and furniture, tassels and prints, then leaving the space to reveal itself. Her colour schemes have character but don't intrude (rich green with pale pink, deep raspberry with royal blue and white or eau-de-nil and ivory) and the new bathrooms are very stylish, the one shower a smart, glass, quarter-circle. Vast *Victor Hugo* is the most château-esque room with its double-draped windows and tasselled wallpaper. Modern comfort in well-respected old surroundings, lots of space, heart-stoppingly peaceful views, a great sloping lawn that beckons, the listed medieval village across the valley calling out to be painted.

Rooms: 4: 3 doubles, 1 suite for 4.
Price: Doubles €60-€74, suite €99.
Meals: Breakfast included; lunch €10-€14; dinner à la carte approx. €26.
Closed: Christmas & New Year.

A16 exit Beauvais Nord. In Beauvais for Mantes la Jolie for about 30km. After Chaumont en Vexin, right on D153 to Reilly. Château entrance on right entering village.

Map No: 4

Château d' Ermenonville

Rue René Girardin
60950 Ermenonville
Oise

Tel: (0)3 44 54 00 26
Fax: (0)3 44 54 01 00
E-mail: chato.ermenonville@wanadoo.fr
Web: www.chateau-ermenonville.com

Christophe Claireau

Walking up to this pure French château you can almost feel the history of the princes who have lived, visited, died here - it has also belonged to Signor Bugatti and the Hare Krishna movement. No wonder Rousseau came to think great thoughts in the 'Baroque' garden - his tomb still attracts literati. The blond building stands like a sculpture in the velvet of fine lawns, tall trees and water; the peace of the place is tangible. There's splendour in the iron-balustraded stone staircase, the vast drawing room's double aspect onto informal parkland and symmetrical courtyard and the dining room with its fine white linen and its stylish, friendly waiters. Rooms all have style too. Be extravagant and take a suite for the full château experience: round, panelled tower bedroom, pure French *salon*, marble fireplace, views over moat and park. The smaller rooms are excellent value, especially on the second floor where lower ceilings make them so cosy; on the deep wooden window seat over the lake you could be in the bows of a boat. Genuine old elegance on a human scale.

Rooms: 49: 47 doubles/twins,
2 suites for 2-3.
Price: Doubles €59-€191, suites
€169-€268.
Meals: Breakfast €13; lunch & dinner
€33-€73.
Closed: Never.

*From north A1 exit 8 for
Chantilly/Senlis. N330 for
Ermenonville. Left into village, then right.
Hotel on left after bridge. Ring at gate.*

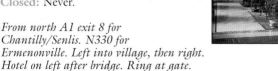

Map No: 4

Hôtel Le Régent

26 rue du Général Mangin
02600 Villers Cotterêts
Aisne

Tel: (0)3 23 96 01 46
Fax: (0)3 23 96 37 57
E-mail: hotel.le.regent@gofornet.com

Mme Thiébault

This is a gracious 18th-century hotel, built around a big cobbled courtyard with a flowering cherry beside a stone well. You wouldn't be surprised to see a carriage come through the archway, with galloping horses anxious for their stable and their cargo ready for supper and bed. No supper now, unfortunately, but there are several restaurants a short stroll away in this attractive, though busy, little town. The only time you might have a problem is on Sunday night. Breakfast is in a somewhat gloomy room with green wallpaper, brightened by pale pink tablecloths. The building actually dates back to the 16th century and is full of atmosphere. The rooms are being carefully renovated and some open onto a covered wooden balcony behind a thick hedge of flowers. A 30-minute drive away is the railway carriage where Marshal Foch signed the armistice at the end of the First World War, while in nearby Pierrefonds is an amazing château with more turrets than Sleeping Beauty's castle. Speaking of which, the (reputedly) real thing is less than an hour away, which could be of great interest to your children.

Rooms: 18 doubles/twins, some with jacuzzis.
Price: €28-€67.
Meals: Breakfast €8. Restaurants within walking distance.
Closed: Some Sunday evenings November-April.

From Pierrefonds on D973 to Villers Cotterêts town centre. Hotel 100m from post office on Rue Général Mangin.

La Tour du Roy
02140 Vervins
Aisne

Tel: (0)3 23 98 00 11
Fax: (0)3 23 98 00 72
E-mail: latourduroy@wanadoo.fr
Web: www.latourduroy.com

M & Mme Devignes

Madame, with references from all over the world, wears the chef's hat here: food is centre-stage, and resoundingly applauded. Monsieur, a delightful character, is wedded to his hotel, which he bought roofless over 30 years ago and has renovated quite beautifully. You arrive in the attractive courtyard with its flower beds and stone fountain. The building has nooks, crannies and corners; swathes of original brickwork and restored stone details. The dining room is, of course, seriously inviting, dressed in wood and marble, pretty antiques and unusual windows and alcoves. The turrets, all that remain of the 11th-century town fortifications where the original building stood, have amazing semicircular bedrooms, stained-glass windows, hand-painted basins, tapestries. Beds are old carved pieces and every room contains a framed menu from a different restaurant - the corridors are lined with framed menus, too! A place to spoil yourself with days of luxurious living and eating. Canal trips, champagne tastings, château visits and steam-train journeys can be arranged.

Rooms: 22: 14 doubles/twins, 8 suites.
Price: Doubles/twins €53-€91, suites €91-€183.
Meals: Breakfast €12; picnic €15; lunch/dinner €27-€76. Restaurant closed Monday & Tuesday lunchtimes except on request.
Closed: Never.

A26 exit 13 to Vervins on N2. Follow Centre Ville signs. Hotel directly on right. Parking through gate, past main building.

Map No: 4

Le Champ des Oiseaux

20 rue Linard-Gonthier
10000 Troyes
Aube

Tel: (0)3 25 80 58 50
Fax: (0)3 25 80 98 34
E-mail: message@champdesoiseaux.com
Web: www.champdesoiseaux.com

Monsieur Boisseau

Only the Museum of Modern Art stands between the Cathedral and this amazingly pure group of 15th-century houses in the centre of lovely, unsung old Troyes. One is dazzled by the astonishing timbers, beams and rafters, inside and out, seduced by the simplicity of the beautifully-jointed stone paving, the wooden floors, the softly luminous natural materials: the owners had their brilliant restoration done by craftsmen who knew the ancestral methods and made it look 'as good as new' ... in 1460. Corridors twist around the creeper-climbed courtyard and little internal garden, staircases change their minds, the place is alive with its centuries. Each bedroom has a personality, some soberly sandy and brown, others frivously floral; they vary in size and status but all are warmly discreet in their luxury and good furniture. And of course, bathrooms are perfect modern boudoirs. The unexpected *salon*, a long, white barrel vault of ancient stones, the original stonemason's craft lovingly revealed, was once a cellar. The Boisseau family can be justifiably proud of their contribution to medieval Troyes.

Rooms: 26: 21 doubles, 5 suites for 2-6.
Price: Doubles €81-€114, suites €130-€145.
Meals: Breakfast €11. Great restaurants nearby.
Closed: Never.

In centre of Troyes, very close to Cathedral.

Château du Ru Jacquier

51700 Igny Comblizy
Marne

Tel: (0)3 26 57 10 84
Fax: (0)3 26 57 82 80
Web: www.rujacquier.com

M Robert Granger

Gatehouse and drive may look a little rough but press on: a sensational little château awaits you, one of those 18th-century gems made of elegantly moulded mellow stone and warmly tiled pepperpot turrets. Nothing too grand though - the door opens onto a family hall in naturally relaxed mood then to the really lovely reception rooms: beams and parquet in glowing condition, open fireplaces and summery florals, a little turet boudoir in the sitting room, it is all unpretentiously smart. Your bedroom will be just as attractive: be it the canopied Louis XIV, the top-floor Blue or any other, its sense of solid quality, secluded space - each one has a proper sitting area - and refined period furnishing will win you over. Your hosts are the same: attentive to every detail, friendly and relaxed without an ounce of affectation, happy to share their skillfully-crafted *table d'hôtes* with you. The big, landscaped gardens are home to a troop of interesting exotic animals to delight all ages, the swimming pool has a sliding glass roof and the Champagne countryside is full of treasures.

Rooms: 7: 6 doubles/twins,
1 suite for 4.
Price: €61-€91.
Meals: Breakfast €6; hosted dinner €23, by arrangement.
Closed: January-March.

A4 Paris-Metz exit 21 for Dormans. There D18 for 7km. Hotel on left 1km before Igny Le Jard.

Le Clos Raymi

3 rue Joseph de Venoge
51200 Epernay
Marne

Tel: (0)3 26 51 00 58
Fax: (0)3 26 51 18 98
E-mail: closraymi@wanadoo.fr
Web: www.closraymi-hotel.com

Mme Woda

What more seductive combination than champagne and culture? Easy to get to from both Reims Cathedral and the champagne vineyards, this cosy hotel has the added attraction of Madame Woda herself. Ever attentive to the comfort of her guests, she purrs with pride in her recent renovation of the Chandon (the other half of Moët) family house. The intricate, pale blue mosaic covering the entrance hall and the hardwood staircase were left alone but her artistic touch is everywhere: in the good beds dressed in vintage linens, the attractive bathrooms with scented lotions and bath salts, the fresh flowers in every room, etchings and paintings from the 1930s, even books of poetry on a shelf. Take a peek at the downstairs bathroom with its cubist paintings and interesting replacement for the usual sink. A champagne aperitif can be organised in a splendid little sitting room with a fireplace and, if weather permits, the buffet breakfast can be taken in the parasoled garden behind the house. Madame Woda will help you organise champagne tastings and has her favourite people to recommend.

Rooms: 7: 6 doubles, 1 twin.
Price: Doubles €125-€143, twin €95.
Meals: Breakfast €14. Lunch & dinner available locally.
Closed: 15 days in February.

From Paris A4 exit Château Thierry. N3 to Epernay.

Château d'Etoges

4 rue Richebourg
51270 Etoges
Marne

Tel: (0)3 26 59 30 08
Fax: (0)3 26 59 35 57
E-mail: etoges1@wanadoo.fr
Web: www.etoges.com

Mme Filliette-Neuville

Louis XIV was impressed by the beauty of the garden, fountains and ponds at Etoges, used as a stopover by various kings of France on journeys east. This moated château was built early in the 17th century and restored as a hotel in 1991 by the family who has lived here for over a century. If you enjoy waking up between beautiful sheets, this is for you. Rooms are all different and two have intriguing little mezzanine bedrooms over the bathroom - presumably originally for servants, now great fun for children. Many rooms have four-posters; all are furnished with antiques and are extremely French. If you fancy breakfast in bed, it will appear on a lace-covered table, with bread, croissants and a bowl of fruit. If you prefer to wander downstairs, choose from the buffet and sit on the terrace if it's warm. This could be a luxurious base for champagne tastings or simply a very pleasant break, convenient if you're heading for eastern France, like Louis XIV or, more likely, meandering south through Reims. It's easy country for cycling or you can try punting if you feel this is more in tune with the surroundings.

Rooms: 20: 17 doubles/twins, 3 suites.
Price: Doubles/twins €80-€190, suites €190.
Special prices for 2-4 nights.
Meals: Breakfast €12; lunch & dinner €30-€60; children's meals €12.
Closed: 27 January-21 February.

From Paris A4 exit at Ferté sous Jouaire, follow signs for Chalons en Champagne. Château in centre of Etoges.

Lorraine
Alsace
Franche Comté

Well loved he garleek, oynons, and lekes. And for to
drinken strong wyn, reed as blood.

Geoffrey Chaucer, Canterbury Tales

A.M.B, CRT Franche Comté

Hostellerie du Château des Monthairons

55320 Dieue sur Meuse
Meuse

Tel: (0)3 29 87 78 55
Fax: (0)3 29 87 73 49
E-mail: accueil@chateaudesmonthairons.fr
Web: www.chateaudesmonthairons.fr

Thouvenin Family

This is not the prettiest or most interesting corner of France, but if you are going this way, or fancy peace and quiet in beautiful grounds, or a spot of fishing, this would be a good choice. Looking just as you would imagine a French château, Monthairons served as an American military hospital in the First World War but was a base for German troops in the Second. It is now run by three couples of the Thouvenin family, who bought it in 1985. One couple looks after the restaurant and food, while the others run the hotel and grounds. Maybe because of this family touch, you will feel at home in the château despite its size. The rooms are classic French and come in all sizes, with some duplex suites which are great for families. The sort of children who love exploring outdoors would be in their element and it is safe to swim or canoe in the Meuse, which meanders through the huge grounds. Apparently a former owner diverted the river especially and a nearby meadow is known as the 'old river'. The restaurant is elegant and full of flowers, but more for a special dinner than a quick meal with the children.

Rooms: 20: 14 doubles/twins, 4 duplexes for 2-3; 2 family rooms for 2-4.
Price: Doubles/twins €82-€135, duplexes & family rooms €134-€185.
Meals: Breakfast €11-€12; lunch, weekdays €20; dinner €29-€71. Restaurant closed Monday and Tuesday lunchtimes.
Closed: January-10 February.

From A4 exit Voie Sacrée for St Mihiel on D34. Monthairons 2.5km on left after village of Ancemont.

Map No: 5

Hotel Merry-Go-Yurt

Parc des Bébés
Meuse

Tel: (0)8 02 16 18 21
Fax: (0)8 30 40 65 82
E-mail: yell@theyurting.com
Web: www.theyurting.com

Yurt Bogarde

The Arabs reached as far as the Loire when they overwhelmed most of Europe in their last major invasion. They were stopped by Charles Martel but their influence lingers on, however, and this brand new, rather 'hip', hotel is really an overgrown yurt. These have become popular with the new century's 'hippy' generation, and not without reason. They are wonderfully cosy, and to sleep in the rounded curves of a yurt is to sleep the sleep of the womb. There is little room, however, for the normal facilities of a hotel, hence the somewhat sober outbuildings, ranged along the fencing outside in a dark, sympathetic green. There you will find the kitchens, loos, billiard-room and staff quarters, leaving you to occupy the whole hotel without disturbance. There you may behave in a proper yurtish way: chanting, meditating, drinking herbal tea, discovering your inner voice, sweating and invoking the spirits of the original yurt-builders. With luck all that may ward off the attentions of the modern park-keepers, who do not appear to have gone through the same spiritual transformation. Their obsession with the regulations is in stark and cruel contrast with the easy-going hospitality of this remarkable little, very little, hotel.

Rooms: 10 single berths, 2 twins.
Price: Dinner, birth and breakfast, 1 midwife.
Meals: On demand.
Closed: Towards the end of the 3rd trimester.

Follow the balloon seller, past the coconut shy, through the haunted house and down the helterskelter. Et voila!

L'Horizon

50 route du Crève-Cœur
57100 Thionville
Moselle

Tel: (0)3 82 88 53 65
Fax: (0)3 82 34 55 84
E-mail: info@lhorizon.com
Web: www.lhorizon.com

Jean-Pascal & Anne-Marie Speck

The house is only 50 years old but its arcading anchors it and Virginia Creeper has crept all over it, clothing its façade in lively warm character. Here is comfortable living in graceful surroundings, as in an elegant private house. A huge terrace envelops the ground floor - from here and from the smart restaurant you have plunging views over Thionville with an astounding, glittering cityscape at night. Some first-floor rooms give onto a balcony over the same view. Despite the surprising hall with its marbled flooring and glamorous tented ceiling, the bedrooms are classic French chic (though carpets may be a little worn here and there and some rooms are smaller than others); bathrooms border on the luxurious. But above all, you will warm to your utterly charming hosts. Monsieur Speck is passionate about Second World War history: the Maginot Line is all around, and Thionville is on the Liberty Road that is marked every kilometre from Cherbourg in Normandy, to Bastogne in Lorraine. He is fascinating on the subject.

Rooms: 10 doubles.
Price: €75-€130.
Meals: Breakfast €11; lunch & dinner €33-€50. Restaurant closed Saturday & Monday lunchtimes.
Closed: January-February.

From A31 exit 40 to Thionville. Follow signs for Bel Air Hospital north of town. At hospital bear left up hill leaving town. Hotel 400m on left.

Map No: 5

Auberge de la Vigotte

1 La Vigotte
88340 Girmont Val d'Ajol
Vosges

Tel: (0)3 29 61 06 32
Fax: (0)3 29 61 07 07
E-mail: courrier@lavigotte.com
Web: www.lavigotte.com

Michel & Jocelyne Bouguerne-Arnould

Michel and Jocelyne are gradually doing up this 18th century farmhouse, with 10 rooms due to be ready by the end of 2001. Michel is full of decorating ideas and Jocelyne teaches English in a local school. Rooms have carved or painted beds and all look out onto fantastic views of the mountains. With tennis, volleyball and a children's play area, this will be a perfect place for families. Yo can also ride, or swim in a lake in the grounds, while in the winter you can go cross-country skiing. Meals are a mix of very traditional and more contemporary: ranging from pigs' trotters to tomatoes with cardamom. An hour from Mulhouse, 700m up, on the gentle slopes of the Vosges, the auberge is set is in densely wooded countryside: total peace and quiet. In winter you will find a roaring fire and a warm welcome, in the summer you can round off your day with dinner out on the terrace. Somewhat off the beaten track for English holidaymakers, this would make a good stop-over, but could also be a great choice for an out-of-doors holiday.

Rooms: 20: 14 doubles, 6 family.
Price: €30-€64. Half-board €38-€53 p.p. for stays of 2 nights or more only.
Meals: Breakfast €6; lunch & dinner €14-€21; children's meals €8. Restaurant closed Tuesdays & Wednesdays.
Closed: 12 November-mid-December.

From Remiremont D23 then D57. Follow white signs to auberge.

Hôtel Anthon
Obersteinbach
67510 Lembach
Bas-Rhin

Tel: (0)3 88 09 55 01
Fax: (0)3 88 09 50 52

Danielle Flaig

Less than mountains, more than hills, the lushly-wooded slopes are pure Vosges Forest, the clear Steinbach snakes its way through pastures, and red rocky outcrops emerge in forbidding contrast to such bucolic enchantment. This little hotel, in the same deep pinky-orange colour as the rocks, is in typical Vosges style. Inside, more warm wood, including a fine carved staircase, echoes the living forest. It is sweetly simple - not basic in any way, just pretty and uncluttered, with carved wardrobes and typical Vosges dining chairs, peachy beige or dull turquoise-green paintwork, coir floors. Bedrooms are not big but, again, prettily done with gingham duvets, starched cloths on round tables, windows onto the quiet night. The first-floor breakfast room is delightful - immaculate white cloths and regional pottery - but the restaurant, definitely in a different class, is the heart of this place. In the big, embracing room with its refined table settings and service, delicious dishes await you - and Madame's huge collection of soup tureens is dazzling.

Rooms: 9 doubles.
Price: €56.
Meals: Breakfast €9.15; lunch & dinner €24-€45; gourmet dinner €61. Restaurant closed Tuesdays & Wednesdays.
Closed: January.

From Haguenau D3 & D27 through Woerth to Lembach (25km); there, D3 through Tannenbrück and Niedersteinbach to Obersteinbach. Hotel in village centre.

Map No: 6

Le Cerf

30 rue du Général-de-Gaulle
67520 Marlenheim
Bas-Rhin

Tel: (0)3 88 87 73 73
Fax: (0)3 88 87 68 08
E-mail: info@lecerf.com
Web: www.lecerf.com

Michel Husser

Michel is the third generation of his family to keep up the Cerf's reputation for imaginatively updated regional food. On his return from the Ecole Hôtèlière his father Robert, who had taken over the kitchen from his own father, 'retired' to the garden. Michel can rely not only on hand picked vegetables and herbs but on a supply of peppery nasturtiums and china-blue borage to scatter on salads. Robert's wife Marcelle and Michel's wife Cathy run the hotel, while the eldest Madame Husser is still fully involved in her 80s, bringing a personal touch to breakfast as well as taking her turn at reception. The hotel encloses a paved courtyard, where tables are set with starched flowery cloths in summer. The cream umbrellas have lights for supper on warm evenings. We often praise places for being light and airy, the Cerf is certainly not gloomy, but with its wood panelling and soft lighting it's more cosy and inviting. Traditional patterned cloths and china make a cheerful breakfast table, while bedrooms have elaborate quilts. Since it is in the middle of the village, there is traffic, but all rooms are air conditioned. A great stopover for a special meal.

Rooms: 12 + 3; 9 doubles/twins;
3 apartments for 2-3.
Price: Doubles & triples €90-€140;
apartments €200.
Meals: Breakfast €15; lunch & dinner
from €53 & à la carte; children €14.
Restaurant closed Tuesdays and Wednesdays.
Closed: Never.

*In centre of Marlenheim, on right when
driving from Strasbourg towards Saverne
(18km west of Strasbourg) on N4.*

Hôtel du Dragon

2 rue de l'Ecarlate
67000 Strasbourg
Bas-Rhin

Tel: (0)3 88 35 79 80
Fax: (0)3 88 25 78 95
E-mail: hotel@dragon.fr
Web: www.dragon.fr

Jean Zimmer

In the heart of old Strasbourg, looking over river and Cathedral, the Dragon is grandly, solidly 17th century on the outside, sleekly, refreshingly 20th century on the inside. Built as a private mansion - where Louis XIV stayed on his way to visit Marie-Antoinette in Austria - it became a hotel ten years ago. The little courtyard received a classically pedimented porch and potted shrubs: a pretty place for an evening drink. Inside, they took a deeply contemporary approach: it is sober, infinitely stylish and extraordinarily restful. Variegated grey and white are the basics: grey curtains on white walls, superb grey pinstripe carpeting, interestingly-laid grey and white tiles in bathrooms, blue and green bedcovers for a dash of colour. And some good abstract paintings hang here and there, to great advantage. After 20 years as a mountain guide, Monsieur Zimmer has returned to his native Strasbourg and intends to make the Dragon as welcoming as it is elegant. He is quiet and gentle and has a predilection for English-speaking guests. *Not all rooms have river views.*

Rooms: 30 + 2 apartments: 30 doubles/twins; 2 apts for 3.
Price: Twins/doubles €75-€107; apartments €130.
Meals: Breakfast €9. Many fine restaurants in town.
Closed: Never.

Across the river from Petite France, off quai St Nicolas.

Map No: 6

Hotel Cardinal de Rohan

17-19 rue du Maroquin
67000 Strasbourg
Bas-Rhin

Tel: (0)3 88 32 85 11
Fax: (0)3 88 75 65 37
E-mail: info@hotel-rohan.com
Web: www.hotel-rohan.com

Rolf & Nicole van Maenen

The atmosphere here is a rare combination: stylish and polite yet utterly friendly, plushly comfortable but not overwhelming. Standing in the historic centre just a stone's throw from the Cathedral, the solid building round its central courtyard in traditional 17th-century Strasbourg layout has been virtually rebuilt, with proper respect for its tall narrow neighbours, three rows of roof windows and tangles of geraniums down the façade. An 18th-century Gobelins tapestry graces the elegant sitting room; the breakfast room, pale and peaceful, feels like a country-house dining room: high-backed cane chairs, ivory cloths, antique chest of drawers. With their pine-clad sloping ceilings and those dormer windows, the top-floor rooms have an ancient air to them. Lower rooms are sober, masculine dark and pale blue or rich, warm ginger and cream or spring-fresh green. They come in 'Rustic' or 'Period' décor, have good velvet or thick contemporary fabrics, clean lines and rich French swag effects. There's a great range of gilt-framed mirrors, the occasional antique armoire and smart marble-and-tile bathrooms. Superb comfort, friendliness and attention to detail are the hallmarks here.

Rooms: 36: 32 doubles/twins,
4 triples. 24 are air-conditioned.
Price: Doubles/twins €63-€122,
triples €118-€129. Child under 15 in
parents' room free.
Meals: Breakfast €11. Restaurants
within 500m.
Closed: Never.

From ring road, exit Place de l'Etoile for Centre Ville and Cathedral to underground carpark Place Gutenberg. Staff will collect luggage from car (until 8pm). No vehicular access to hotel door.

Hotel de la Cathédrale

12 place de la Cathdrale
67000 Strasbourg
Bas-Rhin

Tel: (0)3 88 22 12 12
Fax: (0)3 88 23 28 00
E-mail: reserv@hotel-cathedrale.fr
Web: www.hotel-cathedrale.fr

Alain Cézard

When you sit in the big first-floor breakfast room, that incomparable red Gothic Cathedral is almost in your plate - what a way to start the day. In the Renaissance section of old Strasbourg, this warren of a building carries its history in its bones. The rare and secret spiral staircase, three slim columns holding its centre, is ravishing. M Cézard, one of the gentlest, most committed hotel owners, came late to the profession, delights in his wife's decorating talents, their artist friends' original contributions and his own touches of iconoclastic humour, for instance, the display of now-worthless fortune-promising bonds such as Gold Mines of France. Rooms of varying size, some with that cathedral view, others looking over the pretty Dauphin Restaurant courtyard (closed by midnight), have a soft, relaxed atmosphere, neither too casual nor too formal, with straw-coloured Japanese grasspaper wall-covering and rich carpeting that show respect for both natural things and human comforts. Designer fabrics are a decent balance of colourful and neutral, sheets are pale yellow, bathrooms are pale ivory and towels are rose-window monogrammed. This place breathes humanism and taste.

Rooms: 47 + 5 apartments: 42 doubles, 5 duplexes for 2; 5 apts for 2.
Price: €43-€145.
Meals: Buffet breakfast €9.50.
40 restaurants within 500m.
Closed: Never.

From ring road, exit Place de l'Etoile for Centre Ville and Cathedral to underground car park Place Gutenberg (or staff will park car for you €9). No vehicular access to hotel door.

Map No: 6

Hostellerie Saint Barnabé

68530 Murbach Buhl
Haut-Rhin

Tel: (0)3 89 62 14 14
Fax: (0)3 89 62 14 15
E-mail: hostellerie.st.barnabe@wanadoo.fr
Web: www.hostellerie-st-barnabe.com

M & Mme Orban

The young owners of this angular, 100-year-old, flower-decked hotel are spontaneously smiley, chatty and attentive. He is the chef - he trained with France's best and was chef at Château d'Isenbourg for some years - so food is important here, and good. She is the perfect adviser on what to do between the Vosges hills and the Alsace plain: there are typical Alsatian villages and wine-growers to visit, bike-rides and good fishing places (they also have mini-golf on the spot). The ferny woods are full of paths and burbling brooks and there's skiing in the snow season. There are two sorts of guest rooms: in the main house they are big, decorated with care and individuality (the yellow and white room has an iron-frame canopied bed, the red and white one twin head cushions and super-soft quilts), and have smashing bathrooms and occasionally balconies; in the separate building behind, they are smaller and more old-fashioned (and cheaper!) but are gradually being renovated; bedroom doors will soon all have typically Alsatian hand-painted, floral decoration. A great place for both nature-lovers and gourmets.

Rooms: 24 + 1 apartment: 22 doubles, 2 triples, some in annexe; 1 apt for 2-3.
Price: Doubles €76-€125, triples €139; apartment €183.
Meals: Buffet breakfast €14; picnic €12; dinner €26-€55, gourmet €69.
Closed: Mid-January-February.

From N83 (between Belfort & Colmar) D430 for Guebwiller/Lautenbach; D429 for Buhl then Murbach. Hotel on left.

Hôtel Taillard
Route de la Corniche
25470 Goumois
Doubs

Tel: (0)3 81 44 20 75
Fax: (0)3 81 44 26 15
E-mail: hotel.taillard@wanadoo.fr
Web: www.hoteltaillard.com

M Taillard

Stand on the terrace and let your eye plunge and soar over the thick forests, across the border and into Switzerland - it is gasp-worthy. The building, an 18th-century farmhouse, was turned into a hotel by the Taillard family in 1875; the current Taillard, as well as being a thoroughly charming host, is a very competent painter - his works decorate some rooms. His wife does all the upholstery; her skills are evident too. Using good furniture, some antiques, quiltings and pretty lamps, she has made the bedrooms soft and comforting. But let's start in the warm and inviting lobby where wood panelling, rush matting and a fine old *comtoise* (grandfather) clock greet you. Then to the dining room, which, with its great bay windows grabs those magnificent views and seats you by them in splendour - elegant tables and pretty, splendid food. Outside, the swimming pool seems to float in that sea of woods and mountain pastures that spreads beyond the tame/wild garden. Back indoors, there are temptations such as log fires and billiards, gym and jacuzzi, and just such a welcoming atmosphere.

Rooms: 22: 14 doubles, 8 family.
Price: Doubles €43-€72, family €119-€127, suites €82-€105.
Meals: Buffet breakfast €9; lunch & dinner €20-€53. Restaurant closed Wednesdays Oct-Nov; lunchtimes April-June & September.
Closed: Mid-November-March.

From A36 exit 7 for Montbéliard Sud then D437 for Maîche/Bern. After St Hippolyte D437 left to Goumois. Hotel on right before town.

Le Moulin
25380 Vaucluse
Doubs

Tel: (0)3 81 44 35 18
Fax: (0)3 81 44 35 18

Claire & Camille Malavaux

Lucky guests get one of the balcony rooms, but the whole house oozes personality. It was built in 1930 by an Italian architect for the manager of the sawmill powered by the crystal-clear River Dessoubre that flows at the bottom of the garden. There are private fishing rights for enthusiasts, fabulous countryside for nature-lovers and a beautifully kept walled kitchen garden for fresh ingredients on the table every day. Inside, the house is still deliciously 1930s and the charming elderly Malavauxs have decorated it simply and fittingly in keeping with original features such as floor tiles - those extravagant patterns they loved so much - and fireplaces - wiggly marbles from an Art Deco catalogue. Walls are white, the décor is fairly minimalist with an occasional fling into ruched curtains, and the open stairwell with rooms leading off the landings reminds you that this was a family house. We felt it was just as old-fashioned as it needed to be and the neat, clean rooms were perfect for a very quiet night's sleep. People come back year after year.

Rooms: 6 doubles.
Price: €40-€61.
Meals: Breakfast €6; lunch & dinner €18-€27. Restaurant closed Wednesday lunchtimes.
Closed: 5 January-mid-February; 1st week October.

A36 exit Baumes les Dames for Pontarlier on D50. Left on D464 towards Sancey Le Long/Cours St Maurice for 2km to Pont Neuf. Right for Consolation for 0.5km. Hotel on left.

Burgundy

Without garlic I simply would not care to live.

Louis Diat (1885-1958)

M. Troncy, CDT Saône et Loire

Le Monestier

Le Bourg
71640 Saint Denis de Vaux
Saône-et-Loire

Tel: (0)3 85 44 50 68
Fax: (0)3 85 44 50 68
E-mail: lemonestier@wanadoo.fr
Web: www.lemonestier.com

Margrit & Peter Koller

We almost got lost here, but the valley is a very pretty place to get lost in. You drive into the large grounds through wrought-iron gates, past attractive outbuildings and a swimming pool set in the grass, with huge old trees nearby. It looks a little bit like a Home Counties golf club! But no. Margrit and Peter are Swiss and bought Le Monestier in 1999. Peter can be seen walking round in an apron. He is in charge of the cooking and you can expect some serious eating. Not to say that your host is serious; you will find he has a most un-Swiss sense of humour. The reception rooms are comfortable. One bedroom has its own loo and a bathroom down the corridor, but this is made up for by a private terrace on top of one of the towers. You will be very well looked after here and tennis, fishing, riding and golf are close at hand. More importantly for many: you will be in the very centre of the Côte Chalonnaise region and could go on foot to visit the vineyards of Mercurey, Givry and Rully.

Rooms: 6 twins; 5 with ensuite, 1 with separate bathroom and w.c.
Price: €70-€92.
Meals: Breakfast included; dinner from €18 - be sure to give advance notice for first night.
Closed: Occasionally between mid-November-mid-March.

A6 exit Chalon Nord for Chalon sur Saône; right for Châtenoy le Royal D978 for 9km for Autun. Left at r'bout for Givry. After 50-100m right on D48 for Vallée de Vaux until St Denis. Signposted.

L'Orangerie

Vingelles
71390 Moroges
Saône-et-Loire

Tel: (0)3 85 47 91 94
Fax: (0)3 85 47 98 49

David Eades & Niels Lierow

Ring the bell on the gate, then stroll up through neat gardens alive with colour. Light spills into the sitting room entrance through vine-clad arched windows, and cream walls and Indian rugs add to the simple elegance of this gracious *maison de maître*. Antiques and travel are David's passions, his gentle Irish brogue is enchanting. He not only makes excellent tea imported from Ceylon but his breakfasts are fit for a king (hardly surprising, since he also interviews European royalty for a glossy magazine). Evening meals should be reserved in advance. The grand staircase in the centre of the house could have come straight off a 1930s luxury cruise liner, while interesting paintings and stylish oriental fabrics contribute to a mix of styles that go perfectly together. The bedrooms, with their seersucker linen and antique prints, are lovely, and the bathrooms classically stylish. Being in the heart of Burgundy vineyard country, you are also in the heart of silence. Terraced lawns lead down to the swimming pool, the trees and meadows. Sybaritic, but in the best possible taste. *Cash or French cheque only. No smoking here.*

Rooms: 5 doubles/twins.
Price: €60-€90.
Meals: Copious breakfast included; dinner €30 incl. wine, by arrangement.
Closed: November-March.

From A6 exit Chalon Sud on N80 for Le Creusot; exit Moroges. Signposted from centre of village.

Auberge du Cheval Blanc

71390 Saint Boil
Saône-et-Loire

Tel: (0)3 85 44 03 16
Fax: (0)3 85 44 07 25

M & Mme Jany Cantin

A tonic if you are tired of the standardisation of all things. Everything about it - from the formal furniture, the striped wallpaper, the parquet floors, the great curtains gathered at the waist, to the gravelled courtyard with trumpet vines, white wrought-iron garden furniture, shuttered and dormer windows - is what the French do with such aplomb. Yet, having said all that, Jany and Martine make the place. He is a well-built Burgundian, a fitting descendant of generations of bons viveurs and creator of some spectacular dishes in the restaurant - across the road from the hotel. Martine's generosity and kindness add something very special to the hotel. It is a trifle functional upstairs, perhaps, as is often the case, but very much a *maison de maître* and up the most lovely wooden staircase. On the top floor the beams are exposed, and varnished. The two front rooms up there have charming *œil de bœuf* windows. Bathrooms are all fine, with nothing outstanding to report. Dine under the lime trees in summer and appreciate the survival of such places, and such people.

Rooms: 10 doubles.
Price: €62-€81.
Meals: Breakfast €10; lunch & dinner €29. Restaurant closed Wednesdays.
Closed: 10 February-10 March.

A6 exit Chalon sur Saône Sud on D80 for Le Creusot; D981 Cluny for 10km to St Boil. Hotel on right in village.

Hostellerie La Sarrasine

533 Route de la Madeleine
01750 Replonges-Macon Est
Saône et Loire

Tel: 03 85 31 02 41
Fax: 03 85 31 11 74
E-mail: hotel.sarras@free.fr
Web: www.sarrasine.com

M Bevy

Although close to a main road, La Sarrasine is protected by a high wall, hedges and a wide expanse of well-loved garden with flowering bushes, shady trees, and containers of cascading geraniums. M Bevy's grandparents raised the famous Bresse chickens here on this typical timber-framed farm - perhaps the welcoming committee of chickens are their direct descendants. The present young owners, both graduates of hotel schools, decided to take over the restoration which had already begun under his parents. Keeping close to the original architecture its seven rooms are on the ground floor, all with patio-like doors which open onto the garden or the countryside with sitting-out places adding to the charm. There are puffy peach-coloured coverlets, tapestry headboards and huge comfy ottomans. The bathrooms are not big but perfectly adequate and come in a variety of tiled colours. The restaurant, only open to guests, serves a choice of regional dishes: *escargots de Bourgogne*, Charolais beef - or Bresse chicken, of course.

Rooms: 7 doubles/twins.
Price: €61-€145.
Meals: Breakfast €10-€12; dinner €16-€53. Restaurant closed Wednesdays; also Tuesdays from mid-October-mid-April.
Closed: 7 November-20 December; 9 January-mid February.

From Paris towards Geneva on A40 exit 2 at Feillens. From Marseille A6 exit Macon Sud for Bourg en Bresse N79. Signposted.

Le Grand Monarque

33 quai Clémenceau
58400 La Charité sur Loire
Nièvre

Tel: (0)3 86 70 21 73
Fax: (0)3 86 69 62 32
E-mail: le.grand.monarque@wanadoo.fr

M Grennerat

A feast for the senses awaits you here: the great Loire flows at the feet of the Grand Monarque, her shimmering limpidity enveloping the old bridge and the little medieval town; Monsieur Grennerat's cooking is a treat for eyes, nose and palate. Passionate about food and wine, he actively encourages better taste and smell education among French and foreign, old and young - another warrior against junk food. A historical gold-mine, he will tell the tale of his 17th-century hotel as it shadowed the march of history. The suspended staircase, an architectural marvel, leads to totally French, flocked rooms on the first floor and brighter, more recent rooms on the second. Here, huge old structural timbers, recycled 300 years ago from disused transport boats, jut into bathrooms, embrace beds, frame roof windows. There are some four-posters, one mezzanine bathroom, embossed tiling and floral wallpapers - variety galore. Later, enjoy the 1930s atmosphere of the restaurant, the view of river and bridge, the intense subtlety of the table. France at her cultural best.

Rooms: 15: 12 doubles, 1 triple, 2 family.
Price: €54-€92. Family room price depends upon number of occupants.
Meals: Breakfast €8.50; lunch & dinner €15-€43. À la carte menu also available. Restaurant closed Sunday evenings low season.
Closed: Mid-February-18 March.

From the bridge of La Charité towards Nevers, hotel is 100m on right.

Le Relais Fleuri/
Le Coq Hardi
42 avenue du la Tuilerie
58150 Pouilly sur Loire
Nièvre

Tel: (0)3 86 39 12 99
Fax: (0)3 86 39 14 15

Philippe & Dominique Martin

Ideal for a quick stop, perhaps, rather than a long stay but if you like your French food you'll love it. Monsieur and Madame Martin bought Le Coq Hardi, and its reputation for its restaurant, five years ago and are gradually doing it up. Monsieur gained his experience at the Espérance at St Père-sous-Vézelay - one of France's top restaurants - and judging by the smiles of the customers staggering away at 4 p.m. it is probably worth staying here just for the food. In summer, meals are served on a vine-covered terrace overlooking the Loire. The hotel's original rooms upstairs are a bit gloomy, though some have terraces over the garden. One bathroom is high kitsch: black and yellow tiles and a green basin and fittings. The newly decorated rooms are in what appears to be a boat shed. They are all pleasantly done in blue or yellow but the best thing is the windows: some are arched, others have elegant stained glass. Philippe has added a small *boutique* so you may take away a plate or two with his sign of the cockerel. Ineffably, properly, French.

Rooms: 11: 10 doubles, 1 suite.
Price: €44-€69.
Meals: Breakfast €8; lunch & dinner €17-€40.
Restaurant closed Tuesday evenings & Wednesdays from October-end April.
Closed: Mid-December-mid-January.

From N7 south of Cosne sur Loire, north of Nevers, turn off at Pouilly. Signposted opposite Pouilly wine co-op building.

La Terre D'Or
Rue Izembart
La Montagne
21200 Beaune
Côte-d'Or

Tel: (0)3 80 25 90 90
Fax: (0)3 80 25 90 99
E-mail: jlmartin@laterredor.com
Web: www.laterredor.com

Christine & Jean Louis Martin

Jean Louis can share his love for Burgundy with you in many ways: he can indulge you in wine tasting and explain how those elegant vintages are produced, he can arrange cooking lessons with a local chef, or show you a vestige of Roman art. All this (and more) by bike, horseback, jeep or hot-air balloon. He and Christine have two houses ready for you, both surrounded by a large terraced garden and century-old trees. One is contemporary and multi-levelled, the other is stone-walled and traditional – both have sitting rooms and kitchens with everything that you need. The large bedrooms – each with a separate entrance – have wonderful views of the vineyards of Beaune; some have private terraces or patios. The Martins have used old beams and polished wine-growers tables and chairs. You might have one of your wine classes in the grotto under the house where a river used to run; the stalactites are still there. Jean Louis can also be persuaded to host a barbecue by the pool. This is the kind of place where you book for two nights and end up staying a week... *No smoking here.*

Rooms: 2 houses for 2-8. For parties of 6-12 persons the houses can be reserved exclusively.
Price: Doubles/twins €122-€178. Group price for 3-day theme holiday €686-€762 p.p.
Meals: Breakfast €10; picnic available.
Closed: Never.

From Beaune D970 for Auxerre/Bouze Les Beaunes. After 2km right to La Montagne. Well signposted.

Château d'Ecutigny

21360 Ecutigny
Côte-d'Or

Tel: (0)3 80 20 19 14
Fax: (0)3 80 20 19 15
E-mail: info@chateaudecutigny.com
Web: www.chateaudecutigny.com

Françoise & Patrick Rochet

This is a real castle. It was built in the 12th century to station soldiers guarding the Duke of Burgundy's land from the marauding French. Bits were added over the years but it was abandoned at the end of the 18th-century and fell to ruin, until it was rescued by Françoise and Patrick. The château is a historic monument, with secret passages and Rapunzel towers to prove it, but has been made light, airy and really beautiful inside, without a feeling of having been 'done up'. One room, for example, is in the palest muted colours - not quite pastels - and sparsely furnished with a subtle mix of country pieces and elegant antiques. Bathrooms are large, with cast-iron baths on feet. The floors throughout the château are either mellow terracotta or wood - you won't be walking barefoot on icy stone. Children will love exploring the cellars, stables and farm and Françoise will not be phased by them: she used to run a crèche! This may be why the place runs so smoothly. Comfortable and relaxed despite the grandeur.

Rooms: 6: 5 doubles, 1 suite.
Price: Doubles €76-€107, suite €152.
Meals: Breakfast included; picnic lunch with wine available; dinner €38, including aperitif & wine.
Closed: Never.

From A6 exit Pouilly en Auxois. Follow signs to Bligny sur Ouche, then Ecutigny. Take last turning on right on leaving village.

Map No: 9

Hostellerie des Clos

Rue Jules Rathier
89800 Chablis
Yonne

Tel: (0)3 86 42 10 63
Fax: (0)3 86 42 17 11
E-mail: host.clos@wanadoo.fr
Web: www.hostellerie-des-clos.fr

Michel Vignaud

Not for the faint-hearted; you have to eat dinner. But you may well have come here to do that very thing, in which case you may be close to heaven. (The nuns who lived here until the 1980s presumably were.) Monsieur - handsome, moustachioed, chef-hatted - is an aesthete and a foodie through and through. Eating is serious business, done with charm, intelligence, taste and, above all, professionalism. Some will shy away from the discreet formality, even opulence, but those who stay here are usually thrilled with it. The food upstages the rooms and their bathrooms, but that is no criticism. The dining room is a place of great, orange curtains held open with tassels, flowers on tables, white columns and delicate glassware. The sitting room is where you recover from the gargantuan gastronomic marathons, in formal, striped armchairs and at low mahogany round tables, perhaps before a log fire. It is a 12th-century building of classic beauty with a lovely garden, surrounded by vineyards. Words like 'refinement' spring to mind, even 'prestige' - but that is not our sort of word.

Rooms: 26: 24 doubles, 1 triple, 1 family.
Price: Doubles €48-€84, triple & family €100.
Meals: Breakfast €9; dinner €33-€69.
Closed: 20 December-mid-January.

A6 exit at Auxerre Sud. Hotel well signposted in Chablis.

Petit Manoir des Bruyères

89240 Villefargeau
Yonne

Tel: (0)3 86 41 32 82
Fax: (0)3 86 41 28 57
E-mail: infos@petit-manoir-bruyeres.com
Web: www.petit-manoir-bruyeres.com

Pierre & Monique Joullié

A Rococo place unlike anything you've ever seen. Behind the creeper-clothed façade with only the Burgundian roof as a clue, is eye-boggling glamour; a vast beamed living room, an endless polished dining table, rows of tapestried chairs and shiny ornaments. Upstairs, stagger out of the loo, once you've found the door in the trompe-l'œil walls, to cupids, carvings, gildings, satyrs, velvet walls and clouds on the ceilings. There's a many-mirrored bathroom reflecting multiple magical images of you, marble pillars and gold-cushioned bath; a Louis XIV room with red/gold bathroom with gold/ivory taps; an antique wooden throne with bell-chime flush. *Madame de Maintenon* has a coronet canopy, a long thin *œil de bœuf* window and a shower that whooshes between basin and loo. The 'biscuit' is taken by the deeply, heavily pink suite with its carved fireplace, painted ceilings and corner columns - wild! But such are the enthusiasm of the owners, the peace of house and garden, the quality of comfort, food and wine, that we feel it's perfect for lovers of French extravaganzas.

Rooms: 5: 3 doubles/twins, 2 suites.
Price: €91-€183
Meals: Breakfast included; dinner €38.
Closed: Never.

From Auxerre D965 to Villefargeau; there, right on C3 to Bruyères.

Paris - Ile de France

Since garlic then hath powers to save from death, bear
with it though it makes unsavoury breath. Salerno
Regimen of Health (12th century)

Hôtel des Tuileries
10 rue Saint Hyacinthe
75001 Paris

Tel: (0)1 42 61 04 17
Fax: (0)1 49 27 91 26
E-mail: htuileri@aol.com
Web: www.hotel-des-tuileries.com

Jean-Jacques Vidal

The charming Tuileries feels rather like a family house. The many oriental rugs - most of them on walls - sit well in the quiet old building as its delicate listed façade moves skywards to the rhythm of balconies, arches and mouldings. Great doors give onto a white hall with rugs, mirrors, pictures old and new, leading to the elegant little *salons*. A pretty lightwell illuminates this space and the basement breakfast room; a generous curving staircase leads upwards. The oriental element is general but never excessive: one room is like a soft Persian tent, another has a clever draping of yellow cloth over a white bed, there are Chinese-vase table lamps, paisley fabrics. Colours are skilful - a white room has dark blue carpet, pale blue damask curtains and bedcover, a richly-coloured rug behind the delightful cane bedhead. Lighting is good, there are pretty antiques, country pieces, modern units, good marble bathrooms. One room has a long narrow dressing table in carved painted wood and Empire bed and armchairs, smaller rooms can feel cramped, so splash out for space.

Rooms: 26 doubles/twins; 8 of these can become family rooms for 4.
Price: €139-€183.
Meals: Buffet breakfast €11. Meals available locally.
Closed: Never.

Metro: Tuileries, Pyramides.
RER: Opéra-Auber.
Car Park: Place Vendôme, Marché St. Honoré.

Le Relais du Louvre

19 rue des Prêtres St Germain l'Auxerrois
75001 Paris

Tel: (0)1 40 41 96 42
Fax: (0)1 40 41 96 44
E-mail: au-relais-du-louvre@dial.oleane.com
Web: www.relaisdulouvre.com

Sophie Aulnette

Look down the throats of gargoyles. Soak up the history. The Revolutionaries printed their newsletter in the cellar; it inspired Puccini's Café Momus in *Bohême*; it still rings with the famous carillon next door... and it's an utterly delightful place with charming staff. Antiques and oriental rugs complement the modernity of firm beds and perfect bathrooms (a few singles have showers). Front rooms look onto the church's Gothic windows and flying buttresses and along to the austerely neo-Classical Louvre; others give onto a light-filled patio. Top-floor suites have twin beds and a sofa, pastel walls, exuberant upholstery and heaps of light from mansard windows. The apartment is big and beautiful with fireplace, books, music, old engravings and a superb veranda kitchen. Other, smaller rooms are luminous, fresh and calm - yellow, a favourite colour, brings sunny moods into small spaces. You feel softly secluded and coddled everywhere. The sense of service is highly developed and, as there is no breakfast room, breakfast comes to you. On each floor, two rooms can make a family suite.

Rooms: 20 + 1 apartment: 18 doubles,
2 junior suites; 1 apt for 4-5
Price: Doubles €100-€160,
suites €198-€229, apartment €381.
Meals: Breakfast €9 (in bedroom);
light meals €5-€15.
Closed: Never.

Metro: Louvre-Rivoli, Pont Neuf.
RER: Châtelet-Les Halles.

Hôtel de Notre-Dame

19 rue Maître Albert
75005 Paris

Tel: (0)1 43 26 79 00
Fax: (0)1 46 33 50 11
E-mail: hotel.denotredame@libertysurf.fr

Jean-Pierre Fouhety

A stone's throw from Notre Dame but hidden from the tourist tides in a select little area of unusual shops and smart houses, this fine old frontage opens onto a large lobby adorned with tapestry, bits of antiquity and deep armchairs. Openness reigns - these people genuinely like people and greet you with smiles and humour. If the age of the building (1600s) is evident in its convoluted corridors, contemporary style dictates their smart black dados with tan or sea-green uppers. Bedrooms also mix old and new. There are beams and exposed stones, some enormous, and Cathedral views from the higher floors (through smaller windows). Like the 'porch' over each door, the custom-made desk units are pleasingly curvy and cupboards often have a useful suitcase space at floor level. The new padded upholstery is warm and colourful with contemporary mixes of yellow, red and blue and the translucent Japanese screen doors to bathrooms are an excellent idea for small layouts; not all baths are full size. The black eunuch officially portrayed as Marie-Antoinette's feathered fan bearer lived here...

Rooms: 34 doubles/twins.
Price: €139-€154.
Meals: Breakfast €6.
Closed: Never.

Metro: Maubert Mutualité.
RER: St Michel-Notre Dame (exit 3).

Le Notre-Dame Hôtel

1 quai Saint Michel
75005 Paris

Tel: (0)1 43 54 20 43
Fax: (0)1 43 26 61 75
E-mail: hotel.lenotredame@libertysurf.fr
Web: www.lenotredamehotel.com

Jean-Pierre Fouhety

At the hub of Latin Quarter life, students jostling on the pavements, cars pouring across the Seine, Notre Dame serenely unmovable just there, climb the mirrored staircase from the noisy embankment to the warm welcome inside. The hotel has been magnificently refurbished, reception rooms and corridors brightly decked in red checks, the *salon*-breakfast room extended: your eyes are caught by the plunging views of river, Cathedral and great 'police palace'. Most rooms have at least two windows onto this ancient picture; only the five cheapest, soberly pretty and quieter, give onto a dull courtyard. The very attractive rooms are not huge but uncluttered and full of light. Double-glazing keeps the noise out, air conditioning keeps the air breathable. Excellent fabrics are all from the house of Pierre Frey; a light cherry-wood laminate adorns desktops, bedheads and clever block panelling; hand-enamelled bedside lights from northern France and framed prints from England; dark green marble bathrooms with bright white fittings are extremely smart behind their translucid Japanese-style doors and the top-floor duplex suites are full of character.

Rooms: 26: 23 doubles/twins,
3 suites for 3.
Price: Doubles/twins €149-€198,
suites €244.
Meals: Breakfast €6.
Closed: Never.

Metro: St Michel.
RER: St Michel-Notre Dame (exit 3).

Le Sainte Beuve

9 rue Sainte Beuve
75006 Paris

Tel: (0)1 45 48 20 07
Fax: (0)1 45 48 67 52
E-mail: saintebeuve@wanadoo.fr
Web: www.paris-hotel-charme.com

Jean Pierre Egurreguy

Designer flair pervades this beautifully-refurbished hotel, known and loved during the wilder days of Montparnasse but now very quiet. The atmosphere is of light, unstuffy luxury - quiet good taste in gentle tones and thick furnishings (superb gold and ivory silk curtains). In winter a log fire burns in the old marble fireplace and clients often take a drink to one of the deeply embracing sofas to gaze into the flames. The attentive efficient staff are a vital element in your sense of wellbeing here. It is small and intimate, and so are the bedrooms. The general tone is ancient and modern: lots of white walls, soft colours and contemporary textured fabrics, the pastels modulated by more colourful chintzes and paisleys, at least one antique per room - a leather-topped desk, a walnut dressing-table, a polished *armoire*, old brass lamps - and 18th- and 19th-century pictures in rich old frames. The special *Sainte Beuve* room is extra-big and in dazzling good taste. Bathrooms are superbly modern with bathrobes and fine toiletries. Breakfast is a feast of croissants and brioches from the famous Mulot bakery, and fresh orange juice. *Book early.*

Rooms: 22: 21 doubles/twins
(4 interconnected), 1 suite for 3.
Price: €119-€297.
Meals: Breakfast €13; lunch & dinner
on request €6-€30.
Closed: Never.

Metro: Notre Dame des Champs, Vavin.
RER: Port-Royal.

Map No: 4

Hôtel Louis II

2 rue Saint Sulpice
75006 Paris

Tel: (0)1 46 33 13 80
Fax: (0)1 46 33 17 29
E-mail: louis2@club-internet.fr
Web: www.hotel-louis2.com

François Meynant

Imagination has triumphed in this charming hotel, often to dramatic effect (how about pink satin bamboo wallpaper in the loo?), so that even the smallest rooms (some are very snug with little storage) have huge personality. Two rooms have dazzling wraparound *trompe-l'œil* pictures set into the timber frame by the artist who painted the lift doors. On the top floor, sleep under ancient roof timbers in a long flower-papered room where crochet bed and table coverings are so fitting and there's an old rustic *armoire* or a 1920s cheval glass. One bathroom has brass taps and a yellow cockleshell basin, another has an oval bath and burnished copper fittings. Every room is different, sheets are floral, bath/shower rooms are small but fully-equipped. In the morning, admire the slightly worn elegance of the big sitting/breakfast room with fanned beams to carry the ceiling round the corner, gilt-framed mirrors, fine antiques and candelabras. You will be enthusiastically welcomed by manager and staff and properly cared for: they tend to treat guests like visiting friends.

Rooms: 22: 20 doubles/twins, 2 triples.
Price: €110-€165. Children under 5 free.
Meals: Breakfast €13.
Closed: Never.

Metro: Odéon.
RER: St Michel-Notre Dame.

Grand Hôtel des Balcons

3 rue Casimir Delavigne
75006 Paris

Tel: (0)1 46 34 78 50
Fax: (0)1 46 34 06 27
E-mail: resa@balcons.com
Web: www.balcons.com

Denise & Pierre Corroyer

Yes, it is balconied, and moulded, and corniced. But the delight is the Art Nouveau interior. Denise Corroyer, who teaches *ikebana* and flowers the hotel, copied the voluptuous curves of irises and bindweed from the 1890s staircase windows onto panels, screens and light fittings. There's a touch of humour in the life-size 'Negro boy' smiling on a shelf; a tinge of eroticism in the full-bodied Venus at breakfast; a sense of lightness and pleasure that owners and staff communicate. Service is the key here and Jean-François (Jeff to English-speakers), the owner's son, is enthusiastic about providing an ice machine, a superior selection of bathroom consumables, a clothes line over every bath and a practical meeting room where clients can work or children play. Rooms are not big but judiciously-designed units use the space cleverly and front rooms have, of course, balconies. At the back, you may be woken by the birds. It is all in prime condition with firm beds, good bathrooms, simple, pleasantly bright colours and fabrics. And breakfast is a feast which is free on your birthday.

Rooms: 50: 45 doubles/twins, 5 suites.
Price: Doubles/twins €83-€130, suites €150. Children under 10 in parent's room free.
Meals: Breakfast €9; afternoon tea available in winter from 4pm-8pm.
Closed: Never.

Metro: Odéon.
RER: Luxembourg.

Hôtel de la Tulipe - Tour Eiffel

33 rue Malar
75007 Paris

Tel: (0)1 45 51 67 21
Fax: (0)1 47 53 96 37
Web: www.hoteldelatulipe.com

M & Mme Fortuit

The utterly delightful Tulipe, once a convent, became a hotel for the 1890 *Exposition Universelle* and has rooms around the honeysuckled courtyard or over the quiet street. Most seem small but they all represent at least two cells. There are beams and stone, some yellow-sponged walls with deep red carpets, simple pine or cane furniture, patchwork bedcovers and white curtains, or bright Provençal prints and cream covers. Many bath/shower rooms have blue-pattern, country-style tiling; the renovated ones have bright sunflower-yellow paint. Two rooms, one for disabled guests, lead directly off the patio: it makes them feel specially connected. The breakfast/tea room is utterly charming with its pale stone tiles, blond timbers, slim-legged conservatory furniture and interesting paintings... and croissants fresh from the local bakery. Above all, together with the unpretentiousness of the friendly, intelligent Fortuit family and their hotel, we remember their smiles and relaxed manner. Famous neighbours are: the Poujeran bakery, the market on rue Cler, and the Androuet cheese shop. *The one room without a loo has its own across the landing.*

Rooms: 21: 20 doubles/twins,
1 family suite with two bathrooms.
Price: Doubles €91-€122,
suite €198-€214
Meals: Breakfast €8; lunch & dinner
available locally.
Closed: Never.

Metro & RER: Invalides, Pont de l'Alma, La Tour Maubourg.

Hôtel de Banville

166 boulevard Berthier
75017 Paris

Tel: (0)1 42 67 70 16
Fax: (0)1 44 40 42 77
E-mail: hotelbanville@wanadoo.fr
Web: www.hotelbanville.fr

Marianne Moreau

A deliciously Parisian hotel, with the elegance of inherited style, soft and welcoming like a private home. The Lambert family love their *métier* and are proud of their excellent interior design. The gracious reception area has a bar, deep sofas and a piano beneath Old Masters, mirrors and clocks. Top-floor rooms are magnificent: *Marie*, subtle tones of stone and earth, from palest eggshell to rich red loam, with a gauzily canopied bed, a sitting room onto a delicious little terrace (with Eiffel Tower view) and a brilliant bathroom behind thick, soft curtains; *Amélie*, sunnily feminine in pale yellow and soft ginger, rejoicing in its own balcony and a fine, old-style, bathroom (separate wcs in both). The other rooms, full of light, pale colours and intimacy, have a gentle, airy, soft-quilt-on-firm-mattress touch, period and modern furniture and good bathrooms. Staff - many have been here for years - are as friendly as the owners: the motto of the house might be "Know what they want before they say it".

Rooms: 38: 37 doubles/twins, 1 suite.
Price: Doubles/twins €110-€183,
suite €244.
Meals: Breakfast €11; light meals
€8-€20.
Closed: Never.

Metro: Porte de Champerret, Pereire.
RER: Pereire.

Hôtel Pergolèse

3 rue Pergolèse
75116 Paris

Tel: (0)1 53 64 04 04
Fax: (0)1 53 64 04 40
E-mail: hotel@pergolese.com
Web: www.hotelpergolese.com

Édith Vidalenc

So near the Arc de Triomphe, old Paris gives way to a festival of contemporary design as you pass the intriguing doors: use of light and materials - wood, leather, polished metal - and custom-designed furniture all contribute. Édith Vidalenc works with designer Rena Dumas to keep a sleek but warm, colourful, human hotel. Her own sense of hospitality governs staff attitudes: the team at reception are professional but don't take themselves too seriously - leagues away from the frostiness that often passes for 'de luxe' treatment. Hilton McConnico did the pictures and the brilliant carpet in the bar. An arch shape is the theme: in ash bedheads, lobby sofas before curved glass walls onto the patio, table legs, chrome washbasins. Tones are mutedly smart pastels so the dark-coloured breakfast room is a friendly morning nudge. The fairly small rooms are furnished in ash and leather with thick curtains and white bedcovers of soft skin-like material. The star *Pergolèse* room is a small masterpiece in palest apricot with a few spots of bright colour and a superb open bathroom.

Rooms: 40 doubles.
Price: €170-€320
Meals: Breakfast €12-€15;
snacks from €25.
Closed: Never.

Metro: Argentine.
RER A: Étoile Charles de Gaulle.
RER C: Porte Maillot.
Air France bus: Porte Maillot.

Les Jardins du Trocadéro

35 rue Benjamin Franklin
75116 Paris

Tel: (0)1 53 70 17 70
Fax: (0)1 53 70 17 80
E-mail: jardintroc@aol.com
Web: www.jardintroc.com

Katia Chekroun

Intimate, relaxed, lavish and fun - a listed building with exuberantly Napoleon III décor, when the motto was "Too much is not enough". Behind the bronze-leafed door, two Egyptian torch-bearers salute; muses beckon from landing walls; musical monkeys gambol across doors (all painted by Beaux Arts students). The atmosphere is young and casual - you are greeted by a sweet alabaster Beatrice - but efficiency and service are there, discreet and unobsequious. Lovers of the small and intimate will like it here; so will fans of French style. The gilt-mirrored, bronze-lamped *salon* has pure Second Empire furniture on a perfectly aged marble floor and drinks are served at a genuine custom-made bistro bar, *le zinc*. Don't expect big bedrooms (the 'executive' rooms are larger and very good suites can be organised) but enjoy their soft generous draperies and the genuine ormulu antiques that the owners took such trouble finding; surrounded by marble, luxuriate in your whirlpool bath and fluffy bathrobe, then descend for the 'worldwide tapas' served in the pretty basement dining room.

Rooms: 23: 18 doubles/twins,
5 suites all with whirlpool bath.
Price: Doubles/twins €136-€274,
suites €242-€396.
Meals: Buffet breakfast €15;
lunch & dinner from €15.
Closed: Never.

Metro: Trocadéro.
RER: Charles de Gaulle-Etoile.

Map No: 4

Hôtel Kléber

7 rue de Belloy
75116 Paris

Tel: (0)1 47 23 80 22
Fax: (0)1 49 52 07 20
E-mail: kleberhotel@aol.com
Web: www.kleberhotel.com

Samuel Abergel

The gilt-framed mirrors come from a derelict château - the owners love hunting for such delights. Behind the iron balconies, the atmosphere is determinedly French *Romantique* - witness the gilt-bronze-encrusted curly chests, elaborate lamps (one astounding desk light with hefty bronze stems and three big bunches of electrified (sic) grapes), period paintings and orientalisms (lifesize statues). The suite has a beautiful roll-top desk with Chinese inlay in its generous *salon* (which clients often use as a meeting room), a king-size bed and a kitchenette. All is rich in colour - reds, yellows, blues - and texture, in the smaller rooms too; bedding is new and twins can be zipped into king-size; tiled or mosaic bathrooms have all the necessary bits. The basket of fruit and chocolates in your room is part of Samy's warm welcome. In the refurbished ground-floor area, the breakfast buffet includes home-made jams and croissants as well as cereals, cheese and eggs for a fine start to the day. *English, Spanish, Hebrew, Japanese and Arabic spoken.*

Rooms: 22: 21 doubles/twins,
1 suite for 4.
Price: Doubles/twins €120-€212,
suite €212-€303.
Meals: Buffet breakfast €11.50; lunch
& dinner on request €15-€23.
Closed: Never.

Metro: Kléber.
RER: Charles de Gaulle-Étoile.
Taking avenue Kléber from Place
Charles de Gaulle-Etoile, turn left
at second light.

Hôtel Minerve

13 rue des Ecoles
75005 Paris

Tel: (0)1 43 26 26 04
Fax: (0)1 44 07 01 96
E-mail: minerve@hotellerie.net
Web: www.hotel_paris_minerve.com

Éric Gaucheron & Sylvie Roger

Éric Gaucheron brings all his energy and eagerness to please to his second hotel (his family started with the Familia next door) and that same friendly touch is here, as well as the stimulating university life outside. The red-carpeted, creamy-walled corridors lead to rooms that are not huge but often use the classic, cunning bed alcove for storage space. The higher you are the longer the view (Notre Dame and the Seine, on the street side of course) - top-floor rooms have some wild and wonderful timbers over their quirky shapes and rich red, gold and ivory colour schemes. Walls are decorated with those excellent sepia murals of French monuments, all different. Décor varies from brightly contemporary to soothingly granny, there are damask and satin, timber and tile, some good old bits of furniture and gilt-framed mirrors, some recent built-in cupboards, decent bathrooms that, again, vary in size. The lobby and sitting areas are generously big, light and airy with pleasant repro furniture, tapestries and bookcases. A deserving addition to the Familia's long-standing reputation for value and warm-heartedness.

Rooms: 54: 8 singles, 36 doubles, 10 triples.
Price: €64-€120.
Meals: Breakfast €6.
Closed: Never.

Metro: Jussieu, Maubert Mutualité, Cardinal Lemoine.
RER: Cluny-La Sorbonne.
Car park: Lagrange.

Hôtel des Croisés

63 rue St Lazare
75009 Paris

Tel: (0)1 48 74 78 24
Fax: (0)1 49 95 04 43

Madame Bojena

Not a single crusader (*croisé*) in sight, but one can well believe that the thick-carpeted, finely-carved stone and timber hallway was built as a bank in 1870. It soon became a hotel, and has never looked back. The best rooms carry wonderful legacies of those days of rich dark furniture and log fires: ceramic and marble fireplaces, superbly-crafted cupboards, inlaid beds, carved alcoves - one room even has a 'gazebo'. Not all rooms are as spectacular but choice ornaments are placed here and there and bathrooms are fine, some enormous. Curtains and bedding fit too: heavy velvets, lots of red, some pretty pastel piqués. In the attractive yellow and green breakfast room there's yet another fireplace, two interesting 19th-century busts on the well-garnished buffet table, wicker furniture and a lovely antique bird cage housing two plaster birds. The owner wants to keep the building's historical character, only looking for furniture with 1900-1930 lines. Madame Bojena, a gentle and efficient presence, has known and loved the hotel for years. There's double glazing, though the traffic dies down after 8pm.

Rooms: 27: 19 doubles, 5 twins, 3 suites.
Price: €66-€88; suite €99-€107.
Meals: Buffet breakfast €6.
Closed: Never.

Metro: Trinité d'Estienne d'Orves.
RER: Opéra-Auber.
Car park: 300m: consult hotel.

Hôtel du Danube

58 rue Jacob
75006 Paris

Tel: (0)1 42 60 34 70
Fax: (0)1 42 60 81 18
E-mail: info@hoteldanube.fr
Web: www.hoteldanube.fr

Monsieur Ferrand & Monsieur Sario

Built as a private mansion at the height of the Third Empire, this soft civilised hotel rejoices in a dazzling black and red *salon* (fascinating black-framed cane easy chairs) and a large, white patio where potted palms sit in summer, cast-iron garden tables can be laid for breakfast and elegant façades rise skywards. The quietest rooms look this way. Others have more activity - and more noise - under their double-glazed windows (the higher, the quieter). Style and comfort vary widely, twisty corridors change levels, it's a warm, long-lived-in place. Superb superior rooms have two windows, some very desirable antiques, armchairs and thick, smart fabrics, yet they feel intimate and friendly. Their bathrooms are carefully done too. Standard rooms all have the same blue-laminate bamboo-trim desk units and 'wooden-plank' wallpaper with some quaintly old-style bathroom tiling - but all necessities are there, of course. The attic standard room is in fact the most appealing of these. And everyone meets in the delicious countrified breakfast room and appreciates the bevy of young helpful staff at reception.

Rooms: 40: 34 doubles/twins,
5 suites for 2, 1 suite for 4.
Price: Doubles/twins €115-€160,
suites €191-€198.
Meals: Breakfast €9.
Closed: Never.

Metro: St Germain des Près.
RER: Musée d'Orsay.
Car park: St Germain des Près.

Map No: 4

Hôtel du Quai Voltaire

19 quai Voltaire
75007 Paris

Tel: (0)1 42 61 50 91
Fax: (0)1 42 61 62 26
E-mail: info@hotelduquaivoltaire.com
Web: www.hotelduquaivoltaire.com

Régine Lepeinteur

Oscar Wilde once declared that he "never looked out of the window" - torture for anyone staying here, where only four rooms do not see the Pissarro painting of quintessential Paris through their windows. Baudelaire also stayed here, as did Wagner and Sibelius: the Voltaire was something of an institution and still feels like a well-loved club with its rather worn golden-fringed armchairs in the panelled *salon* and its guests who come back again and again, some for over 30 years. Rooms are small, beds are the standard French 1.4m width, some baths are not for reclining, but mattresses are good, staff are superb old retainers and the welcoming atmosphere is warmly genuine. The manageress is lively, humorous and enthusiastic and has brightened the corridors with fresh paint and changed curtain fabrics so as better to frame that ineffable view. New bathroom fixtures should follow. She loves the contact with guests, old and new. However, you will need earplugs: the price of that view is no protection against riverside traffic noise. *There are three top-floor singles with a bathroom on the floor below at bargain prices.*

Rooms: 33: 5 singles with bath or shower, 2 singles with sinks sharing showers, 25 doubles/twins, 1 triple. *There are two top-floor singles with a bathroom on the floor below at bargain prices.*
Price: Singles €61, doubles/twins €99-€122, triple €145.
Meals: Breakfast €8.

Metro: Rue du Bac, Tuileries.
RER: Musée d'Orsay.
Car park: Musée d'Orsay.

Grand Hôtel de Champagne
13 rue des Orfèvres
75001 Paris

Tel: (0)1 42 36 60 00
Fax: (0)1 45 08 43 33

Madame Lauferon &
Monsieur Herbon

Old, alive with history and timbers, the Champagne was built in 1562 (spot the date on the wooden pillar by reception) on a street corner that was first recorded in the 13th century. Over the ages, it has been a monastery, a school and an inn: rooms were never big, corridors twisted and turned round the corner and the vast expanse of the panelled lobby does not prepare you for the more medieval proportions upstairs. The very smart Louis XIII dining room is big too, in its crimson and gold regalia. This is where you can indulge in a remarkably full and varied breakfast buffet. Bedrooms are sweetly, cosily cottagey, with more timbers and beams, cords and canopy effects, spriggy or stripey wallpapers, the odd little antique and glances at the great periods of French style - Louis XIII, XV and XVI. There are nooks, corners and crannies, as dictated by the ancient layout and the smart suites occupy two or three old rooms each. Bathrooms are imaginatively pretty. It is altogether enfolding and peaceful. Staff and manager are relaxed and smiling - he clearly likes his job and enjoys making clients as comfortable as possible. *No smoking on two floors.*

Rooms: 43: 40 doubles, 3 suites.
Price: Doubles/twins €115-€154,
suites €208-€304.
Meals: Buffet breakfast €11.
Closed: Never.

Metro: Châtelet, Pont Neuf.
RER: Châtelet-Les Halles.
Car park: Belle Jardinière.

Hôtel Nicolo

3 rue Nicolo
75016 Paris

Tel: (0)1 42 88 83 40
Fax: (0)1 42 24 45 41
E-mail: hotel.nicolo@wanadoo.fr

Catherine and her team.

Such a surprise! From the shopping frenzy of the elegant street, dip into the hidden entrance beneath one building, across a courtyard of acacia and evergreen into another. All is hushed, the old mosaic floor smiles at you, French Granny's sitting room opens up on your right, you are greeted by delightful staff who have known and loved the Nicolo for many years. And now new owners have brought new life in the form of many-splendoured furnishings, fabrics, pictures by artist friends that deserve attention - old engravings coloured 'in the manner of', pastels of Port Grimaud, a powerful parrot series - and turned the rooms into stunning sleeping spaces. They all give onto courtyards, of course, quietly. Lovely lacey-carved Indonesian screens have become voluptuous three-arched bedheads with original paintwork, fabric panels or birds and animals. Desks and tables are unusual Dutch, French or oriental antiques; lamps are surprising modern objects; pure white beds have thickly-striped quilts. Here are richness and purity married, and the bathrooms are luscious. A super place to stay.

Rooms: 28: 24 doubles/twins, 4 family rooms for 3-4.
Price: Doubles/twins €78-€89, family €114- €123.
Meals: Breakfast €6.
Closed: Never.

Metro: Passy, La Muette.
RER: Boulainvilliers.
Bus routes: 22 32.
Car park: Next door to hotel.

Hôtel Boileau

81 rue Boileau
75016 Paris

Tel: (0)1 42 88 83 74
Fax: (0)1 45 27 62 98
E-mail: boileau@cybercable.fr
Web: www.hotel-boileau.com

M & Mme Guirec Mahé

Way out west, ideally placed for tennis at Roland Garros, football at the Parc des Princes and family outings to the Bois de Boulogne, the Boileau is a house of peace and memory whose sweet little face is decorated with bright blue gold-lettered awnings. Young, with an easy, welcoming manner, the Mahés have a collection of ancient sewing machines, cash registers and gramophones to delight lovers of early mechanical devices; mirrors, furniture and pictures from Brittany and Morocco to please the traveller; a fresh green patio, humorously supervised by three dwarves, to bring light and air to the sitting and breakfast rooms at the centre of the three low spreading buildings. Rooms are simply delightful, nothing posh, nothing superfluous, just good warm colour schemes, some original painted Breton bedheads, some lamps in Arab filigree work, interesting pictures and good, pretty bathrooms. Oscar the parrot may talk to you at breakfast (a good spread), staff have been here for years and they are such friendly people! Far out perhaps, but excellent value and a perfect spot for those coming from or going to Normandy or Brittany.

Rooms: 30: 12 singles, 15 doubles/twins, 3 triples.
Price: Singles €66, doubles/twins €75, triples €107.
Meals: Breakfast €7.
Closed: Never.

Metro: Exelmans.
RER: Charles de Gaulle-Etoile.
Car park: Avenue de Versailles.

Etoile Park Hôtel

10 avenue MacMahon
75017 Paris

Tel: (0)1 42 67 69 63
Fax: (0)1 43 80 18 99
E-mail: ephot@easynet.fr
Web: www.hotel-etoilepark.com

Sylviane Leridon

This Haussmann-style building and the wide leafy avenue under its windows were built in the 1860s and No 10 has been a hotel, belonging to the same family, ever since. From some of the rooms they say you can see the sun rise over the Arc de Triomphe... and it is anyway a splendid sight up there, proud and solid with its magnificent sculptures. In the time she has been here, Madame Leridon has, with enthusiasm and taste, transformed the sitting area into a warm, unfussy 1930s space, in complete contrast with the grand exterior: natural materials - wood and stone, leather and linen - in plain colours, well-made artificial bouquets and very real cacti, and super pictures by Hilton McConnico. Round the corner is the bar with a discreet television set and the internet machine then, further still, the delightful breakfast room with lively deck-chair-stripe seating and a smooth modern buffet bar. For the moment, the bedrooms are less exciting, even somewhat spartan in their sobriety, and perhaps a little tired. Colour schemes are pale yellow, brown, ivory and dark blue, bathrooms are fine and good engravings hang on the walls. Well-placed and very welcoming.

Rooms: 28: 5 singles, 19 doubles/twins, 4 triples.
Price: Singles €84-€119, doubles/twins €130-€136, triples €151.
Meals: Breakfast €9-€12; meals on request €15-€30.
Closed: Never.

*Metro & RER: Charles de Gaulle-Etoile.
Car park: MacMahon.*

Hôtel Elysées Matignon

3 rue de Ponthieu
75008 Paris

Tel: (0)1 42 25 73 01
Fax: (0)1 42 56 01 39
E-mail: elyseesmatignon@wanadoo.fr
Web: www.elyseematignon.com

Alain Michaud & Jean-François Cornillot

Paris has many imitations of the 1920s Modern Style. The Matignon is superbly genuine 1924. Enter the rectangle-upon-rectangle porch, along the many-rectangled floor, stand under the perfect curves of the moulded ceiling light that grows out of those angles. You will be welcomed by people who are relaxed yet sensitive to your needs, a delightful contrast to the hustle of *Les Champs*. Each bedroom door reveals a large original fresco: landscapes or near-abstract still lifes, they are very proper given the original purpose of these rooms. Bathrooms have Art Deco mod cons and the older ones are being very fittingly renovated. Otherwise, there are discreet dark carpets, heavy curtains, co-ordinated quilted or textured bedcovers and head cushions, black metal bedside lights, fine inner blinds and adequate storage. Rooms, far from enormous, have a lobby (except the junior suites where a larger lobby houses the third bed and the cupboard). An evening venue for the Parisian 'in' crowd (11pm to dawn), the scarlet and black Mathis Bar puts on virginal white cloths for your breakfast - great fun, especially for night-lifers.

Rooms: 23: 19 doubles/twins, 4 suites.
Price: Double/twins €105, suites €198.
Meals: Breakfast €9; lunch & dinner on request €15-€23.
Closed: Never.

Metro: Franklin Roosevelt.
RER: Charles de Gaulle-Etoile.
Car Park: Champs Elysées.

Hôtel de l'Académie

32 rue des Saints Pères
75007 Paris

Pierre Chekroun

Tel: (0)1 45 49 80 00
Toll-free USA: 1 800 246 0041
Fax: (0)1 45 44 75 24
E-mail: academiehotel@aol.com
Web: www.academiehotel.com

When you push the door into this white-rendered, window-boxed building, you leave a bustling street for a cool, quiet haven. Young, shirt-sleeved, relaxed staff welcome you to the old-fashioned atmosphere of an antique-furnished hotel. The plain-painted walls are an excellent foil for old beams and choice pieces of furniture such as a vast two-layered, gilt-framed oval mirror or a grand old ormolu Louis XV chest with elaborate bronze fittings. A couple of little kidney-shaped bedside tables were a delight. The ground-floor breakfast room is cleverly arranged, incorporating an inner lightwell and playing with mirrors and infinite depths. You can have a catered dinner here too if you wish. Bedrooms and bathrooms are biggish, by Paris standards, and storage space has been carefully planned. The feel is of friendly yet professional people doing their best to make sure you return. It's good value for money and, to cap that, Monsieur Chekroun gives our readers up to 30% discount depending upon the availability of rooms.

Rooms: 39: 29 doubles/twins, 10 suites (4 with jacuzzis).
Price: Doubles/twins €99-€229, suites €229-€458.
Meals: Buffet breakfast €14.50; lunch & dinner €23.
Closed: Never.

Metro: St Germain des Prés.
RER: Musée d'Orsay.
Car park: Nearby, ask hotel.

Hôtel Saint André des Arts

66 rue Saint André des Arts
75006 Paris

Tel: (0)1 43 26 96 16
Fax: (0)1 43 29 73 34
E-mail: hsaintand@minitel.net

M Henri Legoubin

The old shop front of this relaxed, low-cost hotel beside the bustling St André crossroads has been known and loved by backpackers and intellectuals for years. They enter to a row of old choir stalls, a listed staircase and Henri, a former philosophy teacher who is happy to talk *philo* and Proust with them. But the old coconut matting has gone from the walls! White paint sets off the old timbers, new carpets are on their way, all windows are new and double-glazed, new little tiled shower rooms are being fitted. But nothing can ever hide how the building twists and turns round the courtyard. Some rooms are very small, one is reached across an interior balcony. Some have immensely high ceilings and great windows, beams, old stone walls, 16th-century style. Practical Rustic French antique furniture is set in a simple, pleasant décor. Breakfast is in the reception area at a wonderful great 'folding' table set on a trompe-l'œil black and white floor that was laid 200 years ago. The neighbourhood is lively, the music sometimes noisy and nocturnal, the atmosphere stimulating. If you feel you would like to join in, book early - it's often full.

Rooms: 31: 3 singles, 14 doubles, 14 triples/quadruples.
Price: Singles €53, doubles, twins, triples/quadruples €60-103.
Meals: Breakfast included.
Closed: Never.

Metro: Odéon.
RER: St Michel-Notre Dame

Map No: 4

Familia Hôtel
11 rue des Écoles
75005 Paris

Tel: (0)1 43 54 55 27
Fax: (0)1 43 29 61 77

Éric Gaucheron & Sylvie Royer

It is well named! And its two 'stars' are outshone by the glow of care and attention showered upon house and guests by Éric, his wife Sylvie, their son Charles and his parents Bernard and Colette. If the hotel looks grand from the outside with its elaborate balconies, their earnest wish is to welcome you as they would their own friends: enthusiastically. Beyond the hall, decorated by an artist friend, is the rich red breakfast/sitting room where the family's collection of leather-bound tomes and the thick oriental rug give a homely feel. This simple atmosphere informs the bedrooms. They are not large or 'Parisian chic' but each has either a lovely fresco of a Paris monument, a wall of ancient stones, an old carved bedhead or a balcony onto the fascinating street life - or a mixture of these. Carpets, wallpapers, bedcovers and curtains seem somehow comfortingly provincial and solid, not brilliantly trendy or stunningly matched. Bedrooms and the small bathrooms are being renovated and it's all spotless. Front rooms look across the wide street to a rich jumble of old buildings with the Ile Saint Louis just beyond. Ask Éric anything - he will answer willingly, at length and in fast English.

Rooms: 30: 27 doubles/twins,
3 family rooms for 3-4
Price: €66-€130.
Meals: Breakfast €5.50.
Closed: Never.

Metro: Jussieu, Maubert Mutualité,
Cardinal Lemoine.
RER: Cluny-La Sorbonne.
Car park: Lagrange.

Hôtel Centre Ville Etoile
6 rue des Acacias
75017 Paris

Tel: (01 58 05 10 00
Fax: (0)1 47 54 93 43
E-mail: hcv@centrevillehotels.com
Web: www.centrevillehotels.com

M Alain Michaud & M Idir Nasser

This tiny hotel has a definite style and tiny has not meant cosy. We like it for its difference. The shiny black desk and the 20-foot ficus tree are in a three-storey galleried well of light - an ingenious and original space - that gives onto a plant-filled *coin* where you can sit out for summer breakfasts. The décor may be a little sombre for some; it is based on an Art Deco style that dictates the black and white theme, with a chromatic glance at American Surrealism in the large original 1930s oil painting. There are prints from American cartoon strips and black carpeting with grey-white stripes like running water. Rooms are small but spaces are well used, though storage remains limited. They can be masculine in brown and black with one red chair or pastelly or elegant white, cream and grey. Bathrooms have white fittings, round basins, grey tiling, lots of mirrors, bathrobes. In contrast, bright red oriental-print cloths (on black tables) and airy Bauhaus wire chairs enliven the basement breakfast room. With so few rooms, staff have plenty of time to be friendly, helpful and really welcoming.

Rooms: 15: 10 doubles, 5 twins.
Price: €105-€151.
Meals: Breakfast €9; lunch & dinner on request €15-€23.
Closed: Never.

Metro: Argentine.
RER & Air France bus: Charles de Gaulle-Etoile.
Car park: 24 rue des Acacias

Hôtel de France

5 rue Colbert
78000 Versailles
Yvelines

Tel: (0)1 30 83 92 23
Fax: (0)1 30 83 92 24
Web: www.hotelfrance-versailles.com

M Laforgue

Bone-tired after a visit to the Château de Versailles? Why not walk across the regal Places des Armes and relax under the linden trees before retiring to your elegant room in this 18th-century town house. It beats fighting for a seat on the commuter train back to Paris and you can rise early the next morning and explore the magnificent gardens which deserve a day all to themselves. Louis XIV made a present of the land to Colbert who built his residence here. Four of the rooms look on to the Places des Armes and the Château itself while the others are perhaps quieter and in the back, some overlooking the indoor terrace of the restaurant. All are light and dressed for the ball, in reds, oranges, golds and yellows, with matching padded headboards, swathed windows and quilted coverlets. The bathrooms are small, very modern and carefully designed with impeccable grey marble counter tops and fresh white tiles with blue trim. Breakfast is served in a wood panelled room off the mirrored lobby - the blue and yellow table cloths blend harmoniously with the blue flower-patterned china service. *Don't miss the Baroque music, bubbling fountains and Versailles grand finale on Sunday afternoons.*

Rooms: 23: 12 doubles, 8 twins, 2 triples, 1 suite.
Price: Doubles, twins, triples €123-€159, suite €213.
Meals: Breakfast €9.
Restaurant next door.
Closed: Never.

From Paris A13 exit Versailles for Château de Versailles/Place des Armes. Stay on Avenue de Saint Cloud. Hotel is at end of avenue in front of Château de Versailles.

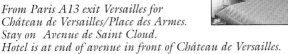

Abbaye des Vaux de Cernay

Route d'Auffargis D24
78720 Cernay la Ville
Yvelines

Tel: (0)1 34 85 23 00
Fax: (0)1 34 85 20 95
E-mail: aby_vau@club-internet.fr
Web: www.abbayedecernay.com

Éric Thomas

It may seem rather large but the buildings are so atmospheric, the place waves such a magical wand of respectful sophistication, that people stop, feel and lose their restlessness. From thriving Cistercian abbey, through Revolution and ruin to Rothschild ownership in the 1870s (the Rothschild suite has an astounding bathroom), Cernay bears the marks of European history. The Savrys have turned it into a luxurious hotel that preserves the spirit and forms of the old place - you can almost hear the monks scurrying along those underground passages while you listen to the Cernay Music Festival in the roofless abbey church or wine and dine in hedonistic splendour under the vaults of the brothers' refectory. There may be little trace of the 'Strict Observance' Trappist rule for daily life that once reigned here - bedrooms have every modern comfort, *salons* are highly elegant, there is a lake for meditation and a 'fitness garden' - but you cannot fail to be deeply influenced by the vibrations from those glowing stones and Gothic arches and glad that the hotel business keeps them alive today. *Various weekend packages available.*

Rooms: 57 + 1 apartment: 54
doubles/twins, 3 suites for 2; 1 4-room
Rothschild apartment.
Price: Doubles/twins €75-€242,
suites & apartment €290-€592.
Meals: Breakfast €12; brunch Sundays
& holidays; weekday lunch from €34;
dinner & weekend lunch €40-€62.
Closed: Never.

From Paris Pont de Sèvres for Chartres.
Exit Saclay for Chevreuse on N306. In
Saint Rémy les Chevreuse D906 becomes
D306 for Chevreuse; signposted in Cernay
La Ville for Auffargis D24.

Map No: 4

Cazaudehore - La Forestière

1 avenue Kennedy
78100 Saint Germain en Laye
Yvelines

Tel: (0)1 39 10 38 38
Fax: (0)1 39 73 73 88
E-mail: hotel@cazaudehore.fr
Web: www.cazaudehore.fr

M Cazaudehore

The rose-strewn 'English' garden is like an island in the great forest of St Germain and it's hard to believe the buzzing metropolis is just a short train journey away. The first Cazaudehore built the restaurant in 1928, the second built the hotel in 1962, the third generation apply their imaginations to improving both and receiving their guests with elegant French charm. The buildings are almost camouflaged among the greenery, summer eating is deliciously shaded under rose-red parasols; hotel guests have the elegant, beamed dining room with its veranda to themselves (there are several seminar and reception rooms). Food and wine are the main focus - the wine-tasting dinners are renowned and chef Jacques Pactol has developed a lighter, more refined version of the Périgord style, skilfully mixing tradition and invention: you will eat supremely well here. But bedrooms are much cared for too, renovated in refined, unostentatious style with good fabrics, original colour schemes - saffron, blue and lightning green, for example - period furniture and prints, and masses of character.

Rooms: 30: 25 doubles/twins, 5 suites.
Price: Doubles €168-€183, suites €229-€244.
Meals: Breakfast €13; lunch & dinner €30-€56; children's meals €20. À la carte also available. Restaurant closed Mondays, except for residents.
Closed: Never.

A13 for Rouen exit 6 for St. Germain en Laye on N186; N184 for Pontoise. Hotel on left 2.5km after château.

Château de Poigny

2 rue de l'Eglise
78125 Poigny la Forêt
Yvelines

Tel: (0)1 34 84 73 42
Fax: (0)1 34 84 74 38

François le Bret

In this big country mansion, the generosity of people and place sing the proper aristocratic poem of nobility and eccentricity. From Morocco, Indonesia and reddest America, this great traveller has amassed carvings great and small, artefacts ancient and modern, inlays and filigrees in brass, lacquer and wood, and filled his family mansion so that it has become a collector's paradise (and a housemaid's hell? It's unbelievably dustless). All is exuberance and love of life and beautiful things, bedrooms are a feast of almost baroque décor: the Coca Cola room is devastatingly... red (surely a unique collection), the Indonesian bed sumptuously rich, the Buddha's room softly, darkly meditative - there's a room for you, whatever your mood. The breakfast table bows beneath dozens of jams, honeys and teas and your vastly cultured host is very good company; on weekdays his delightful assistant Taïeb will take excellent care of you. There is a loo/library and a three-legged cat, exotic fowl who strut and cackle in the garden, stone boars to guard you and remarkable conversations to be had.

Rooms: 6: 5 doubles, 1 suite for 5.
Price: €52-€60.
Meals: Breakfast included. 3 restaurants in village.
Closed: Never.

From N10 north of Rambouillet D937 then D936 & D107 to Poigny la Forêt 5km. Left up road by church; château on right.

Normandy

I must tell you that I have had a whole field of garlic planted for your benefit, so that when you come we may be able to have plenty of your favourite dishes.

Beatrice d'Este, writing to her sister Isabella (1491)

J.F. Lefèvre, CDT Eure

Le Donjon

Chemin de Saint Clair
76790 Etretat
Seine-Maritime

Tel: (0)2 35 27 08 23
Fax: (0)2 35 29 92 24
E-mail: info@ledonjon-etretat.fr
Web: www.ledonjon-etretat.fr

M & Mme Abodib

An extraordinary building, this 1890s concoction of towers, turrets, Gothic windows and battlements all set about with creeping green, in its unforgettable clifftop position above the famous 'Hollow Needle' and pebble shore of Etretat. Its steep landscaped garden of flowers, shrubs and umbrella pines seem to rush down to meet the sea. Le Donjon has a perfectly cluttered eclectic interior to match the 'folly' exterior, an amusing mix of new, old, snazzy and dowdy with the refreshing lift of some good modern art. Three eating areas, one for each meal, all have the soul-gliding view. *Monet*, yellow and beamed, has pretty china and fancy gilt chairs to honour the chef's gourmet Normandy dishes. Here, there and everywhere in the higgledy-piggledy building, the pleasant and cosy bedrooms vary in style, some with canopied beds in Edwardian plush style or whimsically-draped modern metal, three with working fireplaces, nearly all with whirlpool baths. But above all, you will be forever returning to the serenely powerful or spectacularly violent drama of Nature enacted outside your window.

Rooms: 11: 9 doubles/twins, 2 suites for 4.
Half with view of ocean.
Price: Doubles/twins €88-€210,
suites €300-€500.
Meals: Breakfast €11; picnic & poolside snacks
available; lunch & dinner €29-€55.
Closed: Never.

*From Dieppe south on D940 + 17km to Etretat.
Hotel is off a small lane on right before town centre.
Drive runs up a steep hill. Signposted.*

Map No: 3

Auberge du Val au Cesne

Le Val au Cesne
76190 Croix Mare
Seine-Maritime

Tel: (0)2 35 56 63 06
Fax: (0)2 35 56 92 78
E-mail: val_au_cesne@hotmail.com

M Carel

Cupola-shaped cages of parrots, rare chickens, doves and parakeets hint at the exotic; the garden is hidden in an emerald, rolling-hilled Norman valley. Monsieur Carel, a self-made *patron*, will serve a leisurely meal outside on a sunny day - or invite you into the half-timbered farmhouse and place you in one of the two dining rooms separated by the chimney: Monsieur likes mixing locals with visitors, contrary to some owners who segregate the English language speakers. The low ceilings, raw timbers and sepia photographs of his ancestors are an appropriate Norman background for the regional dishes he creates. His customers come in droves now, so the cottage next door has been transformed into five little independent rooms, four of them on the ground floor. Each one has its own personality and the colours are as vibrant as your host's pet ducks: royal blues and reds, canary yellow and iris purple. Padded textiles on the walls make good soundproofing. The last one, lighter and bigger, is at the top of an outside stairway.

Rooms: 5 doubles/twins.
Price: €76.
Meals: Breakfast €8; lunch & dinner from €25. Restaurant closed Mondays & Tuesdays.
Closed: Last 3 weeks of January; last 2 weeks of August.

From Rouen A15/N15 for approx. 20km. Left on D22 to Fréville then D5 for Yvetot for 3km. Don't go into Croix Mare.

Hôtel de la Cathédrale

12 rue Saint Romain
76000 Rouen
Seine-Maritime

Tel: (0)2 35 71 57 95
Fax: (0)2 35 70 15 54
E-mail: arttra@club-internet.fr
Web: www.hotel-de-la-cathedrale.com

Laurent Delaunay

In one of the cobbled streets of historic old Rouen, the Archbishopric looming over it, is the only half-timbered hotel in a city of timber-frame houses. From some windows you see two Gothic marvels: the Cathedral towers and the magnificent tracery of St Maclou - your soul will be safe here. But a wind of material change is blowing over the hotel. The dynamic Delaunays have renovated the rather old-fashioned décor and bathrooms with due respect to the original features. The little half-timbered courtyard is a delight in summer with myriad flower pots and riotous creeper; a lovely spot for breakfast or afternoon tea. The indoor breakfast room has cotton tablecloths and a great old fireplace; it's friendly and fresh with comfortable armchairs. Rooms are simple; the ones overlooking the street the biggest, with old-style double wndows and elaborately-moulded cupboard doors. There are some interesting pieces in the motley mixture of furniture. Laurent Delaunay, attentive, eager to please and keen to put his plans into action, is running a remarkable-value hotel plumb in the middle of a city that cries out to be explored.

Rooms: 25 doubles/twins.
Price: €46-€63.
Meals: Breakfast €7.50; tea room for snacks; meals available locally.
Closed: Never.

In Rouen centre, proceed to Rue St Romain; first street along east side of Cathedral to unload luggage. This is a pedestrian street so park in 'Parking Hôtel de Ville', a 5 minute walk from hotel.

Map No: 3

Le Vieux Carré

34 rue Ganterie
76000 Rouen
Seine-Maritime

Tel: (0)2 35 71 67 70
Fax: (0)2 35 71 19 17
E-mail: vieux-carre@mcom.fr
Web: www.mairie-rouen.fr/fr/tourisme/hotels/carre

Patrick Beaumont

Originally a private town house, then a *maison close*, until as recently as the Second World War when the German officers came to play, the building is gloriously Rouenais, with beams galore and a little courtyard in front. The hotel runs around this space in a straight-sided U-form. The entrance is off-centre with some pretty potted herbs on the doorstep and then there's the reception area - a comfy and relaxing lobby with leather covered armchairs. Behind that is the tea-room where you can have a light lunch of warm braised leeks followed by a grilled sea bass; then pick a cake or fruit tart from the luscious display on the side board. The bedrooms are generally rather small and simply attired: light and fresh with colour combinations of ivory and old pink with 1930s wardrobes - all have bathrooms done mainly in blue mosaic tiles. Most views are over the attractive front courtyard. The roof garden has not yet been done but we have been promised potted apple trees and *chaises longues* here at a later date.

Rooms: 13: 1 twin, 12 doubles.
Price: €53-€61.
Meals: Breakfast €7; lunch & light meals from €12.
Closed: Never.

From autoroute exit Rouen Rive Droite for Hotel de Ville. In centre of town on pedestrian street, 30m from Parking du Palais.

Château de la Rapée
27140 Bazincourt sur Epte
Eure

Tel: (0)2 32 55 11 61
Fax: (0)2 32 55 95 65
Web: www.hotel-la-rapée.com

M Bergeron

You are not lost. It's just a long, winding road - 10km, through 80 hectares of deep forest in the Epte valley. With that in mind, just keep going, the road climbs up and up; not a house, cabin, animal, or road sign to distract you. Finally there is a little plateau at the edge of the world and - Wow! An extraordinary Victorian vision pops into view: a baroque Norman manor of angles, curlicues, overhanging roofed windows, turrets, watchtowers and red brick trim. Monsieur Bergeron *père*, who bought the house many years ago and kept it intact, is quite the gentleman rake; he never uses green in the hotel as it is "not flattering for the ladies". Maybe that is why the circular glassed-in dining room is so feminine with fresh pink cloths and *vieux rose* walls and ceiling. The bedrooms are uncluttered and nicely painted in satiny cream pastels; a canopied bed in one room, good mattresses and linens, carpet on the walls; working chimneys in the dining and sitting rooms. Mad, wonderful, passionate - special.

Rooms: 13 doubles/twins.
Price: €73-€89.
Meals: Breakfast €9; lunch & dinner €26-€35. Restaurant closed February.
Closed: 16-30 August.

From Gisors D915 north for approximately 10km. Signposted.

Map No: 4

Le Moulin de Connelles

40 route d'Amfreville sur les Monts
27430 Connelles
Eure

Tel: (0)2 32 59 53 33
Fax: (0)2 32 59 21 83
E-mail: moulindeconnelles@moulindeconnelles.com
Web: www.moulindeconnelles.com

M & Mme Petiteau

Bring your boater, hop in a green and red-trimmed flatboat right out of a Monet painting, and slip along a quiet arm of the Seine after a morning at Monet's Giverny garden, twenty minutes away. Watery greens, pinks and that scintillating veil of haze that is so particular to this part of Normandy intensify the Impressionist mood. Then look up at the vision of an extraordinary half-timbered, checker-boarded, turreted manor house and you will have to pinch yourself, hard. What's more, you are a treasured guest here. The Petiteau's quiet attentions extend from the tinted glass on the restaurant veranda to the in-house baked croissants and the pre-dinner *amuse-bouches*. Step around to the garden and marvel at the rows of copper pots through the kitchen windows. It's only after a moment that you realise that part of the house is on an island; hidden paths lead through flowering bushes to a private pool and tennis courts. We loved Room Nine with its yellow walls, blue trim and a balcony overlooking the river but our favourite was Suite Seven in the tower, with double exposure. Bring your paintbrushes.

Rooms: 13: 7 doubles, 6 suites for 4.
Price: Doubles €99-€145, suites €138-€191. Half-board €179-€271 for 2.
Meals: Breakfast €12; lunch & dinner €30-€50; children's meals €12.
Closed: January.

From A13 exit 18 on N15 towards Pont de l'Arche for 4km; right to St Pierre du Vauvray, Andé and Connelles. Signposted.

Château de Brécourt

Douains
27120 Pacy sur Eure
Eure

Tel: (0)2 32 52 40 50
Fax: (0)2 32 52 69 45
E-mail: chateau.brecourt@wanadoo.fr
Web: www.chateauxandcountry.com/chateaux/brecourt

Mme Langlais

It's worth a night here just to get the instant access to the Monet's Gardens at Giverny that the miracle-working Madame Langlais will conjure up. On top of that it's quite a fine little place. It is a moated, national historic monument, with a low, raw-beamed dining room that catches the breath and a heart-melting feast of brick and stone. There are chimneys you can hide in, floor tiles polished by centuries of leather soles, a triple staircase with sculpted oak balustrade that would probably not fit into your house, a Louis XV wood-panelled dining room of rare elegance, mosaics on some bathtubs, *tissu* on the walls and, perhaps most importantly, well-worn leather sofas in front of the fireplace. The red of some of the walls is as bold as the blues of the nearby curtains. Needless to say, the bedrooms are gigantic and look over the great park of 20 hectares, enough to lose yourself in if the crowds at Giverny have got to you. On Fridays you can, if you have planned ahead, eat a 17th-century meal; on other days you eat just as well. And everywhere a faint smell of burning logs - perfect.

Rooms: 25 + 5: 25 doubles;
5 apartments for 4-5.
Price: Doubles/twins €76-€165;
apartments €187-€217.
Meals: Breakfast €12; lunch & dinner from €37.
Closed: Never.

From A13 exit 16 onto D181 Pacy sur Eure then immed. left on D75 to Douains. Signposted.

Map No: 3

Hôtel de la Poste

27210 Beuzeville
Eure

Tel: (0)2 32 57 71 04
Fax: (0)2 32 42 11 01

M & Mme Bosquet

Generations ago this was an old postal inn and now the Bosquet family have proudly created a small, solid, very French town-centre hotel. Entering through blue archways you are warmly met in the friendly reception area. From here you are led up a dramatic stairway to carpeted, floral bedrooms with generous double beds. Rooms on the garden side are quiet, but there could be some disturbance at the front on Tuesday, the weekly market day. The restaurant is perfect for the place, in a slightly bistro-ish way - fresh flowers on the tables, views to the newly planted garden and a majestic bar which spans the room. The regional food is specially well cooked and served. Town square activity can be observed from the small terrace in front; dining extends out to the smaller terrace inside the archway. The Bosquets welcome families and their fixed price menus and modest room prices should leave change for future exploration of this rich area. Beuzeville is on the road to Port l'Evêque, ten minutes drive from Honfleur and has some interesting antique shops of it's own. Engagingly, unpretentiously 'correct'.

Rooms: 14: 11 doubles, 2 triples, 1 quadruple.
Price: Doubles €40, triples/quadruple €60-€69. Half-board for 2 €102-€114.
Meals: Breakfast €6.50; lunch & dinner €17-€30. Restaurant closed Thursdays September-June.
Closed: Mid-November-April.

From Paris/Rouen A13 exit 28 left on N175 for Beuzeville.
Between Pont Audemer, Rouen and Pont l'Evêque.

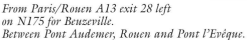

Map No: 3

Hôtel le Petit Castel

Auberge du Cochon d'Or
Place du Général de Gaulle
27210 Beuzeville
Eure

Tel: 02 32 57 76 08
Fax: 02 32 42 25 70
E-mail: auberge-du-cochon-dor@wanadoo.fr
Web: www.le-cochon-dor.fr

Catherine & Olivier Martin

If you are looking for somewhere to stay on the way to or from the boat in Le Havre, this might be just what you are looking for. Our inspector's 'fussy' (surely not…) mother has stayed here four times and loved it, and Olivier and Catherine have built up a group of not very young but very loyal returnees. This is not to say that children are not welcome: they are and the huge sandy beaches are only a short drive away. The grown-ups are close both to the smart shops of Deauville, the shellfish platters in Trouville or the quaint old port of Honfleur. A typical 19th-century town house, almost out of place in this little rural town - large village? Ten rooms look over a pretty garden: try for one of these as the road is rather busy. Rooms may strike you as light, flowery and delightfully comfortable or some are a touch over quilted and padded. The choice of menus in the attractive restaurant is not set in stone: you can pick and choose - within reason - which we thought a nice touch.

Rooms: 20: 13 doubles/twins, 3 family rooms in hotel; 4 doubles above restaurant.
Price: Doubles/twins and family rooms €42-€52. Half-board €52p.p. for a double room.
Meals: Breakfast €6; lunch & dinner €14-€40.
Closed: Mid-December-mid-January.

*From Paris/Rouen A13 exit 28 left
on N175 for Beuzeville.
Hotel in village centre opposite Town Hall.*

Map No: 3

Le Pavillon de Gouffern

61310 Silly en Gouffern
Orne

Tel: 02 33 36 64 26
Fax: 02 33 36 53 81
E-mail: gouffern@chateauxhotels.com
Web: www.chateauxhotels.com/gouffern

Mme Isabelle Ternynck & M Gasnault

More mansion than lodge, Gouffern was built 200 years ago by a wealthy gentleman with plenty of fellow-hunters to entertain. But the scale of this elegant 'pavilion' is perfect for today's traveller. It stands in an estate of 80 hectares and guests can walk, bicycle or ride in the private forest in total peace and seclusion. Inside, the big windows let in lots of soft light to illuminate Isabelle Ternynck's new décor: simple, unfussy elegance with rug-strewn oak floors, antiques and rich fabrics giving a sense of the quiet class of a good country house. Bedrooms, some of them in the well-converted outbuildings, are big and eminently comfortable (smaller on the top floor), functional bathrooms have all the necessary bits and meals are served in the handsome dining room - the food has been much praised. So has your hostess's smile - she and her staff are genuinely pleased to look after you. In the grounds, the delightful Dolls' House, built for children of another age to play in, is now an idyllic suite (honeymoon specials arranged)… and you may play billiards by the fire in the bar.

Rooms: 20: 19 doubles, 1 suite.
Price: Doubles €42-€76, suite €107.
Meals: Breakfast €8; picnic available;
lunch & dinner €15-€28.
Closed: Mid-November-mid-April.

Exit Argentan for Paris on N26.
Hotel is 7km from Argentan in the forest of Silly en Gouffern.

Hôtel Saint Pierre

6 rue de la Liberation
61150 Rânes
Orne

Tel: (0)2 33 39 75 14
Fax: (0)2 33 35 49 23

Françoise & Marc Delaunay

Legend has it that a fairy left a tiny footprint on the top of the tower in this small town. They say she disappeared in a flash upon a forbidden word whispered by her husband, impatient at her tardiness. Madame Delaunay is the keeper of the tower keys and the owner of this large flint stone house, rebuilt in 1953, just across the road. So pocket the keys and explore the castle on your own - the surrounding park makes for a wonderful evening stroll. Monsieur and Madame are justly proud of their Norman heritage and of their region's top class produce. Marc uses these for his regional dishes; you can also buy choice pâtés, tripe, calvados and *pommeau*, a light cognac with strong apple-juice overtones. As for the rooms, much care has gone into the co-ordinated drapes, bedcovers and wallpapers; bathrooms are on the small side. This is a family affair and the Delaunays obviously enjoy the profession and particularly the contact with guests. There is even a baby alarm system and parents can choose to give their children an early dinner and then enjoy a meal on their own, while the little ones join the land of the tiny footprints.

Rooms: 12: 9 doubles, 3 triples. Some rooms interconnect.
Price: €38-€53.
Meals: Breakfast €6.50; picnic available; lunch & dinner from €11-€30. Restaurant closed Friday evenings (simple meal in room available).
Closed: Never.

From Argentan D924 for Flers.
After Ecouche left on D916 to Rânes.
Hotel just off r'bout in town centre.

Auberge de la Source

La Peleras
61600 La Ferté Macé
Orne

Tel: (0)2 33 37 28 23
Fax: (0)2 33 38 78 83

Christine & Serge Volclair

Using reclaimed beams and stone, Christine and Serge built the Auberge de la Source - they did a lot of the work themselves - on the site of his parents' 18th-century apple press. Unfortunately that means no more cider made here, but they serve a superb one made just down the road. Both the restaurants - one smaller and cosier, the other with huge sliding windows - and the bedrooms were designed to make the most of the view down to the lake, which is the hub of a huge sports complex. Apart from windsurfing and a sailing school, there's riding, a climbing wall, archery, fishing and something called 'swing-golf', easy to learn apparently. Children have a play area, pony rides, mini-golf and pedal boats. If you want 'natural' nature the forest is nearby where you will see huge stags without too much searching. The auberge has big rooms catering for families, all cosy with huge beams and chunky antiques mixed in with more modern furniture. The food is simple, centring on steaks cooked over a wood fire, with fresh farm produce to go with them. A great choice for families with either small children or sporty teenagers.

Rooms: 5: 1 double, 4 family.
Price: €46-€76.
Meals: Breakfast included; picnic €8; lunch & dinner €13.
Closed: Never.

From La Ferté Macé, D908 for Domfront Mont St Michel. After 2km right to auberge. Signposted.

Manoir de Courson

Notre Dame de Courson
14140 Livarot
Calvados

Tel: (0)2 31 32 30 69
Fax: (0)2 31 32 30 69
E-mail: gggoy@aol.com
Web: www.manoirdecourson.com

Gérard & Sopheakna Goy

The majestic manor dating back to the 11th century displays its timbered splendours opposite the guest building but you breakfast over there in the handsome beamed dining room by the truly monumental fireplace. Your smiley, eager hosts have put hearts and talent into this restoration of the guest quarters. Gérard's eye for detail and Sopheakna's Cambodian origins inform the décor: Eastern antiques and contemporary art in perfect harmony with the stones and woodwork of the ancient frame; exquisite bedrooms - original crooked beams, painted or plain; seagrass matting and oriental rugs on smooth old terracotta tiles, fabulous, unusual bathrooms. Each unit has it's separate entrance, sitting room and panoramic eyeful of this lovely old (listed) house. The pool is well hidden behind a hedge surrounded by exotic plants in large terracotta pots. When you wake at dawn and find your place on the weathered bench outside your bedroom, all is idyllic silence as you gaze upon apple orchards, woodland and pastures; the cows in the distance are almost immobile in their meditative munchings. Not one mistake: worth every cent.

Rooms: 5: 3 large suites with views of manor; 2 doubles in manor.
Price: €95-€144.
Meals: Breakfast €10; picnic hampers available for lunch or dinner €17.
Good restaurant 1km.
Closed: November-March.

From Paris A13 exit Chaufour (2nd exit after Mantes toll). Through Evreux N13 to Orbec. Through Orbec for Livarot. 10km from Orbec, after water tower, 2nd right; 400m on left.

Aux Pommiers de Livaye

RN 13, Notre Dame de Livaye   Tel: (0)2 31 63 01 28
14340 Crèvecœur en Auge   Fax: (0)2 31 63 73 63
Calvados   Web: bandb.normandy.free.fr

Germain & Marie-Josette Lambert-Dutrait

Some have come for a day and stayed for a fortnight; all have been delighted with the warmth of the welcome and the quality of the food. A long drive bordered by chestnut and apple trees leads to the 300-year-old half-timbered Norman farmhouse smothered in climbing roses and wisteria. The entrance and glassed-in dining room are full of country-farm-style tables and chairs and have a beautiful view of the Lambert's lush green fields where horses, cattle and the occasional deer graze. One wall is lined with home-made jams and dried flowers, and antique plates vie for space above the timbers. The ground floor bedrooms are charming; water-green painted brass beds against pale yellow walls, a joyful selection of pink and green eiderdown coverlets. Marie-Josette judiciously uses *pochoir* patterns to repeat the colours. The towels are prettily presented wrapped with a ribbon - a sweet touch. No tourist office could give you such a personal introduction to the region as do Germain and Maire-Josette; an invaluable asset to guests. They have even mapped out a series of walking tours for you.

Rooms: 5: 1 double, 1 triple,
2 quadruples, 1 suite.
Price: €69-€84.
Meals: Breakfast included; dinner
€15-€23.
Closed: December-March.

*From Lisieux N13 west for Crèvecœur
15km. Hotel 1km before Crèvecœur;
signposted.*

Aux Repos des Chineurs

Chemin de l'Eglise
14340 Notre Dame d'Estrées
Calvados

Tel: (0)2 31 63 72 51
Fax: (0)2 31 63 62 38
E-mail: reposdeschineurs@aol.com
Web: www.au-repos-des-chineurs.com

Mme Claudine Steffen

An excellent stopping place for weary antique hunters (*chineurs*). We wonder if Madame Steffen named it after herself as everything here is for sale. You can finish your paté and fruit tart and walk away with the Lloyd Loom garden chair and the porcelain tea set - the furniture and accessories are mainly English. Built in the 17th century as a relay post, it is highly possible that Henry IV (whose mistress Gabrielle d'Estrées lived in this village) and Louis XV stayed here. The present bedrooms were converted out of the stables and the whole building has an old-fashioned atmosphere: from the old tiled floors downstairs to the exposed stone walls and the heavy oak beams. Our inspector loved the picture postcard gem of a church just up the road and the intimate garden, complete with stream. The bedrooms are cosy cottage style with neat bathrooms, smallish windows, small beds and views towards the church, lush lazy meadows and apple orchards. Roadside rooms might be disturbed during the day but this part of the country goes to bed early. *No smoking here.*

Rooms: 10: 9 doubles/twins;
1 suite for 4.
Price: €58-€100.
Meals: Breakfast €9; light meals and tea time snacks €3-€9.
Closed: January (open by reservation).

From Lisieux N13 towards Caen for 17km; 3km after Crèvecoeur en Auge, right onto D50 at St Jean crossroads. Hotel on left after 1km.

Map No: 3

Hostellerie de Tourgéville

Chemin de l'Orgueuil
14800 Tourgéville-Deauville
Calvados

Tel: (0)2 31 14 48 68
Fax: (0)2 31 14 48 69
E-mail: hostellerie@hotel-de-tourgeville.com
Web: www.hostellerie-de-tourgeville.fr

Wilhelm Stoppacher

There were real stars in the '70s, when film director Claude Lelouch built his glorified 'Norman quadrangle' as a club for friends; now there are just giant photographs. But his adorable private cinema is still here, as are pool, gym and sauna. Timbers and stones are genuinely old; the all-glass ground floor is thoroughly modern. Open-plan sitting and dining areas are in blond oak, soft cushions and warm colours. The chef has an excellent reputation, by the way. Most rooms are soberly decorated with high-quality fabrics, matt satin curtains, beige carpet, the odd antique and those ubiquitous film stars. Ground-floor rooms have small private terraces and triplexes (effectively up-ended suites with the bathroom on a balcony between *salon* and bedroom), fine double-height fireplaces on their stone-flagged floors, plus two deep sofas. The friendly manager is gradually redecorating with a more lively, contemporary touch, interesting, amusing furniture and some superb, strong colour. A very special place to stay; Lelouch calls it "an hotel for people who don't like hotels".

Rooms: 19: 6 doubles, 13 suites.
Price: €100-€137, suites €130-€274.
Meals: Breakfast €13; dinner €31-€48.
Closed: 3 weeks in February or March.

From A13 exit towards Deauville; after Canapville left at r'bout D27 for Caen; 1st left; 1st left D278; 1st right; entrance 600m on left.

Manoir de la Rivière

14310 Saint Louet sur Seulles
Calvados

Tel: (0)2 31 77 96 30
Fax: (0)2 31 77 96 30
E-mail: manoir-de-la-riviere@wanadoo.fr
Web: www.chateaux-france.com/manoirdelarivière

Docteur Jean-Claude Houdret & Aurélien Hourdret

A theatrical place tucked away in the hills of rural Normandy. The outbuildings of this traditional, mellow-stoned 16th-century farmhouse have been converted into guests' extravagantly themed rooms. The *Angel Room* is painted an iridescent white and blue; a fresco of the pyramids graces the *Explorer's Room* - painted by monsieur himself - and the *Colonel's Room* is eccentrically kitted-out with guns, swords, military coins and a life-sized model of a 19th-century soldier. Lots of the artefacts, including the embroidered bathrobes, are for sale. Bathrooms are spotless and immaculate. The guests' sitting room is stone-walled and coir-carpeted, with a wonderful suite of pink, gold and white Louis XV armchairs upon which the Princess of Wales, we are told, once sat, and a big open fire. The *manoir's* warm welcome extends even to your dogs, whose kennels are centrally-heated. More plans are in the pipeline from the unstoppable Docteur Houdret: a concert room, a beauty treatment room, a reception room for grand occasions and yet more improvements to the formal gardens and grounds.

Rooms: 5: 4 doubles, 1 suite for 4.
Price: Doubles €76-€100, suite €122-€152.
Meals: Breakfast included; dinner €23.
Closed: Never.

From Caen N175 to Villers Bocage. There, right to St Louet sur Seulles; pass church - house is second on right up poplar-lined drive.

Ferme de la Rançonnière

Route d'Arromanches
14480 Creully
Calvados

Tel: (0)2 31 22 21 73
Fax: (0)2 31 22 98 39
E-mail: hotel@ranconniere.com
Web: www.ranconniere.com

Mme Vereecke & Mme Sileghem

A matronly farmer was unloading vast quantities of fresh eggs from a wrinkled grey *deux chevaux* as we drove through the crenelated carriage gate, past the 15th-century tower into the vast grassy courtyard around which are the reception, restaurant and bedrooms of the La Rançonnière. Some went into a tiny corner store set in the massive sandstone wall to sit with local cheeses, cream and potatoes. The others were whisked into the oak-beamed, vaulted restaurant laid for lunch; white linen, tiny pink bouquets and a cheerful wood fire at one end. In summer you can dine in the courtyard. Young, efficient Isabelle Sileghem and her husband, with help from a devoted staff, keep this place humming. There are exposed timbers everywhere, and the comfortable bedrooms have small windows and rustic, sometimes heavy furniture. An antique butter churn in the corridor and a well-worn kneading trough in a large family room remind you that this is a working farm. A new annexe in an old farmhouse down the road might be quieter on the weekends. Book ahead for the best rooms. A wonderful old place.

Rooms: 45: 35 doubles/twins, 10 junior suites in 'manoir' 600m away.
Price: Doubles/twins €44-€88, suites €104-€134.
Meals: Breakfast €10; lunch €9-€43; dinner €15-€43.
Closed: Never.

From Caen exit 7 to Creully on D22 for 19km. There right at church for Arromanches on D65. In Crépon, hotel first on right.

Le Château de Sully

Route de Port en Bessin
14400 Sully
Calvados

Tel: (0)2 31 22 29 48
Fax: (0)2 31 22 64 77
E-mail: chsully@club-internet.fr

M & Mme Brault

From the veranda, the view of giant crescent-shaped flower beds filled with flamboyant mixtures of tangled flowers is quite stunning. This elegant 18th-century building combines classical architecture with an exquisite setting, every detail inside and out carefully orchestrated. Yellow is the dominant colour for the formal dining room, while russet reds tone in with the bar and sober leather sofas in the main salon. In another lounge, table-games and a billiard table guarantee some fun too. The first-floor bedrooms looking out over neat lawns are beautifully decorated, and the attic rooms one floor up are cosy and inviting. There are more bedrooms, an indoor pool and fitness centre in the *petit manoir* annexe. There are traces of children's paintings still to be seen in the 16th-century chapel, and lots of outdoor space for today's children. Inside, however, the little darlings will have to resist the temptation to thunder past delicate objects, as well as promise to sit up straight in the dining room. Good value, remarkably, for this really is a most magnificent place.

Rooms: 22: 19 doubles, 2 triples, 1 suite.
Price: Doubles €95-€183, triples €128-€136, suite €160-€183.
Meals: Breakfast €11-€13; lunch & dinner €30-€68. Restaurant closed Monday, Tuesday & Saturday lunchtimes.
Closed: December-March.

From Bayeux D6 for Port en Bessin. Château on right approximately 4km after Bayeux.

Map No: 2

La Chenevière

Escures Commes
14520 Port en Bessin
Calvados

Tel: (0)2 31 51 25 25
Fax: (0)2 31 51 25 20
E-mail: la.cheneviere@wanadoo.fr

M Esprabens

Very near to the debarcation beaches, La Chenevière sits in the middle of a magnificent park with century old trees. The 19th-century manor house has finely-proportioned common rooms all done in soft pastels and honey-coloured hardwood floors. Off-white curtains gently frame the light coming through the French windows which line the length of the corridor of the two *salons* (one for non-smokers) leading into the airy dining room. There are freshly-cut flowers and displays of vermillion wax stamps and architectural drawings on the walls. The rooms, all of which overlook the park, are vast and quiet; the corner ones have double exposition. Some have bright flower strewn beds, some are sober with toile de Jouy patterned wallpaper and impeccable white bedcovers; all have royal bathrooms. A most successful marriage of a country home and a first-class hotel, done with restrained good taste and no surprises. If you turn up for your stay with this book you'll be offered afternoon tea! There are paths galore for walking, biking or riding in the nearby forest of Cerisy.

Rooms: 21: 18 doubles/twins,
3 suites for 4.
Price: Doubles/twins €150-€270,
suites €280-€350.
Meals: Breakfast €15; lunch & dinner
€40-65.
Closed: 3 January-12 February.

From Bayeux D6 northwest to Port en Bessin for 8km. Signposted.

Hôtel du Vieux Château

4 cours du Château
50260 Bricquebec
Manche

Tel: (0)2 33 52 24 49
Fax: (0)2 33 52 62 71
Web: www.hotelrestvieuxchateau.com

Hubert Hardy

It is the *château fort* of the old town's defences - extraordinary, with a fully documented history going back beyond 1066. There may be a gap between expectation and reality, but you come here to wallow in this remarkable piece of history... and the beds and little bathrooms are fine. Actually much of it is fine, with ancient stone walls and plain carpets, beams and the odd bit of good, old furniture. The views onto the floodlit courtyard are to tell your grandchildren about. If the ghost of a previous occupant - the Earl of Suffolk - was about, he could tell them about his imprisonment by Joan of Arc in 1429. There is a fine old dining hall, dressed with candelabra. A suit of armour guards the entrance along with coats of arms, muskets and crossed swords on the walls. It must have been a safe place as it is claimed that Queen Victoria and Prince Albert spent the night in number 2 - a most imposing room. Stay here en route to and from the ferry. It is all very real, and rather endearing.

Rooms: 16: 13 double, 3 family.
Price: Doubles €48-€83, family rooms €97-€101.
Meals: Breakfast €8; lunch & dinner €10-€27. Picnics can be arranged.
Closed: January.

From Cherbourg D900 for Bricquebec for approx. 26km. Hotel in centre of town; look for the high medieval tower dominating horizon.

Map No: 2

Hôtel Restaurant Le Mesnilgrand

Négreville
50260 Bricquebec
Manche

Tel: (0)2 33 95 09 54
Fax: (0)2 33 95 20 04
E-mail: mesnilgrand@wanadoo.fr

James & Pascale Boekee

Deep in the countryside lies a converted 18th-century cider farm, restaurant, small hotel and creative activity centre in one. The owner and chef - both English - of this deeply rural place provide rare opportunities. You could find yourself wild-mushrooming, nature trailing or, chef by your side, seeking the finest fish, cheese or cider from the local market. The energy and creativity of your hosts know few bounds. Le Mesnilgrand has only five bedrooms and you will pay very little extra for children under three. Rooms are comfortable, quiet and simply decorated and have good bathrooms. You can play tennis, paint by the lake or just recline in the English-style long bar. The chef's reputation is big in the area and his organically chosen menu will vary from day to day, or even from person to person. You eat in a setting to match Michael's culinary skills (which he shares on pre-arranged short cookery courses). There are also horse-riding opportunities with or without specialist instruction; everything can be arranged.

Rooms: 5 doubles.
Price: €79. Half-board €57 p.p.
Children under 3 free.
Meals: Breakfast included; dinner
€21-€30, organic whenever possible. Menu
changes daily.
Closed: Very occasionally.

From Cherbourg RN13 exit St Joseph on D146 for Rocheville; 5km after dual carriageway hotel is signposted.

Château de la Roque

50180 Hébécrevon
Manche

Tel: (0)2 33 57 33 20
Fax: (0)2 33 57 51 20
E-mail: mireille.delisle@wanadoo.fr
Web: www.chateau-de-la-roque.fr

M & Mme Delisle

As you come up the poplar-lined drive into the circular courtyard at the end of the day, the windows blink like diamonds. The land falls away to a lake on the other side of this 16th- and 17th-century country house. Your host leads you through the entrance passing collections of precious stones, pictures of ancestors on the farm, leather-covered bellows, a majestic grandfather clock framed by two long windows, Norman statues and a mass of potted plants. Continuing up a circular stone staircase, you reach the large, light bedrooms furnished with the same care for detail, colour and comfort: oriental rugs, an antique writing desk, and good bed linen. The Delisles raise organic chickens, pigs, sheep, cows, turkeys and ducks and make their own bread in a wood-fired oven. Dinner comes after a refreshing glass of their *pommeau* (a Norman speciality of cognac and apple juice). You may ask for a picnic lunch and stroll around their lake or explore the nature reserve nearby. When we visited Raymond and his wife, Mireille, were planning a tandem bicycle trip through England seeing former guests, now friends.

Rooms: 15: 11 doubles/twins, 2 triples, 2 suites for 3-4.
Price: Doubles/twins €69-€77, triples €83, suites €126.
Meals: Breakfast included; dinner €18; wine €3; children's meals €13.
Closed: 2-15 January.

From St Lô D927 for Coutances to St Gilles. In village, D77 for Pont Hébert for 3km; signposted.

Map No: 2

Le Manoir de l'Archerie

Sainte Cecile
50800 Villedieu les Poêles
Manche

Tel: (0)2 33 51 13 87
Fax: (0)2 33 51 33 69
E-mail: bernard.cahu@libertysurf.fr

M & Mme Bernard Cahu

A very short way from the motorway hidden in the deep Norman countryside, this hotel is a lovely, ever-so-French, discovery. An old granite house with immaculately tended gardens and an ancient granite cider press sunk into the lawn. At one side is an old chapel, now bedrooms, on the other is an extension providing a sort of *cour d'honneur* entrance. Some of the furniture is authentically old, though most is solid good quality repro in the 'rustic' Norman style and there are fireplaces to warm body and soul. Rooms are carpeted and comfortable; old tiles, flagstones, and strong dark original beams give a good country-auberge feeling. Mother and daughter Cécile handle the hotel and restaurant service, father and son run the kitchen - they have won several prizes for their culinary efforts. The small number of people running this establishment and the quiet unstressed, unhurried but efficient way they do so, is admirable. The only concession one must make is to arrive before 7pm (no exceptions as they rise at dawn to prepare home-made croissants for breakfast) and the last orders in the restaurant are at 8.30pm.

Rooms: 15: 2 singles, 10 doubles, 3 twins.
Price: Singles €34, doubles/twins €40-€54. Half-board €53-€61p.p.
Meals: Breakfast €6; lunch & dinner €15-€37; children's meals €8. Restaurant closed Mondays except July & August; also Sunday evenings from mid-October-end March.
Closed: Two weeks in November; two weeks in February.

A84 exit 38 Brecey-Villedieu 500m to r'bout for Vire; straight to 2nd r'bout, 2km to main road with 'Président' dairy opp. to left. Cross over, then straight ahead on small lane. Hotel on left, signposted.

Map No: 2

Les Hauts de la Baie du Mont Saint Michel

7 avenue de la Libération
50530 Saint Jean Le Thomas
Manche

Tel: (0)2 33 60 10 02
Fax: (0)2 33 60 15 40
E-mail: leshauts@club-internet.fr
Web: www.chateau-les-hauts.com

André & Suzanne Leroy

You will either really love or hate the inside of this house, with its ornate Art Deco reception rooms and unusual interior design. Everyone, however, will love the spot: perched in a beautiful garden above the sea, with views to Mont St Michel. Madame Leroy is warm, bubbly, chatty and very proud of the house. The beach, 400 metres away, is pebbled but there are others just a short drive away. Madame doesn't do meals, apart from breakfast, but it might keep you going until supper, anyway; a buffet of proper French food, it includes charcuterie, cheese, five different breads, 12 different jams and home-made cake. The bedrooms range from a big room with a canopied four-poster and Art Deco frieze to a delicately pretty room in pale pink, with blue-green paintwork, chintz curtains and bed covers. One room is bold black with white and brown patterns. Some love it, but some might find it too much. The bathrooms have their original 19th-century porcelain fittings. *You can walk across the bay to Mont Saint Michel - at low tide - from the village.*

Rooms: 8: 7 doubles, 1 family
(2 doubles).
Price: €56-€118.
Meals: Copious buffet breakfast included. 3 excellent restaurants within a 5 minute walk.
Closed: Never.

From Cherbourg, N13 to Valognes; D2 to Coutances; D971 to Granville; D911 (along coast) to Jullouville and on to Carolles and St Jean Le Thomas (6.5km from Jullouville).

Map No: 2

Le Gué du Holme

14 rue des Estuaires
Saint Quentin sur le Homme
50220 Ducey
Manche

Tel: (0)2 33 60 63 76
Fax: (0)2 33 60 06 77
E-mail: gue.holme@wanadoo.fr
Web: www.le-gueholme.com

M Leroux

A mouth-watering story can be told about the sea, the meadows, and the orchards of Normandy by dining here on the oysters, *foie gras* with apples and the renowned *pré salé*, lamb grazed on the sea-flooded grass. Michel, the hugely enthusiastic owner-chef, has a deeply rooted commitment to his Norman food - the more local the better. It is hard to spot the simple elegance of Le Gué du Holme from the outside. It was all the more surprising to find the new rooms overlooking a small lavender-spiked, rose-trellised garden. Breakfast is served outside on cheerful pink and white porcelain, sweet Normandy butter under silver cupolas, a delightful mix of breads - a special moment for planning the day or just a relaxing read. The Lerouxs are sensitive to detail and colour; the rooms feel crisp, an exquisite antique trunk lives in the corridor, the warmth and brightness of the welcome is reflected in the dining room with brass light fixtures, wood trim and ochre walls. Well away from the summer crowds, low-key, impeccable.

Rooms: 10: 9 doubles, 1 suite for 3.
Price: €61-€76. Half-board
€76-€91 p.p. minimum 3 days.
Meals: Breakfast €9; lunch & dinner
€23-€59. Restaurant closed Fridays &
Saturday lunchtimes.
Closed: 11-18 November;
2-25 January.

From Caen N175 to Avranches. Exit Cromel at War Museum. Left on r'bout D103. Straight on 2nd r'bout to St Quentin. Hotel opp. church.

Château de Boucéel

50240 Vergoncey
Manche

Tel: (0)2 33 48 34 61
Fax: (0)2 33 48 16 26
E-mail: chateaudebouceel@wanadoo.fr
Web: www.chateaudebouceel.com

Régis & Nicole de Roquefeuil-Cahuzac

The embroidered linen sheets enfold you in a smooth embrace that is a metaphor for the Boucéel experience. The Count's family have lived in the listed château since it was built in 1763 but he and the Countess have worked in Paris and Chicago and theirs is an elegant, unstuffy lifestyle in which you are welcome to join. He, a quietly simple aristocrat, will recount fascinating details from his family history while she, energetic and communicative, prepares a succulent apple cake for your breakfast. The delightful bedrooms, named and portraited for the uncles and grandmothers who slept there, are beautifully done in just the right dusty yellows and misty greys for the original panelling, have superb parquet floors, antiques and personal touches. And if you meet the kindly lady ghost, be properly polite to her, she's a *Marquise*. Breakfast, on fine china, is in the soft green, round, panelled and mirrored dining room with French windows to the lush park, which comes complete with geese, lake and an ancient chapel. It's a treat to stay in this gently grand and gracious château.

Rooms: 4: 2 doubles, 3 suites.
Price: €115-€145.
Meals: Breakfast included.
Restaurant 6km.
Closed: December-January, only by arrangement.

From Avranches for Mont St Michel, exit 34 to N175; exit D40 for Mont St Michel/Antrain. Left for Antrain. After 6km on D40 left for St Senier de Beuvron on D308. Château 800m.

Brittany

A little garlic, judiciously used, won't seriously affect
your social life and will tone up more dull dishes than
any commodity discovered to date.

Alexander Wright, How to Live Without a Woman

C. M. Schulte-Kellinghaus, Phare de Pontusval, Brignogan (9)

La Korrigane
39 rue le Pomellec
35400 Saint Malo
Ille-et-Vilaine

Tel: (0)2 99 81 65 85
Fax: (0)2 99 82 23 89
E-mail: la.korrigane.st.malo@wanadoo.fr
Web: www.st-malo-hotel-korrigane.com

Mme Dolbeau

Small antique daybeds and vast gilt-framed mirrors, carved armoires and ancestral portraits - it's like stepping back into an elegant private mansion of the 1930s, with that deliciously old-fashioned refinement and sense of welcome. The 1990s have contributed all the requisite modern communication and bathroom bits. Madame Dolbeau, enchantingly 'just so', fits utterly into her surroundings and nothing is too much trouble for her. There is elegant stucco in front, solid Breton granite behind, where the peaceful walled garden contains your reading corner or your breakfast table beneath mature trees. In poor weather, the breakfast room is attractive, tall-windowed, chandeliered and the *salon* has comfortable armchairs, log fires and that ever-amazing trick of a window above the fireplace. Bedrooms are big and supremely comfortable, with thick matching covers and curtains, subtle lighting and pretty antiques. Light floods in, there is an irresistible softness, a sense of luxury and good manners - and all this within walking distance of the old walled town and the ferry port.

Rooms: 12: 11 doubles, 1 triple.
Price: Doubles €69-€145,
triple €168.
Meals: Breakfast €10. Lunch & dinner available locally.
Closed: Never.

From ferry port take Quai de Trichet, at r'bout take Rue le Pomellec.

Map No: 2

Hôtel Elizabeth

2 rue des Cordiers
35400 Saint Malo
Ille-et-Vilaine

Tel: (0)2 99 56 24 98
Fax: (0)2 99 56 39 24
E-mail: elizabeth.hotel.st.malo@wanadoo.fr
Web: www.st-malo-hotel-elizabeth.com

Joëlle Dolbeau

Built in 1558, the Hôtel Elizabeth's stone walls look as comfortingly solid against the chilly winds as they were against the pirates who used to make this part of France less than welcoming to outsiders. Apparently the presence of privateers can still be felt in the breakfast room, which is a cave under the house reached by a stone spiral staircase (or a lift if you're feeling prosaic); presumably these are not the kind of privateers who steal your breakfast from under your nose before throwing you off the city walls. You can even call in for breakfast as a non-resident, before walking the plank onto the ferry. The bedrooms have internal wooden shutters and the other accoutrements of history such as 'period' furnishings but also their full complement of 21st-century comforts. Monsieur Dolbeau's welcome is particularly warm to foreigners and this makes an ideal place to treat yourself to a romantic weekend exploring the old stone streets of St Malo or to a night before or after the rigours of the ferry-crossing. *Boat excursions to Jersey/Guernsey.*

Rooms: 17: 4 standard doubles, 13 large doubles/twins.
Price: €66-€120.
Meals: Breakfast €9. Good local restaurants.
Closed: Never.

Enter walled city via Porte Saint Louis and take 2nd right.

Château de la Ballue

35560 Bazouges la Pérouse
Ille-et-Vilaine

Tel: (0)2 99 97 47 86
Fax: (0)2 99 97 47 70
E-mail: chateau@la-ballue.com
Web: www.la-ballue.com

Mme Marie France Barrère

The gardens are reason alone for visiting La Ballue. Saved from suffocating brambles in 1973, restructured by phenomenal topiary in the 17th-century idiom of light and shade, they are a work of modern mannerist art dealing surprises at every turn - 13 green *salons* studiedly peppered with contemporary sculptures. The owners, a relaxed, intelligent couple of aesthetes from the publishing and art worlds, have brought their taste and refinement into the rigorously classical mansion where so many writers and artists have stayed - and renovation continues. The fine reception rooms have panelling and fireplaces, masses of lovely things - antiques, ceramics, modern art and Old Masters - and a soft warm atmosphere. The hugely successful, elegantly understated décor mixes old, oriental and contemporary and the guest rooms are pure château: beautiful woods, fabrics and rugs, deep armoires, top-class mattresses beneath rich draperies, modern bathrooms. A magical place for body and soul. Creep out early when trails of dewy mist still lurk in the maze and haunt the carvings - the vision will never leave you. *Minimum stay 2 nights.*

Rooms: 5: 3 doubles, 2 triples,
1 suite for 5.
Price: €145-€275.
Meals: Breakfast €11; dinner for large
groups by arrangement.
Closed: 20 December-2 March.

*From Avranches A84; N175 to
Pontorson. Continue on N175 to
Antrain; at r'bout head for Dol de
Bretagne 1km; left. Signposted.*

Map No: 2

Hôtel Manoir de Rigourdaine

Route de Langrolay
22490 Plouër sur Rance
Côtes-d'Armor

Tel: (0)2 96 86 89 96
Fax: (0)2 96 86 92 46
E-mail: hotel.rigourdaine@wanadoo.fr
Web: www.hotel-rigourdaine.fr

Patrick Van Valenberg

At the end of the lane, firm on its hillside, Rigourdaine breathes space, sky, permanence. The square-yarded manor farm, originally a stronghold with moat and all requisite towers, now looks serenely out over wide estuary and rolling pastures to the ramparts of St Malo and provides a sheltering embrace. The reception/bar in the converted barn is a good place to meet the friendly, attentive master of the manor, properly pleased with his excellent conversion. A double-height open fireplace warms a sunken sitting well; the simple breakfast room - black and white floor, solid old beams, plain wooden tables with pretty mats - looks onto courtyard and garden. Rooms are simple too, in unfrilly good taste and comfort: Iranian rugs on plain carpets, co-ordinated contemporary-chic fabrics in good colours, some good old furniture, pale bathrooms with all essentials. Six ground-floor rooms have private terraces onto the kempt garden - ideal for intimate breakfasts or sundowners. Good clean-cut rooms, atmosphere lent by old timbers and antiques, and always the long limpid view. We liked it a lot.

Rooms: 19 doubles.
Price: €46-€72.
Meals: Breakfast €6.50. Restaurant nearby in Plouër.
Closed: Mid-November-Easter.

From St Malo N137 for Rennes; after Châteauneuf right N176 for Dinan/St Brieuc; over river Rance; exit for Plouër sur Rance towards Langrolay for 500m; lane to Rigourdaine.

Manoir de La Hazaie

22400 Planguenoual
Côtes-d'Armor

Tel: (0)2 96 32 73 71
Fax: (0)2 96 32 79 72
E-mail: manoir.hazaie@wanadoo.fr
Web: www.manoir-hazaie.com

Jean-Yves & Christine Marivin

Chunks of Breton history - violence, greed and bigotry - happened here where country peace now reigns. The Marivins, she an artist/pharmacist, he a craftsman/lawyer, love every minute of its past and have filled it with family treasures: *La Maison Musée*. The *salon* combines grandeur and warmth, ancient stones, antiques and a roaring fire. Ancestral portraits hang beside Madame's medieval paint and pottery scenes. *Tournemine's* blood-red ceiling inspired a powerfully simple colour scheme, plain furniture and a great canopied bed. Airily feminine *Tiffaine* has wildly gilded, curlicued Polish furniture and a neo-classical bathroom romp: statues, pilasters, a delicate mural of *Girl in Hat*. Baths have sybaritic jacuzzi jets. Rooms in the old mill-house, with fine old floor tiles and lovely rugs, open onto the garden - ideal for families. Row on the pond, glide from Hadrian's Villa into the pool, sleep in luxury, enjoy your hosts' knowledgeable enthusiasm. Past owners have all left their mark: the admiral's anchors, the priest's colours.

Rooms: 6: 5 doubles/twins, 1 suite.
Price: Doubles/twins €91-€183, suite €183-€214.
Meals: Breakfast €11. Lunch & dinner available locally.
Closed: Never.

From N12 Rennes-Brest road exit St René on D81 then D786 for Pléneuf Val André. Just before Planguenoual, right following signs to house (2.2km). Entrance opp. museum 'La Ferme du Laboureur'.

Map No: 2

Manoir du Vaumadeuc

22130 Pleven
Côtes-d'Armor

Tel: (0)2 96 84 46 17
Fax: (0)2 96 84 40 16
E-mail: manoir@vaumadeuc.com
Web: www.vaumadeuc.com

M & Mme O'Neill

The approach down a long drive through mature trees and grass leads to the impressive granite exterior of this 15th-century manor. As you enter through the old, massive wooden door which leads into the manorial hall the whole place seems untouched by time. This is just as it must have been hundreds of years ago - a huge stone fireplace dominates the far end, there's a high vaulted beamed ceiling, an enormously long banqueting table and hunting trophies on the walls. It is easy to imagine former guests feasting and making merry after the hunt. A magnificent staircase leads to bedrooms on the first floor, decorated and furnished in period style - magnificent and comfortable, no frills, quite masculine, à la hunting and shooting fraternity. All rooms are large and some are enormous; one of them has stairs leading down into a room the size of a tennis court. The bathrooms are smart and spotless. Such a courteous welcome from Monsieur O'Neill - his family has owned this listed house for generations and will provide you with good traditional evening meals made with local produce.

Rooms: 13: 10 doubles/twins, 3 suites.
Price: Doubles €90-€183, suites €130-€206.
Meals: Breakfast €8; picnic available; dinner €30, by reservation only.
Closed: November-Easter.

From Plancoët D768 towards Lamballe for 2km. Left on D28 for 7km to Pleven. The Manoir is 100m outside the village.

Château Hôtel de Brélidy

Brélidy
22140 Bégard
Côtes-d'Armor

Tel: (0)2 96 95 69 38
Fax: (0)2 96 95 18 03
E-mail: chateau.brelidy@worldonline.fr
Web: www.chateau-brelidy.com

M & Mme Yoncourt-Pémezec

From upstairs you can see across bucolic fieldscapes to Menez-Bré, Armor's highest spot (302m). The old *chambres d'hôtes* rooms here are cosy, quilty, family-antiqued. Below are the beamed *salon* and billiards room, their vast carved fireplaces built above the two great dining room fireplaces - such strength. The owners have laboured 30 long years to restore 16th-centuty Brélidy, using authentic materials and preserving the sobriety. The worn stone staircase and an iron man fit well; so will you, enfolded in the personal attention that is Brélidy's keynote. In the west wing, on the site of the original open gallery, guests in the suite can parade before waist-high windows like lords and ladies of yore. More modest rooms lie below, carefully decorated with soft colours, enriched with antiques; four have private entrances with little terraces and there's a huge terrace for all up above. In the gentle garden, the converted bakery is ideal for families and there's an indoor jacuzzi. Beyond are two rivers, two ponds with private fishing, and everywhere is utter peace.

Rooms: 13 + 1: 12 doubles,
1 suite for 4; 1 cottage for 2-4.
Price: Doubles €72-€100,
suite €179-€202; cottage €107-€168.
Meals: Buffet breakfast €9.50;
dinner €25-€31.
Closed: November-Easter.

From N12 exit Lannion-Tréguier to Tréguier. D712; D8 then D15 to Brélidy. Hotel signposted.

Map No: 1

Manoir de Kergrec'h

Kergrech'h
22820 Plougrescant
Côtes-d'Armor

Tel: (0)2 96 92 59 13
Fax: (0)2 96 92 51 27

Vicomte & Vicomtesse de Roquefeuil

Come taste the experience of a perfect château as proposed by a perfect couple of *châtelains* whose ancestors bought the place on returning from exile after the French Revolution. Just 200 metres from the sea, exposed to the wild Breton elements, it was originally a Bishop's seat, built with hunks of local granite and fortified as befitted a lord of the 17th-century Church. It is now a vegetable farm, run by the younger Vicomte, with superb grounds and a luxurious interior of marble fireplaces, gilt mirrors, antiques and a classically French *salon* flooded with ocean light. Guestrooms, big, gracious and richly decorated with thick hangings and old prints, have parquet floors, good rugs and lovely family furniture. The tower room, in an older part of the building, is deliciously different, more 'rustic', with its timbers and mezzanine and the new loo fitted to the original, still functioning 14th-century drain! The twin-basined bathrooms are all superb yet respectful of the old frame and breakfast in the more austere dining room is a Breton feast to linger over in good company.

Rooms: 8: 5 doubles, 2 family rooms, 1 suite.
Price: €91-€122.
Meals: Breakfast included. Restaurants in Tréguier 6km.
Closed: Never.

From Guingamp, D8 to Plougrescant. There right after church (leaning spire) and right again 200m along.

Map No: 1

Ti al Lannec

14 allée de Mézo-Guen
22560 Trébeurden
Côtes-d'Armor

Tel: (0)2 96 15 01 01
Fax: (0)2 96 23 62 14
E-mail: ti.al.lannec@wanadoo.fr
Web: www.tiallannec.com

Danielle & Gérard Jouanny

With dozens of English antiques, it is still superbly French - soft and fulsome. An Edwardian seaside residence perched on the cliff, its gardens tumble down to rocky coves and sandy beaches; only breezes through the pine and waves can be heard (the beach club closes at midnight). Inside, a mellow warmth envelopes you in armfuls of drapes, bunches, swags and sprigs. Each room is a different shape, individually decorated as if in a private mansion with a sitting space, a writing table, a good bathroom. Besides the florals, stripes and oriental rugs, the white bedcovers and views onto the sea or ancient cypresses give breathing space. Some bedrooms are big, with plastic-balconied *loggias*, some are ideal for families, with convertible bunk-bed sofas. *Salons* are cosily arranged with little lamps, mirrors, old prints; the sea-facing restaurant serves excellent food. The Jouanny family care immensely about guests' welfare and are deeply part of their community. They create a smart yet human atmosphere, publish a daily in-house gazette and provide balneotherapy in the basement.

Rooms: 29: 2 singles, 22 doubles/twins, 5 family rooms for 3-5.
Price: Singles €70-€87, doubles/twins €130-€229, family rooms €190-€244.
Meals: Breakfast €13; lunch & dinner €19-€62; children's meals €15.
Closed: Mid-November-mid-March.

From N12 Rennes-Brest road, exit 3km west of Guingamp for Lannion onto D767. In Lannion, follow signs to Trébeurden. Signposted.

Map No: 1

Grand Hôtel des Bains

15 bis rue de l'Eglise
29241 Locquirec
Finistère

Tel: (0)2 98 67 41 02
Fax: (0)2 98 67 44 60
E-mail: hotel.des.bains@wanadoo.fr
Web: www.grand-hotel-des-bains.com

M Van Lier & M Dufau

Marine purity on the north Brittany coast: it's like a smart yacht club where you are an old member. The fearless design magician has waved a wand of natural spells - cotton, cane, wood, wool, sea-grass: nothing synthetic, nothing pompous. Sober lines and restful colours leave space for the scenery, the sky pours in through walls of glass, the peaceful garden flows into rocks, beach and sea. Moss-green panelling lines the deep-chaired bar where a fire leaps in winter. Pale-grey-panelled bedrooms have dark mushroom carpets and thick cottons in stripes and checks of soft red or green or beige or blue. Some have four-posters, some have balconies, others are smaller, nearly all have the ever-changing sea view. Bathrooms are lovely, with bathrobes to wear to the magnificent indoor sea-water pool and spa treatment centre. Staff are smiling and easy, the ivory-panelled dining room with its sand-coloured tablecloths is deeply tempting and children are served early so that adults can enjoy the superb menu. The luxury of space, pure elegant simplicity and personal attention are yours for the booking.

Rooms: 36 doubles/twins.
Price: €84-€162
Meals: Breakfast included; lunch & dinner €23-35. Excellent wine cellar. Restaurant closed for lunch in low season.
Closed: 8 January-7 February.

From Rennes-Brest N12 exit to Plestin les Grèves, continue to Locquirec. Hotel in centre. Through gate to car park on right.

Le Brittany

Boulevard Sainte-Barbe
29681 Roscoff
Finistère

Tel: (0)2 98 69 70 78
Fax: (0)2 98 61 13 29
E-mail: info@hotel-brittany.com
Web: www.hotel-brittany.com

Patricia Chapalain

A very convenient place to stay for those travelling to or from Plymouth or Cork. This is an old Breton manor house with an imposing, rather austere looking façade which overlooks the harbour and is far enough away from the terminal buildings so that views are of the lovely Ile de Batz, only a short boat ride away. We must prepare you for the entrance to the hotel from the car park at the rear - quite a surprise. You come in onto a balcony on the first floor overlooking the reception area and look down onto a huge chandelier, an expanse of marble floors, lovely rugs and curtains which hang down two stories. Behind the reception is a photograph of Mme Chapalain shaking hands with Prince Charles: he might have just had an excellent meal of locally caught fish in the dining room, with its arched windows and magnificent views of the harbour, or just had a brew in the bar sitting in one of the leather chairs. A warm welcome is a priority here, even to a jug of fresh flowers and a bowl of strawberries in the bedrooms.

Rooms: 27: 25 doubles, 2 suites.
Price: Doubles €79-€136, suites €120-€183. Special half-board prices for thalassotherapy treatments.
Meals: Breakfast €11; lunch & dinner €30-€54. Restaurant closed Saturday & Thursday lunchtimes & Mondays during low season.
Closed: 20 October-21 March.

Exit Morlaix from N12. From ferry terminal right for 300 metres.

Map No: 1

Manoir de Moëllien

29550 Plonévez-Porzay
Finistère

Tel: (0)2 98 92 50 40
Fax: (0)2 98 92 55 21
E-mail: manmoel@aol.com

M & Mme Garet

The sheer strength that pours from this stern stone manor was designed to withstand Atlantic storms, the decorative bits to demonstrate status. Now swishing pines protect the drive, hydrangeas bloom in October and the young garden of lawns and pond flourishes. Rooms are neatly arranged in converted outbuildings, each with its own entrance and little terrace. In the block of suites and duplexes, splendid luminous colour schemes are perfect foils for some delicious Breton antiques; fabrics are strong, bathrooms excellent, finishes unfussy. The 'older' rooms, although smaller and less contemporary, are perfectly comfortable, excellent value - and soon to be redecorated. The eating halls in the manor are superb in their deep-windowed, high-beamed authenticity and huge carved fireplaces. Your host, the chef, is as enthusiastic about his dinners as he is about his wife's décor and gardening plans. The two-ton granite cider-press fountain is his own, most successful, design. Modern dynamics married to solid old stones in a place of peace.

Rooms: 18: 10 doubles/twins,
8 suites.
Price: Doubles/twins €56-€113,
suites €75-€116.
Meals: Buffet breakfast €8; lunch &
dinner €19-€38. Restaurant closed
Wednesday & Thursday lunchtimes
except mid-June-September.
Closed: Mid-November-April.

*From Quimper north for Locronan on D39,
D63 for 17km. Left on D7 for Douarnenez
and Kerlaz for 3km; right on D107 to Plonévez.
Manoir signed on right (20-25 mins).*

Map No: 1

Château de Guilguiffin

Le Guilguiffin
29710 Landudec
Finistère

Tel: (0)2 98 91 52 11
Fax: (0)2 98 91 52 52
E-mail: chateau@guilguiffin.com
Web: www.guilguiffin.com

Philippe Davy

The bewitching name of the rough knight who became first Baron in 1010 (the King rewarding him royally for battle services with a title and a swathe of wild, remote Brittany), the splendidness of the place, its vast, opulent rooms and magnificent grounds, seduced us utterly: it is a powerful experience, grand rather than intimate, unforgettable. Built with stones from the ruined fortress that originally stood here, the present château is a jewel of 18th-century aristocratic architecture. Philippe Davy, the latest descendant, knows and loves old buildings, his ancient family seat in particular, and applies his energy and intelligence to restoring château and park. He repairs, decorates and furnishes in all authenticity; bedrooms are richly, thickly draped and carpeted; reception rooms glow with grandeur and panelling; superb antiques radiate elegance. In the park, he has planted thousands of bulbs and bushes and cleared 11km of walks. He likes to convert his visitors to his convictions and is a persuasive preacher. Guilguiffin is deeply, fascinatingly unusual.

Rooms: 6: 4 doubles, 2 suites.
Price: Doubles €114-€137,
suites €168-€198.
Meals: Breakfast included. Good choice of restaurants nearby.
Closed: December-February, but open by arrangement.

From Quimper D785 for Pont l'Abbé until airport exit. Then D56 5km to D784 for Audierne. 3km before Landudec look for signs.

Map No: 1

Manoir de Kerhuel

Route de Quimper
29720 Plonéour-Lanvern
Finistère

Tel: (0)2 98 82 60 57
Fax: (0)2 98 82 61 79
E-mail: manoir-kerhuel@wanadoo.fr
Web: perso.wanadoo.fr/manoir-kerhuel

M & Mme Lanvoc

The new managers are keen to make Kerhuel thoroughly welcoming. Breakfast is copious, in the intimate breakfast room for the few or, for the many, through some lovely carved panelling in the splendid banqueting room (once the stables), scanned by windows and tapestries. Your smilingly busy host and chef serves other meals in the pleasing modern restaurant that joins the old house to the old stables. This Manoir is just 100 years old, whence its rather stolid form in a flourishing green mantle of great trees and rhododendrons. The round, stone-walled, yellow-tented Bridal Chamber in the old dovecote is a tiny hideaway - go easy on the champers, though, the bathroom stairs are steep. Families are brilliantly catered for: bunk beds behind curtains, swings in the garden, a shallow children's pool beside the big one. Some rooms are pretty big, some have small high windows, beds may be canopied and quilted, there's plenty of storage space behind sliding doors. You will find gentle colours, good repro furniture, the odd antique, space and a very easy atmosphere.

Rooms: 26: 21 doubles/twins, 5 suites for 2-4.
Price: Doubles €58-€88, suites €78-€140.
Meals: Buffet breakfast €9; lunch & dinner €17-€41. Restaurant sometimes closed, please check when booking.
Closed: Mid-November-mid-December; January-March.

From Quimper D785 for Pont l'Abbé for 10km; exit Plonéour-Lanvern on D156 for 4km. Hotel on left.

Map No: 1

Manoir du Stang

29940 La Fôret Fouesnant
Finistère

Tel: (0)2 98 56 97 37
Fax: (0)2 98 56 97 37

Hubert Family

There is ancient grandeur in this 'hollow place' (*stang*) between the remarkable dovecote arch and the wild ponds. On the tamed side: a formal French courtyard, a blooming rose garden, rows of trees, some masterly old stonework. But the welcome is utterly natural, the rooms not at all intimidating. The Huberts like guests to feel at home in their family mansion with a choice antique here, an original curtain fabric there, an invigoratingly pink bathroom to contrast with a gentle Louis Philippe chest - always solid, reliable comfort and enough space. Views are heart-warming, over courtyard, water and woods, the peace is total (bar the odd quack). Communal rooms are of stupendous proportions, as befits the receptions held here. The dining room can seat 60 in grey-panelled, pink-curtained splendour, its glass bays looking across to the gleaming ponds. Masses of things sit on the black and white *salon* floor - a raft of tables, fleets of high-backed chairs, a couple of sofas, glowing antique cupboards - and you still have space and monumental fireplaces. A magnificent place.

Rooms: 24 doubles/twins.
Price: €75-€145.
Meals: Breakfast €8; dinner €29.
Restaurant closed September-June.
Closed: October-May; occasionally at other times.

From Quimper N165 exit Concarneau/Fouesnant on D44 then D783 for Quimper. Entrance by private road on left.

Château-Hôtel Manoir de Kertalg

Route de Riec sur Belon
29350 Moëlan sur Mer
Finistère

Tel: (0)2 98 39 77 77
Fax: (0)2 98 39 72 07
Web: www.manoirdekertalg.com

M Le Goamic

So many contrasts. Driving through thick woods, you expect the old château in its vast estate, but the hotel is actually in the big, blocky stables, built in 1890 for racehorses (who even had running water): it became a hotel in 1990 when the tower was added. The *salon* is formal and glitzy with its marbled floor, modern coffered ceiling, red plush chairs - and intriguing dreamscapes by Brann. You will be welcomed with polished affability by the charming young owner, and possibly by visitors come for tea and ice-cream, a favourite summer outing. Even the 'small' bedrooms are big; château décor is the rule: brocading, plush lace, satin and gilt-framed mirrors. The 'big' rooms are exuberant: one has the full Pompadour treatment in gold, pink and white, another is richly Directoire in curved cane and coffee-coloured velvet. The tower rooms are cosier, old-fashioned posh, but have space for a couple of armchairs. Some bathrooms are to be modernised, yet all are solid good quality and the value is remarkable. Wild woodland walks beckon and there's a helipad - two worlds meet and embrace.

Rooms: 8: 7 doubles/triples, 1 duplex for 4.
Price: Doubles/triples €80-€160, duplex €190.
Meals: Breakfast €10. Five restaurants within 2-8km.
Closed: November-March; open for Easter.

From N165 westwards exit Quimperlé Centre to Moëlan sur Mer; there, right at traffic lights for Riec and follow signs (12km from N165).

Château de Kerlarec

29300 Arzano
Finistère

Tel: (0)2 98 71 75 06
Fax: (0)2 98 71 74 55

Monique & Michel Bellin

The plain exterior belies the 19th-century festival inside - it's astonishing. Murals of mountain valleys and Joan of Arc in stained glass announce the original Lorraine-born baron ('descended from Joan's brother') and the wallpaper looks great, considering it too was done in 1830. In the gold-brocade-papered *salon*, Madame Bellin lavishes infinite care on every Chinese vase, gilt statuette and porcelain flower: sit in an ornate black and green chair by the red marble fireplace and soak up the atmosphere. Staircase and bedrooms have more overflowing personality, mixing fantasy with comfort, some fascinating furniture, lovely old embroidered linen on new mattresses and bathrooms of huge character. On the top floor, slip through a 'slot' in the rafters from sitting to sleeping space and discover a gold and white nest. Expect porcelain and silver at breakfast and reserve your *crêpes* or seafood platter for a candlelit dinner one night. Your enthusiastic hostess lavishes the same attention on her guests as on her house - and the bassets will walk with you in the park.

Rooms: 6: 1 double, 5 suites.
Price: €76-€89.
Meals: Breakfast included; lunch & dinner €23-€34, crêpes or shellfish platter by arrangement.
Closed: Never.

From Quimperlé D22 east to Pontivy for 6km; château on left - narrow gate.

Map No: 1

Château du Launay

Launay
56160 Ploërdut
Morbihan

Tel: (0)2 97 39 46 32
Fax: (0)2 97 39 46 31
E-mail: info@chateaudulaunay.com
Web: www.chateaudulaunay.com

Redolfi-Strizzot Family

A dream of a place, another world, another time, beside bird-swept pond and quiet woods. Launay marries austere grandeur with simple luxury, fine old stones with contemporary art, rich minimalism with exotica. In the great white hall, an Indian monk shares the Persian rug with a bronze stag. The staircase sweeps up, past fascinating art on the huge landing, to big light-filled rooms where beds are white, bathrooms are plainly, beautifully modern, light and colour are handled with consummate skill. The second floor is more exotic, the corridor punctuated with an Indian gate, the rooms slightly smaller but rich in carved colonial bed, polo-player armchairs, Moghul prints. For relaxation, choose the gilt-edged billiards room, the soberly leather-chaired, book-filled library or the stupendous drawing room, stuffed with pieces including a piano (concerts are given), a giant parasol and many sitting corners. A house of a million marvels where you take unexpected journeys and fabulous parties are thrown. Your charming young hosts know how to receive - and food is deliciously varied.

Rooms: 10 doubles/twins.
Price: €91-€114.
Meals: Breakfast €6; dinner €21,
by reservation only.
Closed: January-February.

*From Pontivy D782 (21km) to Guémené; D1 for
Gourin to Toubahado, 9km. Don't go to Ploërdut. In
Toubahado right on C3 for Locuon, 3km. Entrance
immediately after 'Launay' sign.*

Château de Talhouët

56220 Rochefort en Terre
Morbihan

Tel: (0)2 97 43 34 72
Fax: (0)2 97 43 35 04
E-mail: chateaudetalhouet@libertysurf.fr
Web: www.chateaudetalhouet.com

M Jean-Pol Soulaine

Arrival here is as dramatic as a suspense film: you drive up a gloomy, bumpy, muddy lane smelling of moss and fungi, then suddenly: Wow! You come upon a 16th-century granite manor house dominating views of fields terraced down to the distant Aze valley and the sandstone cliffs of Rochefort-on-Terre. Jean-Pol bought the ruined house, built by the crusader Talhouët family in 1562, 12 years ago, fulfilling a dream he had nurtured for many years. He has also restored the grounds, which vary from woodland to open fields, with a series of fascinating walled gardens: English, formal French and a wild flower meadow. Inside, floors are stone worn to satin with the years or polished wood with Persian rugs. The sitting room manages to be both cosy despite being enormous, with old rose panelling, antique chairs and soft, deep sofas. You can browse through the giant bookcase or a tempting selection of magazines and Jean-Pol will join you for a drink to discuss dinner. This is cooked by a charming young chef who will prepare a delicious choice. The bedrooms are up an impressive stone staircase. You will find a canopied bed, softly painted beams and well-chosen *toile de Jouy* and will awake to birds and a peaceful view.

Rooms: 8 doubles.
Price: €110-€155.
Meals: Breakfast included; dinner €39.
Closed: January.

From Redon D775 through Allaire 9km; right D313 through Malansac to Rochefort en Terre; D774 for Malestroit 4km; left onto small road 2km. Entrance on left; Château another 500m.

Le Logis de Parc er Gréo

9 rue Mané Guen
Le Gréo
56610 Arradon
Morbihan

Tel: (0)2 97 44 73 03
Fax: (0)2 97 44 80 48
E-mail: logisparc.er.greo@wanadoo.fr
Web: members.aol.com/morbihan1/hotels.html

Éric & Sophie Bermond

The neat new building is a metaphor for Breton hospitality. The front is a high north wall - it may seem forbidding but once inside you know that it shelters house and garden from the wild elements, that fields, woods, sea and the coastal path are just yards away. Éric prepares itineraries for guests, boating is on the spot, swimming a little further away. Warm colours, oriental rugs and fine family pieces sit easily on the tiled floors of the many-windowed ground floor, Éric's father's watercolours lend personality to all the rooms, and the unusual candlesticks in the hall and ancestral portraits, including a large Velazquez-style child in a great gilt frame, are most appealing. *Salon* and dining room open widely onto terrace and garden - wonderful places to relax or play with the children on the big lawn. Rooms, attractive in shades of red, green and salmon, are functionally furnished. Your hosts, their charming young family and their enthusiasm for their project - to stop being clients in boring hotels and do things properly themselves - make this an easy, friendly place to stay.

Rooms: 12 doubles/twins; some connecting to become family rooms for 4-5.
Price: Doubles €66-€95.
Meals: Breakfast €9.
Closed: Mid-November-mid-March (open at Christmas).

From Vannes D101 for Ile aux Moines. Ignore left turns to Arradon, left to Le Moustoir then on to Le Gréo and follow signs.

Western Loire

And, most dear actors, eat no onions nor garlic,
for we are to utter sweet breath.
William Shakespeare, A Midsummer Night's Dream

B. Krebs

Auberge du Parc

La Mare aux Oiseaux
162 Ile de Fédrun
44720 Saint Joachim
Loire-Atlantique

Tel: (0)2 40 88 53 01
Fax: (0)2 40 91 67 44
E-mail: aubergeduparc@aol.com
Web: www.auberge-du-parc.com

Éric Guérin

A perfect little inn in a low-lying village deep in the watery wilderness of the Brière Regional Park - people even come for lunch by boat; it has the charm and simplicity of a remote staging post and the exquisite sophistication of an increasingly reputed table. Éric Guérin, an adventurous and attractive young chef, trained with the best in Paris and now applies his lively culinary creativity on his own account. Appropriately in this amphibious land, he delights in mixing earth fruits and water creatures - he calls it "good French traditional with a zest of young Parisian". His pretty, low-ceilinged dining room, with rough rustic walls and smartly-dressed chairs, is the ideal setting for this experience; bedrooms under the thatch are for quiet nights after days of marshy discoveries and evenings of gourmet pleasure. Éric's art-world background is evident in his choice of gently contemporary, uncluttered décor and country antiques. He has some modern but approachable art, too. The garden is green, the canal watery, the welcome genuine and the food... out of this world.

Rooms: 5 doubles/twins.
Price: €58. Half-board €137 for 2.
Meals: Breakfast €7. Lunch & dinner €30-€40. Restaurant closed Sunday evenings & Mondays except July & August.
Closed: March.

From Nantes towards La Baule, exit Montoir de Bretagne for Parc Naturel Brière to St Joachim. In St Joachim, left at lights to Fédrun (2km). Auberge opposite La Maison du Parc.

Hôtel Villa Flornoy

7 avenue Flornoy
44380 Pornichet
Loire-Atlantique

Tel: (0)2 40 11 60 00
Fax: (0)2 40 61 86 47
E-mail: hotflornoy@aol.com
Web: www.villa-flornoy.com

Luc Rouault

Villa it is, a large one, in a quiet road just back from the vast sandy beach and protected from the sea-front bustle. Built as a family boarding house in the 1920s, Flornoy still stands in the shade of a quieter age: high old trees, nooked and crannied seaside villas in stone, brick and wood. Inside it is just as peaceful. After being greeted by the delightful young owner and admiring the clock over the desk - his family have made clocks for generations - enjoy sitting in the *salon*: garden view, four tempting 'corners', well-chosen marine prints and the occasional interesting *objet*. Rooms - mostly a good size, a few with balconies - have a pretty, fresh, padded feel, nothing frilly, just plain or Jouy-style wall fabrics, co-ordinated colours and patterns, good modern/traditional furniture, excellent beds and white bathrooms with fine new fittings. It is simple, solid, attractive and extremely comfortable and in the morning you will be glad to breakfast, generously, in the light dining room or under the trees in the green and blooming garden. Really good value and relaxedly welcoming.

Rooms: 20: 13 doubles/twins,
7 triples.
Price: €50-€84, triples €58-€92.
Meals: Breakfast €7; dinner €19-€22.
Restaurant closed October-April.
Closed: November-mid-February.

In Pornichet Centre Ville in big market place, right onto av. Général de Gaulle for 300m; av. Flornoy on right just after Hôtel de Ville on left.

Saint Christophe

Place Notre Dame
44502 La Baule
Loire-Atlantique

Tel: (0)2 40 60 35 35
Fax: (0)2 40 60 11 74

Calixte Jouon

An easy walk from the "finest beach in Europe", the exceptionally attractive Saint Christophe is a trio of 1920s seaside villas with a family-house atmosphere where you never feel the weight of 30+ rooms. There are no corridors, just hallways and landings, each one an opportunity for a fine old table, a glass-fronted cabinet with family treasures or a deep sofa with a good reading light: books are an essential part of this exceptionally civilised hotel. Your host, a charming, urbane and humorous man of great height and much heart, and his artist wife, whose works enliven many walls, genuinely enjoy people. They "cultivate the informal", provide excellent food in the invigoratingly red and electric-blue dining room, fresh flowers and space for families (five rooms have bunk beds). Rooms vary greatly in size but each has at least one old piece of furniture, one object or picture to arouse your curiosity. Décor varies too - there are stripes and florals, pastels and powerfuls, patchwork and *piqué*, all put together in a personal, relaxing style. One does indeed feel at home here.

Rooms: 33: 28 doubles/twins, 5 family.
Price: Doubles/twins €59-€90, family €65-€114. July & August: half-board only €145-€180 for 2.
Meals: Breakfast €8. Lunch & dinner €22-€30.
Closed: Never.

In La Baule to Centre Ville. At Place des Victoires, right on Avenue de Gaulle to sea front. Right along beach; second right (Avenue des Impairs); hotel 100m facing you.

L'Abbaye de Villeneuve

Route de la Roche sur Yon
44840 Les Sorinières
Loire-Atlantique

Tel: (0)2 40 04 40 25
Fax: (0)2 40 31 28 45
E-mail: abbayevilleneuve@aol.com
Web: abbayedevilleneuve.com

M Choblet

This ancient foundation has waxed and waned for 800 years. Today's hotel is the abbey's 18th-century hostelry. One corridor is atmospherically frugal in its coconut matting and deep brown curtains held by heavy unbleached ropes - a cypher for a monk's sandals, robe and belt. The rich-coloured, thick-curtained rooms are less austere. Even the sober-*saloned* suite with ancient chest and grey plush chairs, has a bedroom warmly clothed in old rose and a capacious bathroom. Warm fabrics, armoires, marble-topped tables and French armchairs abound, with not a single furbelow. 'Standard' rooms are small, well decorated, warmly beamed. Down the superb barrel-vaulted staircase you come to the authentic touch of the public rooms: hung with blue or red cloth, flaunting carved fireplaces and beamed ceilings, they hum with history - and the scent of good food. The quiet 'cloister' garden with its round swimming pool balances the duck pond by the fairly busy road (we gather it's less so at night) at the bottom of the drive and banishes all memory of the plastic cloches opposite!

Rooms: 17 + 3: 17 twins/doubles; 3 apartments for 2.
Price: €75-€190.
Meals: Breakfast €11; lunch & dinner €21-€58.
Closed: Never.

From Nantes A83 South exit 1 for La Roche sur Yon; right D178 to Viais.

Map No: 2

Le Palais Briau

Rue de la Madeleine
44370 Varades
Loire-Atlantique

Tel: (0)2 40 83 45 00
Fax: (0)2 40 83 49 30
E-mail: palaisbrio@aol.com
Web: welcome.to/palais-briau

Thérèse & François Devouge

A glorious Palladian house perched high on the hillside overlooking the Loire valley. Built in the 1850s by François Briau, an early industrialist who made his fortune building railways, the house is palatial, lovingly restored and saved from commercial modernisation by the present owners. Faithful to the era in which the house was built, they have even held on to Briau's original furniture and fittings (of which he was immensely proud). Madame radiates exuberance and charm; Monsieur is an artist and designer whose impeccable taste has been stamped on every interior. A remarkable colonnaded stair sweeps up to the guests' sitting and dining rooms - pure Napoleon III. Bedrooms are light and large; three are blessed with magnificent views, all have separate dressing-rooms. Exquisite wallpapers, brocade canopies above polished mahogany beds, fine linen, flowers - all elegant and glamorous. Bathrooms are sumptuous and orientally-tiled. The grounds too are fabulous; large areas are completely wild and overgrown and contain the remains of a vast *orangerie*. A breathtaking place.

Rooms: 4: 3 doubles, 1 suite for 2 with children's bed.
Price: €84-€130.
Meals: Breakfast included. Good restaurants nearby.
Closed: Never.

From Angers N23 for Nantes. Château is signposted left at r'bout as you enter Varades.

Hôtel du Martinet

Place de la Croix Blanche
85230 Bouin
Vendée

Tel: (0)2 51 49 08 94
Fax: (0)2 51 49 83 08
E-mail: hotel.martinet@free.fr

Françoise Huchet

Madame Huchet describes the Martinet as a country hotel that is by the sea. It's a fair description: sitting by the pool in the garden you feel very much in the country, but the sea is just down the road. Halfway down the Vendée coast, Bouin is a working seaside village - the pretty church was built in the 14th and 15th centuries - not somewhere that has sprung up for the tourists. Madame Huchet's son Emmanuel runs oyster beds off the village, and busy little fishing ports are clustered along the coast. This is a real family hotel and Emmanuel is also the chef, specialising, unsurprisingly, in fresh fish and seafood. Meals are either in a cosy blue-panelled dining room or a more summery one in a veranda looking onto the garden. The rooms are simply but attractively decorated, some in the main house and some like little cottages alongside the swimming pool. A great place to bring children for a holiday: the hotel is relaxed and informal, there are country walks as well as beaches and Emmanuel will be happy to take you to see his oysters. *No smoking here.*

Rooms: 30: 23 doubles/twins, 1 triple,
6 duplexes for 4-6.
Price: Doubles/twins/triple €46-€91,
duplexes €58-€95, half-board for 2 €48-70 p.p.
Meals: Breakfast €6; lunch & dinner €19-€23.
Closed: Never.

*51km south-west of Nantes on D751 past Bouaye,
then D758 through Bourgneuf en Retz towards
Noirmoutier for 9km.*

Map No: 11

Hôtel du Général d'Elbée

Place du Château
85330 Noirmoutier en l'Ile
Vendée

Tel: (0)2 51 39 10 29
Fax: (0)2 51 39 08 23
E-mail: general-delbee@wanadoo.fr
Web: www.esprit-de-france.com

M Philippe Savry

The General in question came to a sorry end, shot on the square for raising an army of Vendéen royalists against the Revolution, but was allowed, as an officer, to face the firing squad in his armchair. This house is where the rebellion was planned, a solid, powerful building down by the bridge, just below the castle, at the heart of life on Noirmoutier. The sea air makes the colours soft and limpid, the land and seascapes are flat and bewitching (Renoir was very taken with this spot), the inner garden and swimming pool were a haven for the general's privileged guests. Inside, the atmospheric old building is fittingly furnished with excellent country antiques, 18th-century fireplaces and fresh flowers. Bedrooms in the wing over the garden have been recently redecorated and are very pleasant indeed. Those in the 18th-century part, which also has a big terrace over the canal, may be in need of a little face-lift. But all bathrooms are excellent, the suites under the rafters on the second floor are ideal for families and a quiet, careful welcome is waiting for all.

Rooms: 27: 23 doubles,
4 suites for 3-4.
Price: Doubles €91-€136, family
rooms €113-€182, suites €168-€258.
Meals: Breakfast €10. Dinner available
locally.
Closed: Mid-October-April.

*From Nantes ring road south west D723,
D751, D758 to Beauvoir sur Mer. Road
to Noirmoutier via Le Gois only possible
at low tide. Otherwise take bridge.*

Hôtel Fleur de Sel

Rue des Saulniers
85330 Noirmoutier en l'Ile
Vendée

Tel: (0)2 51 39 09 07
Fax: (0)2 51 39 09 76
E-mail: info@fleurdesel.fr
Web: www.fleurdesel.fr

Pierre Wattecamps

Noirmoutier has a personality all its own: this group of simple white buildings in its Mediterranean garden is typical. Built in the 1980s, it sits peacefully between sea and salt marsh, long sandy beach and little yachting harbour. It is perfect for family holidays, with tennis court, golf driving range, big pool and superb outdoor jacuzzi. Bedrooms are good too, some in classic cosy style with country pine furniture and fabrics, others more bracing with ship-shape yew furniture and yachting motifs; several have little ground-floor terraces. The delightful, caring owners have humour and intelligence; their daughter's paintings are sometimes shown here. The chef has worked with the very best in Paris and meals are served by courteous waiters in the airy, raftered dining room or on the oleander-lined terrace. It is all clean-cut, sun-warmed, impeccable and welcoming. There is a bridge, but try and come by the Passage du Gois causeway, open 3 hours twice a day round low tide: an unforgettable 4km drive 'through the sea' where shellfish-diggers cluster. The island is, of course, very popular in summer.

Rooms: 35: 30 doubles, 3 triples, 2 family.
Price: €64-€113.
Meals: Breakfast €9; lunch €23; dinner €30-€36.
Closed: 2 November-12 February.

From Paris A11 for Nantes. 82km south-west of Nantes D751 Bouaye then D758 Bourgneuf en Retz, Beauvoir sur Mer to cross Passage du Gois at low tide or Pont de Fromentine. Hotel 500m behind church.

Map No: 11

Château de la Flocellière

85700 La Flocellière
Vendée

Tel: (0)2 51 57 22 03
Fax: (0)2 51 57 75 21
E-mail: erika.vignial@wanadoo.fr
Web: www.flocellierecastle.com

Vicomte & Vicomtesse Patrice Vignial

You really need to see La Flocellière from a helicopter: the aerial view is the most striking. Funnily enough, the origin of the name is apparently 'Flower of the Sky'. The castle – although the part the family live in looks like a 'château', the rest is definitely a 'castle', complete with towers and battlements – was built in around 1090 and is listed as a *Monument Historique*. If you are coming as a family, the best option would probably be a week in either the Tower or the Louis XIII Pavilion, each sleeping about eight, with your own garden and use of the big swimming pool. Otherwise, stay in the château itself: rooms are vast, gracious and opulent, with huge windows on two sides onto the gardens and park. You can lounge around in the drawing room or the library or explore the park. If you like, you will be given a full tour of the estate and the château. If you want to eat in, dinner is either with the Vicomte and Vicomtesse or en famille if you prefer. Lots to see round about: the historical enactment at Puy du Fou is only 7km away so you can pretend the last few centuries never happened. *Special rates for long stays.*

Rooms: 8 + 2: 1 single, 6 doubles,
1 suite; 2 houses for 8.
Price: Doubles €100-€130,
suite €130-€185.
Houses €1,067-€1,524 per week.
Meals: Breakfast €8; dinner by
arrangement €45.
Closed: Never

*A11 Paris for Angers; N160 to Cholet;
D752 for Pouzauges until St Michel
Mont Mercure.
Signposted.*

Le Domaine de Mestré

49590 Fontevraud l'Abbaye
Maine-et-Loire

Tel: (0)2 41 51 75 87
Fax: (0)2 41 51 71 90
E-mail: domaine-de-mestre@wanadoo.fr
Web: www.dauge-fontevraud.com

Dominique & Rosine Dauge

History oozes from every corner of Mestré. A Roman road, a cockleshell for the pilgrims who stayed en route to Compostela, part of a 13th-century chapel - and the mill and tithe barn remind us that monks farmed here when Mestré was part of the vast Abbey. Most of the present building is 18th-century: the family have farmed here for 200 years and keep the traditions of French country hospitality. Monsieur runs the eco-conscious farm, milking by hand. Madame makes fine natural soaps, and cooks; two daughters help out. All take pride in providing wholesome, home-grown food and elegant service. Big, rustic-style rooms are furnished with old family furniture, some of it well lived in - huge *lits bateaux* or brass beds with wool-stuffed mattresses and fluffy eiderdowns; armchairs, including a pair of fine old American rocking chairs - and some have great views over to the wooded valley. The sitting room is pure 'Victorian parlour' with its dark panelling, red wallpaper, card table and leather-bound books; the dining room is simply delightful. A sense of timeless welcome and class enfolds the privileged guest.

Rooms: 12: 2 singles, 8 doubles/ triples, 2 suites.
Price: Singles €39, doubles/triples €53-€63, suites €95.
Meals: Breakfast €7; dinner €24, by arrangement.
Closed: 20 November-February. Open weekends only in March.

From Saumur D947 for Chinon; right in Montsoreau for Fontevraud l'Abbaye; 1st right 1.5km after Montsoreau; signposted.

Hôtel Anne d'Anjou

32 quai Mayaud
49400 Saumur
Maine-et-Loire

Tel: (0)2 41 67 30 30
Fax: (0)2 41 67 51 00
E-mail: hotel-anneanjou@saumur.net
Web: www.hotel-anneanjou.com

Jean-René Camus

Any malign inhabitants of the château could have tossed rocks onto the roof of this elegant townhouse. It is just below, on the banks of the Loire in a picture-book position. The main staircase is listed and has a fine wrought-iron balustrade and trompe l'œil that gives the impression of a dome. The main reception area, big and filled with light, has just a discreet desk to welcome you. The bedrooms on the first and second floors look either onto the river and the road, or onto the courtyard and château. Two of the rooms are especially fine: the listed *Salle Empire* has terracotta panelling and moulded friezes, and the *Salle Epoque* has a splendid old chequered tiled floor and grey panelling. Another room has a fine parquet floor and a balcony overlooking the river. Top floor rooms have solid old ceiling beams and views of the château through dormer windows. Some front rooms are plainer and look over the road, but the traffic is light, especially at night. The new owners are breathing fresh life into this lovely old building, and doing so with a mixture of dynamic (ex-naval) efficiency and Seychellois flair.

Rooms: 43 + 2 apartments: 41 doubles/twins, 2 family; 2 apts for 4.
Price: €72-€159.
Meals: Buffet breakfast €9; lunch & dinner €29-€55; restaurant closed Sundays from October-Easter.
Closed: Never.

From Saumur follow signs to Saumur Centre. Continue along south bank of Loire on Chinon-Fontevraud road. Hotel below château 500m after theatre.

Château des Briottières

49330 Champigné
Maine-et-Loire

Tel: (0)2 41 42 00 02
Fax: (0)2 41 42 01 55
E-mail: briottieres@wanadoo.fr
Web: www.briottieres.com

François de Valbray

This heavenly *petit château* has been in the same family for 200 years and is now occupied by the relaxed and endearing Monsieur de Valbray, his wife and six children. *La vieille France* is alive and well here and your hosts love to share it with guests. A magnificent library/billiard room leads into a small sitting room, but if it's grandness you're after, share your pre-dinner aperitif with Monsieur in the huge, and hugely aristocratic *salon*, furnished with family portraits, tapestries and fine antiques. Sweep up the marble staircase to the bedrooms on the first floor, feel the comfort of the beds (the newest are king-sized), relish the park views. Several bedrooms have been recently redecorated but traditional furniture and fabrics prevail. Some beds are charmingly canopied, while the sumptuous family suite includes a small governess's room. Some bathrooms are marbled; the more expensive sport towelling robes. In the grounds is a delightful country-style *orangerie*, let out as a *gîte*, and a large swimming pool in the walled garden. It is the perfect aristocratic retreat.

Rooms: 15 + 1: 12 doubles, 3 suites; 1 cottage for 4-6.
Price: Doubles €128-€300; suites & cottage €257-357, breakfast included.
Meals: Breakfast €10; dinner €46, including aperitif & coffee. Restaurant closed December-mid-March.
Closed: Two weeks in February.

From A11 exit 11 at Durtal onto D859 to Châteauneuf sur Sarthe, then D770 to Champigné, D768 for Sablé; left after 4km to Les Briottières. Signposted.

Map No: 2

Château du Plessis Anjou

49220 La Jaille Yvon
Maine-et-Loire

Tel: (0)2 41 95 12 75
Fax: (0)2 41 95 14 41
E-mail: plessis.anjou@wanadoo.fr
Web: www.chateau-du-plessis.com

Claude-Eric & Valérie Vadot

Built in the 16th century, Le Plessis has always been in the family and has been taking guests for 14 years. Though large and very elegant, the château, set in 14 hectares of wooded park is inviting rather than imposing, with curving tiled roofs, white walls and creeper-covered shutters. You can play tennis or fish or sail off from the grounds in a balloon; two of the best *Sons et Lumières* are within easy reach, so are the châteaux and wineries of the Loire. Dinner, at a long table in a rather ornate dining room with Roman friezes, could include salmon, pork fillet with apricots, cheese and a crisp fruit tart. Although a grown-up sort of place, children would be made welcome; the owners are particularly friendly and Valérie has a young child herself. While one bedroom is very striking, with a lofty beamed ceiling and beds set in a deep turquoise alcove, some of the others are less so. *An English-speaking guide is available for many activities: wine tasting, cycling, visits to châteaux and gardens.*

Rooms: 8 doubles/twins.
Price: €100-€150.
Meals: Breakfast included; hosted dinner €46, including drinks.
Closed: November-March, except by arrangement.

From A11 exit Durtal on D859 to Châteauneuf sur Sarthe; D770 for Le Lion d'Angers for 18km. Right on N162 for Château Gontier. After 11km right on D189 for La Jaille Yvon.

Auberge du Roi René
53290 Saint Denis d'Anjou
Mayenne

Tel: (0)2 43 70 52 30
Fax: (0)2 43 70 58 75
E-mail: info@roi-rene.fr

Marie-Christine & Pierre de
Vaubernier

Monsieur is the original *bon viveur*, and looks the part. He's also a fund of culture and wit and a passionate believer in the art of good living. Madame has no airs and graces either: she is friendly, straightforward and chief gastronome. Food is a way of life here: Marie-Christine has passed muster with several top chefs, the Trois Gros brothers included, and cooks a *cuisine d'amour*. An attractive grassy courtyard fronts the restaurant. The stately Auberge, which dates from the 15th century, lies in the centre of St Denis, a delightful village (let Monsieur be your guide). The bedrooms on the first floor are reached via ancient stone stairs in the tower and have magnificent old oak doors and terracotta floors; they are narrow, cosy, charming, well lit. There are two dining rooms to choose from: one in the medieval part, warm-carpeted with a huge and handsome stone fireplace; the other, pure 18th-century, elegant gracious and light. It is everything that an auberge should be, and more.

Rooms: 4: 3 doubles, 1 suite.
Price: €53-€84.
Meals: Breakfast €8; dinner €12-€38.
Closed: Never.

From Sablé sur Sarthe D309 to St Denis d'Anjou. Auberge in centre of village.

Château de Craon

53400 Craon
Mayenne

Tel: (0)2 43 06 11 02
Fax: (0)2 43 06 05 18

Comte Louis de Guebriant, Comte & Comtesse Loïk de Guebriant

Natural authentic elegance informs both place and people at Craon with its innumerable expressions of history, taste and personality: an oval room with curved doors to the dressing room and a lift down to its own sunken marble bathroom, a dear little children's room tucked in above the bathrooms, a romantic canopied double bed, superb reception rooms (occasionally open to the public), a magnificent stone staircase. Outside is the perfect château park: a formal terraced bit with pool and fountain (a mini-Versailles?), a carefully casual English-style bit, some really wild corners beyond. Monsieur le Comte, devoted to his garden, particularly the huge walled *potager* (a mini-Villandry?), is the sprightly, intelligent patriarch of this very close family which will extend to include you. Loïk and Hélène, the younger generation and parents of six, have a wonderful sense of humour and welcome their guests with spontaneous ease. Teresa Berganza stayed and practised with her pianist at the grand piano - she too enjoyed the gracious, natural sense of hospitality. A very special place.

Rooms: 6: 2 doubles, 1 twin, 3 singles. Extra space for children.
Price: Singles €45-€70; Doubles €100-€140.
Closed: Mid-December-mid-January.
Meals: Breakfast included. You can picnic in the park. Lunch and dinner available in village.

From Château Gontiers N171 to Craon. Château clearly signposted as you enter town.

Le Tertre
72270 Dureil
Sarthe

Tel: (0)2 43 92 46 12
Fax: (0)2 43 92 46 12
E-mail: kalker-gerson@infonie.fr
Web: www.letertre.com

David & Corrine Kalker-Gerson

David and Corinne think of this as a bed and breakfast, but Le Tertre is definitely at home in this book. Corinne is from Annecy, while David is a larger than life mix of French and American, with a pet wolf he brought back from a reintroduction programme in Colorado. The three rooms, all with garden views, can be booked separately or as a whole, giving you your own country house in 40 acres of wooded farmland, within reach of the châteaux. Breakfast is brought to your room, or served on the terrace. You can order a delicious picnic complete with chilled fruit and wine, and in the evening can either cook in the well-equipped kitchen shared by the guest rooms (maid service can be arranged) or David and Corinne will suggest somewhere delicious. If you are staying for five nights, you will be invited for dinner the first evening with David and Corinne. David is proud of his wines and the menu will have been inspired by the local farmers' market and their own organic produce. They will also organise riding or leisurely trips down the river.

Rooms: 3 + 1: 1 single, 2 doubles; 1 cottage for 6-8
Price: Single €99, doubles €183-€213; whole cottage €274-€305. Weekend rates available.
Meals: Breakfast included; picnic €12; hosted dinner €38 incl. aperitif, wine and digestive, by arrangement.
Closed: Never.

A11 for Nantes; exit Sablé La Flèche; D306 for Sablé; D23 through Bailleul/Arthezé; D8 for Parcé. 2km after sign 'Les Belles Poules', C1 right to Dureil. House on left.

Château de Saint Paterne

72610 Saint Paterne
Sarthe

Tel: (0)2 33 27 54 71
Fax: (0)2 33 29 16 71
E-mail: paterne@club-internet.fr
Web: www.chateau-saintpaterne.com

Charles-Henry & Segolène de Valbray

A twentieth century fairytale: this 15th-century château and park was abandoned by its owners for 30 years, rediscovered by the heir who left sunny yellow Provence for cool green Normandy to resurrect the old shell. He and his wife are a charming young couple and have redecorated with refreshing taste, respecting the style and history of the building, adding a zest of southern colour to panelled, antique-filled rooms, pretty country furniture before ancient fireplaces and hand-rendered, rough and 'imperfect' finishes - nothing stiff or fixed. Sitting, dining and first-floor bedrooms are in château-style (plus a South-American rug on a parquet floor); the *Henri IV* room (he had a mistress here, of course) has thrillingly painted beams; ancestors and *objets* adorn but don't clutter. The attic floor is fantasy among the rafters: nooks, corners and split levels, a striking green and red bathroom, another bath sunk below the floor. Your host, an excellent, unfrilly cook, uses exotic vegetables from his Laotian-tended kitchen garden. A brilliant, attractive mixture of past and present values and superb hosts.

Rooms: 7 + 1: 5 doubles, 2 triple;
1 cottage for 2/3.
Price: €85-€137.
Meals: Breakfast €9; dinner €38,
including aperitif and coffee.
Closed: Mid-January-mid-April.

*From Alençon D311 for
Chartres/Mamers. St Paterne on
outskirts of Alençon. Through village;
entrance for château on right opposite
garage (Elf).*

Hôtel Haras de la Potardière
72200 Crosmières
Sarthe

Tel: (0)2 43 45 83 47
Fax: (0)2 43 45 81 06
E-mail: haras-de-la-potardiere@wanadoo.fr

Mme Benoist

Marie-Yvonne Benoist's mother inherited La Potardière from her father and in 1990 entrusted her daughter with taking care of it – and making it pay for its keep. Luckily her husband François is an architect, specialising in restoring old buildings. They live in a creeper-covered wing of the château with their four children: Camille, Alexis, Noëlle and Emeline. In fact one of the most appealing features of La Potardière is a brochure-cum-history written in the form of a letter from all six of them. Marie-Yvonne's grandfather built up a successful centre for training show jumpers alongside an established thoroughbred stud. After ten years of empty stables, in 1992 La Potardière began taking stallions from the prestigious *Haras National* for the summer months, when owners bring mares from all over France. Most of the rooms look out onto peacefully grazing horses. Bedrooms – seven in the chateau and 10 in the farm - are just as you would hope: a graceful mixture of pretty and elegant, wood and flowers. What a place for a horse-mad child! But all children will love it: fields, a safe pool and even a Wendy house full of toys.

Rooms: 17: 4 doubles/twins, 1 triple, 2 family suites in château; 7 doubles/twins, 1 triple, 2 family suites on farm.
Price: Doubles €60-€100, triple €76, suites €92-145.
Meals: Breakfast €8.
Closed: Never.

From Paris, leave A11 at exit 10 and D306 for La Fleche. Right in village of Crosmières and follow signs.

Map No: 7

Château d'Esclimont

28700 Saint Symphorien le Château
Eure-et-Loir

Tel: (0)2 37 31 15 15
Fax: (0)2 37 31 57 91
E-mail: esclimont@grandesetapes.fr
Web: www.esclimont.com

Stéphane Jitiaux

The château that has everything: built in 1543 by the Archbishop of Tours, owned by the Rochefoucauld family until 1968, it was then transformed into an impressive hotel. Superb architectural features, swish décor and a great setting - not only the immediate moat, gardens and mature parkland but Paris only an hour away. The La Rochefoucauld motto *"C'est mon plaisir"* could have been devised for the present staff; they are immensely courteous and genuinely seem to have guests' best interest at heart, whether they arrive by helicopter for a business meeting or come for a romantic weekend. Bedrooms and bathrooms, especially those in the château itself, are pretty splendidly comfortable, as you would expect; there is always renovation work in progress, Forth Bridge-style. Dining rooms are plushly traditional (and have menus to match) with chandeliers, padded chairs and carefully restored *cuir de Cordoue*. Eat on the terrace or by the pool. There are musical evenings and cookery courses, tennis courts, bicycles and boating on the lake - you'll need the exercise. Less than 1 hour from Paris and 20 minutes from Chartres.

Rooms: 47 + 6: 47 doubles/twins;
6 apartments for 4-5.
Price: €168-€991.
Meals: Breakfast €18; buffet breakfast €24; lunch €35-€79; dinner €59-€79; children's meals €21.
Closed: Never.

A10/A11, exit 1 Ablis. N10 for Chartres. After 6km right on D168.

Loire Valley

No cook who has attained mastery over her craft ever apologizes for the presence of garlic in her productions.
Ruth Gottfried, The Questing Cook (1927)

D. Chauveau, Conseil Général du Loiret

Auberge du Port des Roches

Le Port des Roches
72800 Luché-Pringé
Sarthe

Tel: (0)2 43 45 44 48
Fax: (0)2 43 45 39 61

Valérie & Thierry Lesiourd

If you can see yourself sitting at the edge of slow green water of an evening, perhaps watching out for the odd fish, this is the place for you. Not grand or anything – this is the Loir not the Loire, an altogether less glamorous river – but we can hear you saying: "Oh, what a pretty spot". Valérie and Thierry have been here about five years, are young, very friendly though a touch shy, and full of enthusiasm for their auberge. Their main business is probably the restaurant, they can seat about 50 people in two rooms, but Valérie is justly proud of the effort she has put into the bedrooms – and into the way everything positively sparkles. Rooms are not large but done in fresh colours, sky blue, for example, with crisp white bedcovers. At the front you will have a view over the Loir. A small road does run past the hotel, but windows are double glazed. Not a place to bring children for a long stay, as they wouldn't have much room to run about, but they would be very happy for a stopover. This is a very quiet, very French place to stay, in easy reach of the châteaux but less expensive.

Rooms: 12: 9 doubles, 2 twins, 1 triple.
Price: €39-€48.
Meals: Breakfast €5.50; lunch & dinner €18-€32; picnic available. Restaurant closed Sunday evenings & Mondays.
Closed: February; 1 week in autumn.

From La Flèche N23 to Le Mans for 5km; right on D13 to Luché-Pringé. Through village for 2km, right on D214. Signposted.

Domaine de Courtalain

Château de Courtalain
28290 Courtalain
Eure-et-Loir

Tel: (0)2 37 98 80 25
Fax: (0)2 37 98 84 64
E-mail: courtalain@libertysurf.fr
Web: www.chateau-de-courtalain.com

Comte de Gontaut-Biron

An architectural kaleidescope is what the owners call their great pile, first built in 1483 when turrets and lookouts were the thing, added to down the centuries culminating, in the late 1700s, with a smallholding with colonnaded farmhouse where lords and ladies played farmers like their masters at Versailles. The last estate of the great Montmorencys, this was once a self-sufficient community with its own staging post. Three of the beautiful outbuildings now house the soberly welcoming guest rooms; they have elegant inside shutters, some antiques and parquet, timeless peace pouring in from the park. The suite in the château is in the rich bed canopy and high windows class, of course. Your host, the young count, is friendly and active; his father is fully occupied with the agricultural side of the family business - they make a good team. There are also splendid reception rooms (the orangery is a wonderful wedding hall), a duck-swum lake, squirrels dashing across the vast expanses of lawn and up the ancient trees of the impressive gardens, and... three meteorites to be investigated. *No smoking here.*

Rooms: 29: 3 singles, 19 doubles/twins, 5 triples, 2 family.
Price: Singles €67, doubles/twins €79, triples & family €95-€105.
Meals: Breakfast €7; dinner €34.
Closed: Mid-December-3 January.

A11 for Le Mans exit 4, then D955 for Brou. At Brou D15 for Arrou; D927 to Courtalain. Entrance opp. petrol station. Signposted from Brou.

Map No: 7

Château de Beaujeu

18300 Sens Beaujeu
Cher

Tel: (0)2 48 79 07 95
Fax: (0)2 48 79 05 07
E-mail: info@chateau-de-beaujeu.com
Web: www.chateau-de-beaujeu.com

M & Mme Wilfrid de Pommereau

Sweep up the tree-lined avenue, pass the stables and the dovecotes in the yard, step back in time: your turretted 16th-century château has been in the family since the French Revolution. Monsieur de Pommereau is elderly and hard of hearing and stays in the background, but will recount reams of family history when asked. And every item tells a story: the stags' heads on the wall were shot by his grandmother a century ago. It is a rare pleasure to spend a night under the roof of a château so untouched by modernity. No carefully renovated 'features' here - everything is as it was. The paintwork may be peeling, the wallpapers faded, but the colours are original and refreshingly unsynthetic. The trompe l'œil on the walls is all of a piece, in spite of the cracks. Downstairs rooms are filled with generations of possessions, including magnificent Aubusson tapestries on the walls. Bedrooms are comfortable, with gracious windows overlooking the park; bathrooms, with '60s fittings, slightly eccentric. The suites in the tower are lovely, with splendid mouldings, windows and doorways in curved glass. *No smoking here.*

Rooms: 4: 2 doubles/twins, 2 suites.
Price: Doubles €110, suites
€120-€150.
Meals: Breakfast included; dinner €38, by arrangement.
Closed: November-Easter.

From Sancerre D955 for Bourges. Right on D923 for Aubigny sur Nère. Left on D7 to Sens Beaujeu. In village left at fountain, D74 for Neuilly en Sancerre. Down hill, château at end of drive.

Château d'Ivoy

18380 Ivoy le Pré
Cher

Tel: (0)2 48 58 85 01
Fax: (0)2 48 58 85 02
E-mail: chateau.divoy@wanadoo.fr
Web: perso.wanadoo.fr/chateau.divoy/

Marie France Gouëffon-de Vaivre

Every antique bed is appropriately canopied (Kipling: frothy mosquito net on carved Anglo-Indian bed; Lord Drummond: the Olde-English feel), every superb bathroom a study in modern fittings on period washstands. Ivoy is home to an interior designer who has achieved miracles since buying it from a famous entomologist who had planted a tropical rainforest in one stateroom, now the fine-furnished 'Spode' dining room. It was built for Mary Stuart's Purser, Drummond: the Stuarts were allowed to create a Scottish duchy here that lasted 200 years and it became the Drummond family seat after the battle of Culloden. The front is stern, the back opens wide onto sweeping lawns, park and hills - all bedrooms face this way. The house radiates refinement and your hostess's infectious delight. She will welcome you in her grey-green hall with its lovely sandstone floor and ceramic stove, invite you to use the library (home to a huge spider... imprisoned in a glass paperweight) or the *salon*, and will then retire discreetly. A very special place to stay. *Children over 12 welcome. No smoking here.*

Rooms: 6-7: 5 doubles, 1 twin, all four-poster beds. Can combine some rooms to make suite for 3.
Price: €125-€170. Extra small bedroom €61.
Meals: Breakfast included. Lunch & dinner available locally.
Closed: Never.

From A10 exit Salbris D944 for Bourges to Neuvy sur Barangeon; left on D926 to La Chapelle d'Angillon; D12 to Ivoy. Château on right after church.

Prieuré d'Orsan

18170 Maisonnais
Cher

Tel: (0)2 48 56 27 50
Fax: (0)2 48 56 39 64
Web: www.prieuredorsan.com

Patrice Taravella & Sonja Lesot

The priory was originally built in 1107 - mostly to house the unwanted wives of the local nobility who were forced to take the veil - and stands in rural France at its most unspoilt. The oldest remaining buildings, probably the refectory and dormitory, are from the 16th century and form three sides of a square, enclosing beautifully restored gardens, which are open to visitors. Patrice and Sonia, both architects, saved the house from long abandon ten years ago and have preserved the sense of harmonious calm associated with a convent: there is no 'hotel' feel to the place at all, and the visitors to the gardens don't make it feel busy either. Subdued colours and a contemporary, minimalist style work perfectly here: the striking black and beige striped curtains providing a dramatic touch in the sitting room. You will eat either in a large dining room or a smaller, more intimate one, or in a pergola under the vines when it's warm. Bedrooms have pine-panelled walls, shutters and windows and doors painted in a soft grey-green. You will look out onto the wonderful garden and each find a little teddy bear warming your bed.

Rooms: 6: 3 doubles, 3 triples.
Price: €99-€191.
Meals: Breakfast €14; lunch €30; dinner €45
Closed: November-April.

From Paris exit 8 from A71 to St Amand Montrond; D925 towards Lignières; D3 towards Le Chatelet then D951 to Maisonnais.

Le Manoir des Remparts

14 rue des Remparts
36800 Saint Gaultier
Indre

Tel: (0)2 54 47 94 87
Fax: (0)2 54 47 94 87
E-mail: willem.prinsloo@wanadoo.fr

Ren Rijpstra

Behind imposing gates and high walls - the house is built on the outside of the old city ramparts - lies this charming 18th-century manor. The place is a gem: a gravelled courtyard and wisteria-clad barn at the front, a large, tree-filled walled garden with summer house at the back. Your hospitable and punctilious Dutch hosts have renovated the house with sympathy and style, preserving the beautiful fireplaces, the parquet floors and the marvellous oak staircase. Bedrooms are really comfortable. The style is essentially Provençal - Ren is an interior designer - with *soleado* and *toile de Jouy* wallpapers, country antiques, old paintings and pillows decked in fine antique linen. One room has a metal-framed four-poster with red check curtains. Bathrooms are sumptuous, the traditional fittings offset by sea-grass flooring and elegant drapes. Dine on *mille-feuille* of salmon in the dining room in the next door barn; retire with a book to the guests' sitting room which is warm and inviting with its book-lined walls, soft lighting and ancient beams. *The two-bedroom apartment has balconies and ground floor terraces. No smoking here.*

Rooms: 4 + 1 apartment: 3 doubles, 1 suite; 1 apt for 4.
Price: Doubles & suite €99-€114; apartment €1,068 per week.
Meals: Breakfast included; dinner, 5 courses, €24, by arrangement.
Closed: 15 December-2 January.

From Châteauroux A20 for Limoges, N151 Le Blanc/Poitiers. Entering St Gaultier stay on Le Blanc road; cross 2 sets of lights; right, then immed. left across Le Blanc road. Pass supermarket towards Thenay, continue for 500m. Manoir on right.

Château de Boisrenault

36500 Buzançais
Indre

Tel: (0)2 54 84 03 01
Fax: (0)2 54 84 10 57
E-mail: boisrenault@wanadoo.fr
Web: www.chateau-du-boisrenault.com

Yves & Sylvie du Manoir

Built by a 19th-century aristocrat as a wedding present for his daughter - well overdue, she'd had two sons by the time it was finished - this is a turretted, customised, Renaissance château. Noble and imposing on the outside, it's very much a family home within. Furniture, objects, pictures, all have a tale to tell and there are plenty of hunting trophies and stags' heads on the walls. Reception rooms are lofty, with huge fireplaces. One sitting room has a baby grand; another, smaller and cosier, is lined with books. Each bedroom is an adventure in itself. Named after the family's children and grandchildren, the rooms feature a hotchpotch of pieces from different periods, including some excellent antiques. A couple of stuffed pheasants make unusual lampshades in *Hadrien's* room and offset the yellow walls beautifully. Breakfast and dinner are shared with other guests at a vast table in the dining room. A delicious pool is discreetly tucked away behind trees in the grounds; table tennis and table football are a godsend on rainy days. A super place for a family stay.

Rooms: 6 doubles.
Price: €69-€96.
Meals: Breakfast included. Other meals available locally.
Closed: January.

From A20 exit 11 on D8 to Levroux; D926 for Buzançais; château on left 3km before town.

La Petite Fadette

Place du Chateau
36400 Nohant
Indre

Tel: (0)2 54 31 01 48
Fax: (0)2 54 31 10 19
Web: www.aubergepetitefadette.com

M Bernard Gabriel Chapleau

Just off the main road, this tiny unspoilt village takes you back two centuries to George Sand's quiet country childhood, whence she proceeded to make her name, rather noisily, as an early advocate of feminism and free love (with Chopin, Musset, et al). Opposite her elegant house, this pretty country inn fits the scene perfectly. A cluster of village houses of age and character, it has been in the Chapleau family for generations, houses their fine period furniture and feels like home. Arched doors open into the simple tea room where pink-clothed tables lead to the grand piano (they often have recitals) and the old oak stairs up to the bedrooms. Under the stairs is a luxurious loo for diners and beyond is a sophisticated restaurant whose vaulted wooden ceiling and magnificent fireplace frame elegantly-laid tables, ready for the chef's tempting dishes. The attractive bedrooms are all different, cosily done in traditional style with antiques, good fabrics and highly up-to-date bathrooms. Both village and inn have exceptional atmosphere that may make you stop and wonder.

Rooms: 9: 8 doubles, 1 suite.
Price: €53-€107.
Meals: Breakfast €8; lunch & dinner €15-€38.
Closed: Never.

From Chateauroux D943 for La Châtre. 5km before La Châtre left into Nohant. Hotel in centre of village opposite church.

Map No: 8

La Rabouillère

Chemin de Marçon
41700 Contres
Loir-et-Cher

Tel: (0)2 54 79 05 14
Fax: (0)2 54 79 59 39
E-mail: rabouillere@wanadoo.fr
Web: rabouillere-ifrance.com

Martine & Jean-Marie Thimonnier

Monsieur - a construction engineer by profession - built the traditional Solonge farmhouse himself. This building, with its timber frame and herringbone brickwork, and his first project, the delicious little house next door, bring together old and new: traditional materials, modern comforts. Monsieur is constantly planning improvements and is a most civilised and articulate host. Madame is charming too, and has thoughtfully furnished the interiors. The first-floor suite of the main house is large and splendid, decorated in pretty Laura Ashley fabrics and with fine views over woodland and park. Other rooms are quite a bit smaller, but sympathetically decorated too, with good sized bathrooms (towels are changed every day, bed linen every other), communicating doors between two sets of rooms should you need them, and shared kitchenette. Some lovely old family pieces decorate the smaller house next door, which has a more rustic feel. Breakfasts are served in the spacious guests' dining/sitting room at tables beautifully laid with English china, and include eggs from the farm and home-made jam.

Rooms: 5 + 1: 4 doubles, 1 suite; 1 cottage for 2-5.
Price: Doubles €55, suite €84; cottage €107-€137.
Meals: Breakfast included. 3 good restaurants less than 10km. Can picnic in garden.
Closed: Never.

Leave A10 at Blois for Vierzon onto D765 to Cheverny; D102 for Contres. Chemin de Marçon is 6km beyond Cheverny on left.

Map No: 7

Hôtel Château des Tertres

Route de Monteaux
41150 Onzain
Loir-et-Cher

Tel: (0)2 54 20 83 88
Fax: (0)2 54 20 89 21
E-mail: chateau.des.tertres@wanadoo.fr
Web: www.chateau-tertres.com

Bernard Valois

A classic mid-19th-century nobleman's house surrounded by mature wooded parkland in the Loire valley - but all is not traditional inside. The young and energetic Monsieur Valois is an artist, and his sense of fun pervades this lovely place. Many of the rooms *are* period pieces, including the sitting rooms and the largest of the bedrooms, some of which are remarkably ornate. The smallest rooms, though, are minimalist - symphonies of creamy yellow and white. That a creative spirit is at work is evident, too, in the gardener's lodge whose four guest rooms have been furnished with panache: one with a massive Italian four-poster, another with a perspex bedhead and a row of medieval steel helmets lined up on the wall! Older children will love it here. Your host is extremely hospitable and will let you in on the secrets of the château if you ask: before it was restored to its original elegance it had an amazingly chequered career, having been a German military headquarters, a school for metal workers and a chicken farm in first three of its former lives.

Rooms: 18 doubles, including 4 in gardener's lodge.
Price: €70-€105.
Meals: Breakfast buffet €8. Other meals available locally.
Closed: Mid-November to week before Easter.

From A10 exit Blois. N152 for Amboise/Tours. Right to Onzain opp. bridge to Chaumont. Left in village for Monteaux. Château 1.5km on right.

Le Moulin de Saint Jean
Saint Jean Saint Germain
37600 Loches
Indre-et-Loire

Tel: (0)2 47 94 70 12
Fax: (0)2 47 94 77 98
E-mail: millstjean@aol.com

Andrew Page & Sue Hutton

A deliciously watery home. We love this place - a restored mill on an island. Having breakfast on the veranda over the mill stream is not the only reason guests return. Sue radiates generosity and charm; Andrew, equally relaxed and friendly, is an excellent cook. Dinners are extremely convivial affairs, shared with your hosts. All is ups and downs, nooks and crannies, big rooms and small ones, character and variety. The guests' sitting room upstairs has French windows opening onto a balcony overlooking the river. Comfy chairs and colourful cushions set the scene; bedrooms, too, are full of personality, and all different. Attractive, high-quality fabrics, interesting pictures and much evidence of Sue's spongeing and stencilling skills. Add a shady garden, a pool, the temptation of about 1,000 paperbacks and the colourful presence of a blue and yellow macaw. Everywhere there is the gentle murmur of running water - which is why this site, however idyllic, is not the most relaxing place for parents of very young children.

Rooms: 5: 3 doubles, 1 twin, 1 triple.
Price: €60-€70.
Meals: Breakfast included; hosted dinner €25, including aperitif, wine & coffee.
Closed: December-January.

From Loches N143, for Châteauroux; pass Perusson, left at sign to St Jean St Germain; house over bridge, last on left.

Le Cheval Blanc
5 Place de l'Eglise
371501 Bléré
Indre-et-Loire

Tel: (0)2 47 30 30 14
Fax: (0)2 47 23 52 80
Web: www.lechevalblancblere.com

Michel & Micheline Blériot

Set in the flowered, cobbled and car-free church square of old Bléré, the *White Horse Inn* has been known for years as one of the best tables in the highly gastronomic Royal Valley and Michel Blériot is keeping that reputation very much alive. He calls his cuisine "lightened classical" and plans his creations around fresh seasonal ingredients. Eating is either in the utterly traditional French atmosphere of original beams, high, rich-draped windows, pale Louis XVI chairs, tall-stemmed glasses and fresh flowers on snow-white cloths, where a certain formality reigns in honour of the fine food, or in warm weather outside in the delightful creeper-clad courtyard. The professional yet delightful staff give really good service. Sleeping is done upstairs in rooms that are all fairly similar in their beamed ceilings, quilted floral prints and dinky lamps. Swimming is at the bottom of the pretty ornamental garden - a rare treat for an urban hotel. The atmosphere is altogether light, fresh and attractive and Bléré is a perfect base for château-crawling - but come above all for the food.

Rooms: 12: 10 doubles/twins, 2 triples.
Price: €57-€85.
Meals: Breakfast €8; weekday lunch €17; dinner €38-€53. Restaurant closed Sunday evenings all year also Mondays during low season.
Closed: January-mid-February

From Tours towards Chenonceaux D140; 4km before Chenonceaux left on D3 to Bléré.

Hôtel du Bon Laboureur et du Château

6 rue du Docteur Bretonneau
37150 Chenonceaux
Indre-et-Loire

Tel: (0)2 47 23 90 02
Fax: (0)2 47 23 82 01
E-mail: laboureur@wanadoo.fr
Web: www.amboise.com/laboureur

Isabelle & Antoine Jeudi

This little hotel, in the middle of the village of Chenonceaux, a short stroll from the château, started life as a coaching inn in the 18th century. Now it has expanded into an adjoining building, the old village school and into a somewhat grander building with a rather pretentious tower known tongue-in-cheek as 'the Manor'. The bedrooms are all light and airy with plenty of space and are kept in tiptop condition. One is in psychedelic green and yellow, another is more traditional in pink and another, smaller, in fresh blue and white. A good spot for seeing the châteaux with children as there are family rooms and the garden has a pool. The heart of the hotel is in the original building, with an elegant 18th-century style dining room and a simpler, more relaxed one next to it. In summer, tables with starched white cloths, candles and flowers are set on the terrace under the trees. Amboise, Chaumont, Chambord and other châteaux are within easy reach so you will have time for a swim and a cocktail before dinner. A large potager behind the hotel supplies vegetables.

Rooms: 22 + 4: 22 doubles;
4 apts for 4.
Price: Doubles €61-€91,
apartments €107-€152.
Meals: Breakfast €8; picnic €8;
dinner €26-€56. Restaurant closed
Wednesday lunchtimes & Thursdays
during low season.
Closed: Mid-November-mid-December;
January.

From Blois, cross Loire onto D751 then D764 to Montrichard. Follow signs to Chenonceaux. Hotel on right in village centre.

Map No: 7   144

Château des Ormeaux

Nazelles
37530 Amboise
Indre-et-Loire

Tel: (0)2 47 23 26 51
Fax: (0)2 47 23 19 31
E-mail: chateaudesormeaux@wanadoo.fr
Web: www.chateaudesormeaux.com

Emmanuel Guenot

The charming owners of Des Ormeaux were happy to swap the small-town mentality of Savonnières for the grandeur of their turreted 19th-century château in its 67 acres. They live in 'cave' rooms built into the rock face behind the hill-top château. Corner bedrooms on two floors - original panelling on the first floor, sloping ceilings on the second - have tiny little *boudoirs* off the main room in the turret; all are named after classical composers. A decent size, with elaborate bedcovers and drapes and massive bathrooms, they are very grand in a turn-of-the-century way. One room, blue and gold, has a marble fireplace and an *armoire à glace*, a wall of mirrors hidden behind an apparently ordinary cupboard; another, decorated in ochre and maroon, a crystal chandelier and plushly canopied bed. Yet more crystal chandeliers in the dining room, where evening meals, shared with one or more of your hosts - there are six in total - are enhanced by background Bach and candlelight. Best of all, from wherever you stand (or swim) the valley views are superb.

Rooms: 6: 3 doubles, 3 twins.
Price: €107-€115.
Meals: Breakfast included; hosted dinner €38, by arrangement.
Closed: Never.

From Tours N152 for Blois. After Vouvray, left to Noizay and from there D1 for Nazelles. Château on left about 2km after Noizay.

Le Manoir Les Minimes

34 quai Charles Guinot
37400 Amboise
Indre-et-Loire

Tel: (0)2 47 30 40 40
Fax: (0)2 47 30 40 77
E-mail: manoir-les-minimes@wanadoo.fr
Web: www.amboise.com/les-minimes

Éric Deforges & Patrice Longet

Every detail has been thought out with tender care, lovingly-chosen antiques and *objets* placed to create a light sophistication. A far cry from the *Minimes* order who had a convent here until it was destroyed in the French Revolution; then this noble townhouse took the site. Between majestic Loire and historic castle, the manor has 18th-century grace and generous windows that look onto its big courtyard, the castle and the lustrous river. Before opening Les Minimes in 1998, the charmingly young and enthusiastic Éric Deforges was a fashion designer, hence his faultless eye for fabric, colour and detail. Exquisitely-decorated rooms are big - slightly smaller on the top floor, with beams and river views from their dormers - and have luxurious bathrooms. The masterpiece is the suite where the *toile de Jouy* wall fabric seems to be one single piece. The elegant chequered hall leads to a series of interconnecting *salons*. There's a smaller, more intimate television room and a breakfast room in soft yellow and grey. With fresh flowers everywhere, this feels more like a classy home than a formal hotel.

Rooms: 13: 11 doubles, 2 suites.
Price: Doubles €80-€150, suites €190-€375.
Meals: Breakfast €11.
Closed: December-mid-March; Sundays.

From A10 for Amboise. Cross Loire, right on D751, for town centre. Hotel on left approaching town centre.

Map No: 7

Château de la Bourdaisière

25 rue de la Bourdaisière
37270 Montlouis sur Loire
Indre-et-Loire

Tel: (0)2 47 45 16 31
Fax: (0)2 47 45 09 11
E-mail: labourd@club-internet.fr
Web: www.chateaux-france.com/-bourdaisière

Prince P.M. de Broglie

A superlative, princely experience, it belongs to the National Tomato Conservatory. The brothers de Broglie grow 200 aromatics and 500 types of tomato - taste a selection in salad with a glass of Château Bourdaisière. Their history-heavy estate has formal garden and native woods, a Renaissance château on the foundations of a medieval fortress, vaulted meeting rooms and a little boudoir for intimacy as well as a bright, floral breakfast room onto the garden, recently redecorated by manager Madame de Roquefeuil. Guest rooms? *Francois 1* has a bathroom the size of a bedroom, rich dark green beams and quantities of old books in his magnificent terrace suite; *Gabrielle d'Estrées* is gorgeously feminine as befits a mistress of *Henri IV*, who wears rich, regal red (cheaper rooms are less grand). The drawing room is the Princes' own - they drop by, their books lie around, their family antiques and paintings furnish it. Authenticity and good taste are rife, the place is genuinely special yet very human and your hosts are charmingly friendly. *Well-behaved children welcome.*

Rooms: 19: 11 doubles, 2 suites in château; 6 doubles in pavilion.
Price: Doubles €115-€199, suites €148-€207.
Meals: Breakfast €11; light lunch €15 (April-September); dinner €30, by arrangement.
Closed: Never.

From A10 exit Tours Centre for Amboise, then D751 to Montlouis sur Loiret. Signposted.

Map No: 7

Le Fleuray Hôtel

37530 Cangey - Amboise
Indre-et-Loire

Tel: (0)2 47 56 09 25
Fax: (0)2 47 56 93 97
E-mail: lefleurayhotel@wanadoo.fr
Web: www.lefleurayhotel.com

Peter & Hazel Newington

Perfect if, like most of our readers, you have a helicopter - or a hot-air balloon. Pretty perfect, too, for ordinary mortals, for Peter and Hazel have created a haven of pure peace. The raw material was ideal: a solid, handsome old manor-house with duck-pond and barns, mature trees and bushes; all that was needed to persuade them to settle. The rooms in the barn are just right for families; slightly cut off from the rest, their French windows open onto the garden, so children may roam unfettered. The Newingtons are unstuffy and easy-going, genuinely enjoying the company of visitors. They have created a slightly English mood, with lightly floral sofas into which you can sink, bookcases, flowers and prints - and a plain carpet in the sitting room. The bedrooms are big and fresh; one, for example, has white cane furniture and floral covers on the huge bed. It must be fun to dine outside, under the old roof and its arched entrance; or under huge parasols, on pink tablecloths and green chairs. It is fun in the winter, too, with an open fire and Hazel's superb cooking.

Rooms: 14: 9 doubles/twins, 5 family.
Price: €76-€92.
Meals: Breakfast €11; dinner €25-€35; childrens' meals €13.
Closed: February school holidays; 1st week in November; Christmas.

From A10 exit 18 Amboise/Château Renault. D31 to Autrêche. Left on D55 to Dame Marie Les Bois. Right on D74 for Cangey.

Domaine des Bidaudières

Rue du Peu Morier
37210 Vouvray
Indre-et-Loire

Tel: (0)2 47 52 66 85
Fax: (0)2 47 52 62 17
E-mail: infohote@bidaudieres.com
Web: www.bandb-loire-valley.com

M & Mme Pascal Suzanne

In the three years they've been here, Sylvie and Pascal Suzanne have made their mark on this classic, creamy-stoned ex-wine-grower's property. Unstuffy and outgoing, this young couple lend a stylish sophistication to the place and have begun to produce a small quantity of their own wine, having planted new vineyards to the terraced rear. Cyprus trees planted on the hillside behind give an Italianate feel. Bedrooms are fresh and contemporary, each wall-papered and carpeted differently, each immaculate. All are light, south-facing and have valley views. The dining room, where the kitchen used to be, was actually built into the rock - a hugely attractive, stone-floored room with a low rocky ceiling, a sitting area and an open fire at one end. Guests can idle away the afternoon in the elegant swimming-pool on the lower terrace which lies alongside the carefully restored *orangerie*. Families are welcome to stay in the more rustic 'troglodyte' apartment nearby.

Rooms: 4 + 1 apartment: 3 doubles,
1 suite for 3; 1 apartment for 4.
Price: Doubles € 105, suite € 120,
apartment € 114.
Meals: Breakfast included. Lunch &
dinner available locally.
Closed: Never.

*From Paris, A10 exit 20 Vouvray onto
N152 for Amboise. In Vouvray D46 for
Vernou sur Brenne. House second on left
after railway bridge.*

Map No: 7

Château de Montgouverne

37210 Rochecorbon
Indre-et-Loire

Tel: (0)2 47 52 84 59
Fax: (0)2 47 52 84 61
E-mail: info@montgouverne.com
Web: www.montgouverne.com

Laurent Gross

The attentive, dynamic new owner of Montgouverne is full of plans for his mansion up on the vineyard-striped hillside above the Loire. He loves this smart, almost lavish 18th-century château with its listed walled garden where stupendous old trees and box hedges grow, and serves a magnificent breakfast buffet in the wrought-iron conservatory that he has built overlooking this fine horticultural sight. Some rooms are in the château - you climb lots of stairs to the top room but what a view when you get there - some in the pretty little 17th-century outbuilding near the pool; one has a dramatic oval window onto the setting sun. The superb décor is a harmony of lovely materials, subtle colours, fine furniture, attention to origins and sumptuous bathrooms. One more 'monastic' room (humbly plain walls, exposed brick and timber) contrasts pleasingly with the overall classy plushness. The heated outdoor swimming pool looks as if it grew here on its grassy terrace and the limpid air is birdsung peaceful. A high-class château where you feel you can live normally while enjoying a moment of luxury.

Rooms: 5 + 1 apartment: 3 doubles, 2 suites in the château; 1 apt for 2-4 in the closerie.
Price: Doubles €95-€140, suites €140-€170, apartment €140-€220.
Meals: Breakfast included; dinner €40 including aperitif and coffee.
Closed: Never.

From Tours N152 for Blois 4km. At St George left and follow signs to château.

Prieuré des Granges

37510 Savonnières
Indre-et-Loire

Tel: (0)2 47 50 09 67
Fax: (0)2 47 50 06 43
E-mail: salmon.eric@wanadoo.fr
Web: www.chateauxcountry.com

Éric & Christine Salmon

An oasis in an encroaching sea of suburbia, Le Prieuré is a dream. Hidden away in three acres of landscaped gardens and mature trees, the main building, long, low, ornate, is 400 years old, but behind its magnificent stone walls there's a refreshing lightness of touch and lack of pretension. The dining room, sitting room and breakfast room - long, light, painted white and blue - are discreet, comfortable and very charming. The generous bedrooms are equally elegant affairs, each one with a character of its own, and the occasional rustic touch. One has its own bread oven. Stone floors are softened with Persian rugs; ceilings are beamy; bathrooms are large, mostly white and luxurious. Downstairs rooms open onto their own little courtyards. At the back is a large grassy garden with a pool. Your host, a relaxed anglophile with a taste for fine beer, takes huge pleasure in making sure his guests have everything they need. Éric and Christine have achieved the near impossible: that elusive mix of the sophisticated and the down-to-earth. *Cash or French cheque only.*

Rooms: 6: 1 single, 2 doubles, 1 suite for 2, 1 suite for 4.
Price: Single/doubles €65-€95, suites €115-€170.
Meals: Breakfast included. A light meal available upon request in the summer. A good choice of restaurants nearby.
Closed: December-February.

Leave A10 at exit 24 Joué lès Tours for Villandry. In Savonnières, left at Hôtel Faisan towards Ballan Miré. On left after approx. 1km. Signposted.

Château du Vau
37510 Ballan-Miré
Indre-et-Loire

Tel: (0)2 47 67 84 04
Fax: (0)2 47 67 55 77
E-mail: chateauduvau@chez.com
Web: www.chez.com/chateauduvau

Bruno & Nancy Clement

Philosopher Bruno and Titian-haired Nancy, an intelligent and engaging couple with four young children, have turned his family château into a delightful, harmonious refuge for the world-weary traveller. The demands of children to be taken to dancing lessons and guests needing intellectual and physical sustenance are met with quiet composure and good humour: the cosy, book-lined, deep-chaired sitting room is a place where you find yourself irresistibly drawn into long conversations about music, yoga, art... The sunny breakfast room is charming with its stone-coloured floor tiles and pretty fabrics. Generations of sliding children have polished the banisters on the stairs leading to the large, light bedrooms that are beautifully but unfussily decorated - splendid brass bedsteads, Turkish rugs on parquet floors or seagrass matting, old family furniture, pictures and memorabilia - the spirit of Zen can be felt in the search for pure authenticity. On fine summer evenings you can take a supper tray to picnic *à la* Glyndebourne in a favourite corner of the vast grounds.

Rooms: 5: 4 doubles, 1 triple.
Price: €84-€99.
Meals: Breakfast included; picnic €15.
Dinner available on Saturdays.
Closed: Never.

From Tours D7 towards Savonnières &
Villandry. Left at Renault garage 2km
before Savonnières. Continue for 2km to
crucifix. Right & château 500m.

Map No: 7

Le Castel de Bray et Monts

Place du Village
37130 Bréhémont
Indre-et-Loire

Tel: (0)2 47 96 70 47
Fax: (0)2 47 96 57 36
E-mail: cooking-class-infrance@wanadoo.fr
Web: www.cooking-class-infrance.com

M & Mme Rochereau

This pretty manor house on the edge of the Loire was built by Louise de Valois as a holiday home in the 18th century. Pollarded lime trees lead up to the house, through a garden full of flowers and huge ancient magnolias while a stream, fed by the river, meanders through the garden. The head gardener from the Château de Villandry comes each year to prune the roses! The first thing you see inside is an amazing wooden, double-spiral staircase: apparently the only one of its kind in France. There are almost as many flowers in the house as in the garden: in vases, pots and on the walls - some traditional wallpapers, some well-chosen Laura Ashley. Some walls are hung with beautiful antique patchwork quilts: a sample of an impressive collection that Madame Rochereau built up while living in the US. Monsieur is a successful chef; he once worked at The Ritz in Paris, but recently decided to give up the restaurant business to concentrate on cookery classes for guests. Most bedrooms look onto the garden, but not the river as the embankment is too high. Children have a corner of the garden with swings and a place to play boules.

Rooms: 9 + 1 apartment: 7 doubles, 2 duplex suites; 1 apt for 4-6.
Price: Doubles €47-€111, suites €95-€190, apartment €145-€175.
Meals: Breakfast €7.50; dinner €30.
Closed: 20 November-20 February.

From Tours N152 to Langeais. Cross river & right after bridge onto D16 to Bréhémont. Left after church. Signposted.

Map No: 7

Le Vieux Château d'Hommes

37340 Hommes
Indre-et-Loire

Tel: (0)2 47 24 95 13
Fax: (0)2 47 24 68 67
E-mail: levieuxchateaudehommes@.fr
Web: www.hotelrestvieuxchateau.com

Hardy Family

The moat and the ruins of the old castle, with one little tower still standing, make a thoroughly idealistic setting for this great house, originally the tithe barn built just outside the castle wall. Inside, a vast baronial hall and fireplace welcome you and the atmosphere becomes more formal. In the big, luxurious bedrooms, antique furniture (beautifully Italian in one case) goes hand-in-hand with the lavish bathrooms. Two rooms give onto the fine courtyard bounded by outbuildings containing a couple of gîtes; two look out to open fields and woods. In contrast, the stone walls and terracotta tiles of the Tower Room, which overlooks the moat, give it a more rustic feel - its bathroom is down a narrow spiral staircase. In an area not particularly renowned for stunning countryside, the courtyard setting is certainly splendid, and the Hardys are interesting though they are often away, leaving daily management to permanent staff. Villandry and Azay le Rideau nearby.

Rooms: 6: 2 twins, 3 doubles, 1 suite.
Price: Doubles/twins €94, suite €121.
Meals: Breakfast included; dinner €27, including aperitif, wine & coffee.
Closed: Never.

From Tours N152 for Saumur. In Langeais D57 to Hommes. There, D64 for Giseux. Château on right as you leave village.

Château des Réaux

Le Port Boulet
37140 Bourgueil
Indre-et-Loire

Tel: (0)2 47 95 14 40
Fax: (0)2 47 95 18 34
E-mail: reaux@club-internet.fr

Jean-Luc & Florence Goupil de Bouillié

Two white swans and two white Indian ducks patrol the moat, while rows of simple topiary - pyramids of various sizes - stand guard round the château. It looks like a castle in a fairytale: with a tower, turrets and resplendent in red and white checks. It has been in the same family for more than a century; Jean-Luc and Florence Goupil de Bouillié are still very involved, but their son and his enthusiastic New Zealand girlfriend Nicky are handling much of the day-to-day management. They can arrange garden tours and cookery courses, even taxi you to a nearby restaurant. The hotel is in the fertile Loire flood plain, in the middle of both wine and château country. Rooms are either in the château or in a cottage, which looks out to the early Renaissance château on the other side of the moat. The cottage is charming, with a pretty, fresh yellow sitting room, but you can hear the odd train from here. The rooms in the château are grander and in very definite styles: the Bishop's suite is all done in purple; the Provençal has sliding windows on three sides. It could have been pompous and pretentious, but it is enchanting, elegant, and sophisticated.

Rooms: 11 + 1 apartment: 7 doubles, 4 suites for 3; 1 apt for 4.
Price: Doubles €69-€152, suites & apartment €168-€213.
Meals: Breakfast €11; lunch & dinnner: gourmet €40-€59, regional €20-€25.
Closed: Never.

From Paris A85 exit 5 Bourgeuil and take D749. At traffic lights, right on N152 towards Saumur. Château is signposted on right after 1km.

Hôtel Gargantua

73 rue Voltaire
37500 Chinon
Indre-et-Loire

Tel: (0)2 47 93 04 71
Fax: (0)2 47 93 08 02
E-mail:
hostelleriegargantua@hostelleriegargantua.com
Web: www.hostelleriegargantua.com

M Michel Giraud

You are treading in the footsteps of Rabelais here: built as a bailiff's court in the 15th century, his father was once the bailiff. Halfway down the oldest street in Chinon – don't wear your stilettos, cobblestones are easier on the eyes than the feet – the Gargantua is a tall, narrow building in local white tufa-stone with a small look-out tower at one corner of the steep slate roof. Tucked beneath the high walls of the château, the hotel looks down to the river and valley beyond. The stone walls, lofty beams and stag's head give a medieval atmosphere as you go in. A striped canopy keeps up the theme in the dining room. Access to all bedrooms is up a central spiral stone staircase. The first two floors were covered in patterned stone a century ago to make them smoother but the top flight is now listed and is very well trodden. Friendly new owner Michel is carefully re-doing the rooms: *Louis XVI* has an unusual oriental *toile de Jouy*, while *Gargantua* has an old four-poster and a splendid view. In summer you can eat under the wisteria in a paved courtyard, looking up to the château.

Rooms: 8 doubles/twins.
Price: €53-€91.
Meals: Breakfast €8; lunch & dinner €18-€34. Restaurant closed Thursdays and Friday lunchtimes off season.
Closed: Last 2 weeks of January; first 2 weeks of March.

From Tours D751 to Chinon. In town, park by river and walk up one of the side streets to rue Voltaire. Hotel half-way along.

Manoir de la Rémonière

37190 Cheillé - Azay le Rideau
Indre-et-Loire

Tel: (0)2 47 45 24 88
Fax: (0)2 47 45 45 69
E-mail: pcarole@wanadoo.fr

Carole & Chantal Pecas

Come for the remarkably authentic 15th-Century château - behind the mullioned windows there are regal rooms, genuine antiques, four-posters, thick rich drapes - and you may decide to sleep in the stables next time. Rémonière stands on 2000 years of history: the lovely stable block overlooks the 4th-Century gallo-Roman remains so its guest spaces have mosaics, ochre-sponged walls, very effective murals of Roman scenes, roof windows to the archaeology. A delight, in brilliant contrast to the enchanting main house, so perfectly restored and furnished. Here, breakfast is at a long, candelit table by a huge carved fireplace; the corridor has royal red carpet and old portraits; the levels change with the centuries; the atmosphere enters your blood. The lively, welcoming mother-and-daughter team, passionate about their house, prove this. Through a clearing the view to Azlay le Rideau is unsurpassed, the quiet is broken only by birds singing in the great trees, the owl wheezing behind the children's turret and the friendly black Thai pig trotting round the courtyard. A dream.

Rooms: 9: 6 doubles/twins, 1 suite for 4, 2 duplexes in annexe.
Price: Doubles €86-€122, duplexes & suite €100-€162.
Meals: Breakfast included. Gourmet restaurants 1km & 4km.
Closed: Never; open by reservation only November-end April.

A10 exit Joué les Tours, D751 for Chinon. Through Azay past Château to Cheillé. Left on D17; entrance 250m on left. Signposted.

Map No: 7

Domaine de la Tortinière

Les Gués de Veigné
37250 Montbazon
Indre-et-Loire

Tel: (0)2 47 34 35 00
Fax: (0)2 47 65 95 70
E-mail: domaine.tortiniere@wanadoo.fr
Web: www.tortiniere.com

Xavier Olivereau

It seems unreal, this pepperpot-towered château on a hill above the Indre, the bird-filled woods where wild cyclamen lay a carpet in autumn and daffodils radiate their light in spring, the view across to the stony keep of Montbazon - an exceptional spot with tennis, a heated pool, fishing or rowing on the river. Bedrooms are perfect, decorated with flair and imagination, be they in the château or in a converted outbuilding. One of these, an adorable Renaissance dolls' house, has two smaller rooms and a split-level suite; the orchard cottage, for playing shepherdesses *à la Petit Trianon*, is big and beautifully furnished - the desk invites great writings. Bathrooms are luxurious, some smaller than others. Guests enjoy taking the underground passage to the orangery to dine in simple elegance, inside or on the terrace. Soft lighting, panelled reception rooms, deep comfort, discreet friendliness are the marks of this real family-run hotel: the warm, humorous owners are genuinely attentive, their sole aim is to make your stay peaceful and harmonious.

Rooms: 29: 22 doubles, 7 suites.
Price: Doubles €88-€200, suites €260.
Meals: Breakfast €14; picnic €15; dinner €47. Restaurant closed Sunday evenings from November-March.
Closed: 21 December-March.

2km north of Montbazon. From Tours N10 south for Poitiers for 10km. In Les Gués, right at second set of traffic lights. Signposted.

Poitou-Charentes

Garlic used as it should be used is the soul, the divine
essence, of cookery. The cook who can employ it
successfully will be found to possess the delicacy of
perception, the accuracy of judgement, and the dexterity
of hand which go to the formation of a great artist.

Mrs W.G. Waters, The Cook's Decameron (1920)

CDT Charente, Vignes à Cressac

Chalet de Venise

6 rue Square
86280 Saint Benoît Bourg
Vienne

Tel: (0)5 49 88 45 07
Fax: (0)5 49 52 95 44

M & Mme Mautret

St Benoît is a pretty little village with a fine Romanesque church and, despite being just outside the suburbs of Poitiers, has managed to keep its village atmosphere. Set in the wooded valley, on the edge of a rippling stream, the Venise was completely rebuilt in 1994. It is a low, rendered building with stone balconies curving round following the stream, a wide terrace spread out below its balustrades. The smallish bedrooms have French windows onto the balcony and are decorated with apricot sponged walls, floral fabrics in contrastingly dark colours and stained wooden beds and dressing tables, all in neat, new contemporary style. But most people come here for the food, which is superb. Monsieur Mautret is the chef, Madame manages the restaurant - they are a delightful and excellent team. Service is elegant, almost reverential (silver cloches) but quick. Madame welcomes children and says they enjoy eating in the lovely big, light dining room or out on the terrace. The breakfast room is attractive too in soft blue and peach with Turkish rugs, good prints and plenty of plants.

Rooms: 12 doubles.
Price: €53-€58.
Meals: Breakfast €7; dinner €23-€45.
Closed: Two weeks in February; one weekend in August.

From A10 exit Poitiers Sud to Poitiers. At traffic lights head for Limoges/Châteauroux. Right after 1km. Right at lights to St Benoît Bourg (careful: there are 4 St Benoîts in the area!). Hotel in village centre.

Map No: 7

Château de Périgny
La Chapelle
86190 Vouillé
Vienne

Tel: (0)5 49 51 80 43
Fax: (0)5 49 51 90 09
E-mail: info@chateau-perigny.com
Web: www.chateau-perigny.com

Philippe Binni & Didier
Broquerault

Don't worry about the featureless countryside as you drive along the main road: you turn off to the chateau and find yourself in a secluded wooded valley, with a stream winding its way through water meadows. Périgny was rebuilt in cream stone with steep slate roofs in the 16th century, on the site of an older house and sits with woods at its back looking out onto the peaceful meadows. Rooms in the main building are newly but harmoniously decorated, ranging from an elegant suite on the ground floor to less elaborate rooms upstairs, some in contemporary fabrics, others in *toile de Jouy*. Immaculate farm buildings form a square round a huge courtyard dotted with islands of grass and trees and secluded white tables and chairs. The flowers are white too. The outbuildings house some conference facilities and simpler rooms, often home to wedding guests. On the sunny side is another terrace with a 20-metre heated pool. Once again, the umbrellas and loungers are miles apart, with one end kept for meals. Philippe was a musician for many years before opening a bistro with his wife Jeanine and taking on Périgny two years ago. They will make sure you are really looked after: you can even ride here, a comfy stable will be ready for your horse.

Rooms: 43 + 3: 37 doubles, 6 suites for 4-5; 3 cottages for 3-6, all with private terrace.
Price: Doubles & suites €64-€125; cottages €140-€183.
Meals: Breakfast €11; lunch from €22-€33; dinner from €27-€36.
Closed: Never.

Poitiers exit 29 - Poitiers Nord. On ring road follow green signs for Nantes/Angers. Head for Nantes. Right at roundabout for Nantes/Vouillé N149 for 5km. Château 5 min on left.

Château Clos de la Ribaudière

10 place du Champ de Foire
86360 Chasseneuil du Poitou
Vienne

Tel: (0)5 49 52 86 66
Fax: (0)5 49 52 86 32
E-mail: ribaudiere@ribaudiere.com
Web: www.ribaudiere.com

Philippe Bini & William Migeon

Imposing wrought-iron gates are the entrance to this solid early 19th-Century mansion in the centre of a sprawling village that is ideally placed for visits to old and new Poitou, Romanesque treasures and high-tech Futuroscope. The builder's grand designs are still clear in the stone-balustraded fishpond, the gardens leading down to the little river and a couple of remarkable architectural curiosities: the first floor landing appears to be an old chapel with its high stained-glass window, mirrored ceiling and dark walls, and there's a fascinating gallery with floor to ceiling leaded windows onto the park. Downstairs, two of the dining rooms have magnificent painted ceilings while the ten elegant, château rooms are astonishingly high and decked in period furnishings. All the others are in a converted lodge and the new extension beyond it. They are pleasantly comfortable with all mod cons, lots of light and, of course, modern soundproofing. Staff are welcoming and efficient, the owners pride themselves on their food and the château is a favourite for wedding receptions and seminars.

Rooms: 41: 38 doubles, 3 suites.
Price: Doubles €79-€110, suites €125-€140.
Meals: Breakfast €9.50; lunch & dinner €20-€45.
Closed: Never.

Leave A10 at Futuroscope exit; follow signs to
Chasseneuil centre. Hotel is signposted in town.

Le Relais du Lyon d'Or
4 rue d'Enfer
86260 Angles sur l'Anglin
Vienne

Tel: (0)5 49 48 32 53
Fax: (0)5 49 84 02 28
E-mail: thoreau@lyondor.com
Web: www.lyondor.com

Heather & Guillaume Thoreau

In one of France's most beautiful villages, this old hotel owes its revival to Heather and Guillaume's herculean efforts: they bought it half-ruined in 1994 as a place for their wedding, new home and business, then left their high-flying London careers to do it up. They now run renovation courses, with practical advice from their epic experience of problems with red tape, labour, time and money. Each room was rebuilt round its old flagstones, doors and beams, then decorated in warm natural colours with Heather's beautiful paint effects (ragged, distressed, veiled), patinas and stencils - she also gives courses in paint finishes, using her rooms as living examples. Marvellous they are too, in their rich fabrics, intriguing details and individuality, small, not overdone, with delicious bathrooms. It's like staying in a country house with delightfully relaxed and friendly hosts. The menu is varied and refined - they have an excellent chef; generous breakfasts are served in the pretty yard in summer. And there's *La Source* for steam baths, massages, face and body care.

Rooms: 10: 9 doubles, 1 suite for 4.
Price: Doubles €56-€69, suite €91.
Meals: Breakfast €6; lunch & dinner €17-€29.
Restaurant closed Monday & Tuesday lunchtimes.
Closed: January & February.

A10 exit Châtellerault Nord D9/D725 east through La Roche Posay onto D5 to Angles sur l'Anglin; hotel in village centre.

Map No: 7

Hôtel les Orangeries

12 avenue du Doctuer Dupont
86320 Lussac les Châteaux
Vienne

Tel: (0)5 49 84 07 07
Fax: (0)5 49 84 98 82
E-mail: orangeries@wanadoo.fr
Web: hotel-lesorangeries.com

Olivia & Jean-Philippe Gautier

Even before you step inside, the fabulous pool beneath the mature trees of the landscaped garden at the back will convince you that these people have the finest sense of how to treat an old house and garden: the harmony of the deep wooden deck, raw stone walls, giant baskets and orange trees (*naturellement*) draws you in. The young owners fell in love with the place and applied all their talent – he's an architect – to giving it an authentic 18th-century elegance in contemporary mood. Indoors, stripped oak doors, exposed stone walls, warm wood or cool stone floors are radiant with loving care, like valued old friends. Each lovely, uncluttered bedroom has just the right mix of vibrant pastels, pretty hangings on brass fittings, new-stained old furniture and a super bathroom. The rooms over the road are soundproofed with double windows. The Gautiers' passion includes the old-fashioned games they have resuscitated for you: croquet and skittles outside, two kinds of billiards, backgammon, mahjong in the vast games room inside. Their delightful enthusiasm for this generous house is catching.

Rooms: 10 + 3 apartments: 10 doubles/triples; 3 apts for 4-5.
Price: Doubles/triples €55-€90; apartments €90-€115.
Meals: Breakfast €9; picnic available; dinner in summer season €24. Restaurants in town.
Closed: Mid-December - mid-January

Exit Poitiers for Limoges on N147 to Lussac les Châteaux. Town is 35km from Limoges. Ask for route via Châtellerault if arriving from north.

Château de Saint Loup sur Thouet

79600 Saint Loup Lamairé
Deux Sèvres

Tel: (0)5 49 64 81 73
Fax: (0)5 49 64 82 06
E-mail: chdb@compuserve.com
Web: www.chateaudesaint-loup.com

Comte Charles-Henri de Bartillat

This château inspired Perrault to write *Puss in Boots!* It has an ancient and fascinating history. The Black Prince incarcerated John the Good here after the Battle of Poitiers in 1356. It was rebuilt in the 17th century by the Marquis of Carabas, whose magnificence so impressed the fairytale writer. Charles-Henri de Bartillat visited the château on Christmas Eve 1990, fell in love with the place and 10 days later had bought it. Saint Loup is a Historic Monument and both the château and the gardens are open to the public. The count, charming and passionate about his home, is painstakingly restoring the house and the grounds (using the plans drawn up by Jacques Boyer de la Boissière in the early 18th century). If you are a gardener, you won't know where to turn: to the orchard with 75 ancient varieties or to the enormous *potager*, recreated in 1998. This is where you will have an aperitif with Charles-Henri or it will be served in the library if there is a bit of a chill. The guest rooms are just as full of atmosphere with beautiful old beds and fine antiques.

Rooms: 15: 2 singles, 13 doubles.
Entire château can be rented.
Price: Singles €100, doubles
€130-€190.
Meals: Breakfast €11-€15; dinner
including wine €55, by arrangement,
in main dining room of medieval keep.
Closed: Never.

From Airvault D46 to St Loup Lamairé.
Château visible as you enter village.

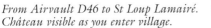

Hôtel Le Chat Botté
2 place de l'Eglise
lle de Ré
17590 Saint Clément des Baleines
Charente-Maritime

Tel: (0)5 46 29 21 93
Fax: (0)5 46 29 29 97
Web: hotelchatbotte.com

Mmes Massé-Chantreau

A perfect seaside house, pine-panelled, pale-chaired, decorated with pastels and peace, this is part of a family network: one sister is your hotel hostess, another has her beauty salon right here where you can be wrapped in seaweed and reflexologised, a third has a B&B nearby and two brothers have a restaurant each, one of them next door. So things are well-organised, all is spotless and you can choose to have your *énergétique* breakfast on the sweet little patio in the flowery garden or the grey-blue dining room before shiatsu and a bicycle tour of the island. The garden provides fresh flowers for the house, the sea and sky provide the limpid light that filters into the simple country-furnished, quilted bedrooms which give onto the church square or the garden or the patio - we preferred the patio aspect but all are havens from the heat of the summer beaches. Bathrooms and linen are of excellent quality. The island has lots to offer - salt marshes, one of Europe's biggest bird sanctuaries, the Baleines lighthouse for a stupendous view (257 steps up) - and peace at your hotel.

Rooms: 19 doubles/twins.
Price: €52-€98.
Meals: Breakfast €8-€11.
Family-owned restaurant next door.
Closed: 1-15 December; 6 January-8 February.

From A10 exit 33 onto N248 then N11 for La Rochelle. Cross bridge to Ile de Ré and take northern itinerary towards Le Phare des Baleines. Hotel opposite church.

Hôtel de l'Océan

172 rue Saint Martin
17580 Le Bois Plage en Ré
Charente-Maritime

Tel: (0)5 46 09 23 07
Fax: (0)5 46 09 05 40
E-mail: ocean@iledere.com
Web: www.re-hotel-ocean.com

Martine & Noël Bourdet

Seasoned travellers, Martine and Noël tried to find a hotel that felt like a home. Although they had worked in antiques and interior design, after a spell running a restaurant they realised this was what they should be doing - but where? They knew it had to be on an island and after toying with Corsica and the Ile de Ré, they stumbled upon a rather sad old hotel, the Océan, and knew they had found 'their' hotel. Set back from the dunes in a garden pungent with rosemary and lavender, the hotel has 24 bedrooms: some around an inner courtyard, others like tiny cottages among the hollyhocks. They are all different. Children will love the curtained cabin bed set in a buttercup yellow alcove. Floors are covered in sisal matting and Martine and Noël's ships, lighthouses and shells are dotted around against cool, soothing colours. After your *pastis* on the decked terrace, your supper will involve a lot of fresh fish and herbs. The dining room is another success, with cream boards on walls and ceiling and palest greeny-grey carved chairs. It's fresh without being cold and clean without being clinical.

Rooms: 24 doubles.
Price: €61-€91.
Meals: Breakfast €9; lunch & dinner €21-€30. Restaurant closed Wednesdays except during school holidays.
Closed: 5 January-5 February.

A10 exit 33 for La Rochelle. N248 then N11 Rocade round La Rochelle for Pont de l'Ile de Ré. At Le Bois Plage hotel is in town centre.

Map No: 11

Domaine de la Baronnie

21, rue Baron de Chantal
17410 Saint Martin de Ré
Charente-Maritime

Tel: (0)5 46 09 21 29
Fax: (0)5 46 09 95 29
E-mail: info@labaronnie-pallardy.com
Web: www.labaronnie-pallardy.com

Pierre & Florence Pallardy

Creaky back? Or simply looking for some effective pampering? Pierre is a successful author, osteopath and dietician who runs a summer practice here and a winter one in Paris. This secluded retreat is only 100 metres from the bustling nightlife and fun beaches of St-Martin so you can either come here with others sharing your plans or with large or small people whose idea of a good time is sandcastles or bodysurfing and hanging out. Walking down the side street from the port you could easily miss the Baronnie. The Ile de Ré is a very busy, though charming, place in the summer but the big iron gates lead to a clam green haven. Built as government premises in the 18th Century, La Baronnie became a private house but passed from owner to owner, becoming gradually more dilapidated. The imposing house was rescued in 1996 by Pierre and Florence - a former model who has been coming to the island for 35 years - and turned into a sanctuary for healthy living. You can come for a 'normal' seaside holiday, with the odd massage, or you can book a special package with a week of treatment and advice. Minimum 2 nights stay.

Rooms: 6: 3 doubles, 3 suites.
Price: €120-€169.
Meals: Breakfast €12. Many restaurants in town.
Closed: November-March.

Over bridge from La Rochelle to Centre Ville St Martin. Street 2nd on right going down to port.

Résidence de Rohan

Parc des Fées
Route de Saint Palais
17640 Royan (Vaux sur Mer)
Charente-Maritime

M & Mme Seguin

Tel: (0)5 46 39 00 75
Fax: (0)5 46 38 29 99
E-mail: info@residence-rohan.com
Web: www.residence-rohan.com

A gloriously peaceful place: the pool sits lazily on the low cliff, the gardens drop down to the sea, you can lie secluded under the umbrella pines with the sea lapping below or enjoy the fashionable beach. The hotel, built in typical *Belle Époque* style by the Rohans as a seaside cottage, has many of its original features - floors and fireplaces, cornices and carvings, a seductive staircase twisting up to the top floor - and smells deliciously of floor polish. The owners, as affable, warm and open as their house, welcome families and their pets into their lovely home. There are polished *armoires* and upholstered chairs in the big recently-decorated rooms, skilfully-matched fabrics and wallpapers and excellent bathrooms with big old-style basins. Breakfast at low tables indoors or out; dine in small, exclusive Vaux or big, bustling Royan - much favoured by Parisian families. There's masses to do: take bike and ferry to the Médoc vineyards, visit "the best zoo in Europe" at La Palmyre or historic La Rochelle. There's even a surfable Atlantic wave on the *Côte Sauvage*.

Rooms: 41: 35 doubles/twins,
6 triples.
Price: Doubles/twins €82-€122,
triples €118-€129.
Meals: Breakfast €9. Many restaurants
nearby.
Closed: 11 November-April.

A10 exit 35 Saintes for Royan, then
Pontaillac Plage. Continue to Vaux sur
Mer and St Palais. Résidence de Rohan
on sea side of D25 in private estate
called Parc des Fées.

Château de la Tillade

Gemozac
17260 Saint Simon de Pellouaille
Charente-Maritime

Tel: (0)5 46 90 00 20
Fax: (0)5 46 90 02 23
E-mail: la.tillade@t3a.com

Vicomte & Vicomtesse Michel de Salvert

You can tell that Michel and Solange, the present Vicomte and Vicomtesse, like people and love entertaining. Their impressive château sits at the end of an avenue of lime trees alongside the family vineyards that have produced grapes for Cognac and Pineau des Charentes (a local aperitif) for over two centuries. Much of the original distillery equipment is on display and well worth a visit. Your hosts make you feel instantly at ease in their comfortable, friendly home, even if you're secretly terrified of dropping the fine bone china. Solange's talents as an artist (she also holds painting courses in her art studio) are reflected in her choice of fabrics while traditional French beds with rolled headboards capture the elegance of your surroundings. Meals are a delight, with good conversation (in English or French) round the family table while you are waited on lavishly but without stuffiness. The de Salverts provide colourful descriptions of local sites or restaurants to visit, and golfers, too, will be spoilt for choice.

Rooms: 5: 4 doubles, 1 triple.
Price: Doubles €69-€80, triple €100.
Meals: Breakfast included; hosted dinner €31, including aperitif, wine, liqueur & coffee.
Closed: Never.

From A10 exit 36 right for Gémozac. At r'bout: Gémozac bypass for Royan, right on D6 for Tesson. Entrance about 3km on left, signposted (château not in village, but on D6).

Map No: 11

169

Château des Salles

17240 Saint Fort sur Gironde
Charente-Maritime

Tel: (0)5 46 49 95 10
Fax: (0)5 46 49 02 81
E-mail: chateaudessalles@wanadoo.fr
Web: www.chateauxhotels.com/dessalles

Sylvie Couillaud

A pretty little château with great personality, Salles was built in 1454 and scarcely touched again until 1860, when it was 'adapted to the fashion' (profoundly). 100 years later, the enterprising Couillaud family brought the estate guest house, its vineyard and stud farm into the 20th century. Behind its fine old exterior, it exudes light, harmony, colour and elegant informality with spiral stone stairs, boldly-painted beams and warm, well-furnished bedrooms bathed in soft colours and gentle wallpapers. Salles is a friendly family affair: sister at guest house reception, brother at vines and horses, mother at her easel - her watercolours hang in the public rooms, her flowers decorate bedroom doors - and in the kitchen. At dinner, refined food made with local and home-grown produce is served with estate wines. Sylvie Couillaud will help you plan your stay - she knows it all and is almost a mini tourist office. It's a congenial, welcoming house: people come back again and again and one guest said: "She welcomed us like family and sent us home with goodies from her vineyard".

Rooms: 5: 4 doubles, 1 triple.
Price: Doubles €69-€84, triple €91.
Meals: Breakfast €8.50; dinner €27.50.
Closed: 15 October-April.

A10 exit 37 Mirambeau. Château is between Lorignac and Brie sous Mortagne at junction of D730 and D125.

Maison Karina

Les Métairies
16200 Jarnac
Charente

Tel: (0)5 45 36 26 26
Fax: (0)5 45 81 10 93
E-mail: hotelkarina@easynet.fr
Web: www.hotelkarina.co.uk

Austin & Nikki Legon

This old house was built as a cognac distillery and the bar is arranged around the copper stills. The Legons have done an excellent conversion, the garden is most successful and they are still planning to extend the pool, plant more trees and create better seminar facilities. The dining room has many-shaped tables clothed in many-coloured cloth and plate-laden dressers in a lovely converted barn with a huge open fireplace giving off the aroma of wood fires. In summer, they do barbecues where they join their guests and they're eager for people to have a good time. Some come back year after year, the village council meets here and many locals come for the restaurant. Inside, family photographs, knick-knacks and pictures have a welcoming, homely air. The bedrooms are a good size and very pretty; some chintzy, some flowery, some plainer, with lacey white bedcovers, oriental rugs on wooden floors, moulded ceilings or rafters, exposed stone walls or sober wallpaper and plenty of space in chests and armoires. And there's lots to see in the area.

Rooms: 10: 6 doubles, 2 suites for 3, 2 suites for 4.
Price: €49-€76. Half-board €101-€136 p.p.
Meals: Breakfast €5-€10; picnic lunch €7-€13; lunch & dinner €14-€23.
Closed: 10 December-20 January.

From Cognac N141 to Jarnac; over bridge to traffic lights, left D736 for Sigogne; bear right; Les Métairies signs in village: right, 1st left, 1st right, house on left.

Map No: 7

Hostellerie du Maine Brun

Asnieres sur Nouère
16290 Hiersac
Charente

Tel: (0)5 45 90 83 00
Fax: (0)5 45 96 91 14
E-mail: hostellerie-du-maine-brun@wanadoo.fr
Web: www.hotel-mainebrun.com

Sophie & Raymond Menager

The only sounds to wake you in your luxurious bedroom come from the birds and the water gushing beneath the hotel, a 16th-century mill, sympathetically remoulded in the 1930s. You may even forget you are in an hotel at all. The rooms have a mix of French 18th- and 19th-century furniture, expensive wallpaper and heavily draped curtains loaded with gold and cream. The flowers look as if they have been freshly picked from the garden. Raymond and Sophie have managed the trick of making the Moulin sumptuous without being stuffy. The only modern touches are in the bathrooms, designed for wallowing rather than a mere splash. Children are welcome, but unless yours are period items - more seen than heard - they may not blend in. There is a big pool, however, with plenty of sunshades and chairs. You can breakfast in the sunny dining room or on the terrace, and if you are planning to explore - Cognac is nearby and Oradour-sur-Glan, preserved as the site of a horrific civilian massacre in the Second World War.

Rooms: 20: 18 doubles, 2 suites.
Price: Doubles €96-€116,
suites €160.
Meals: Breakfast €10; lunch & dinner €17-€34. Restaurant closed Mondays.
Closed: October 15-February.

From Angoulême N141 for Cognac for approx. 8km. D120 right for Asnières sur Nouère. Hostellerie just along on left.

Aquitaine

A garlic caress is stimulating. A garlic excess soporific.

Curnonsky (1872-1956)

P. Laplace, Tourisme de la Gironde

Château Le Lout

Avenue de la Dame Blanche
33320 Le Taillan - Medoc
Gironde

Tel: (0)5 56 35 46 47
Fax: (0)5 56 35 48 75
E-mail: chateau.le.lout@wanadoo.fr
Web: pro.wanadoo.fr/chateau.le.lout/

Colette & Olivier Salmon

If the dusky pink walls, first-floor loggia and green windows give Le Lout more the look of a somewhat patrician Italian villa than a French château, this is because its original owner chose an architect from Siena to build his country retreat. When Colette and Olivier bought it, the house had been empty for 18 years and was in need of a lot of attention. Colette not only brought a feel for period detail but plenty of elbow grease: she did much of the work herself and should feel very pleased with it. A flight of stone steps leads to a white stone hall, sparsely decorated with tapestries and the odd old chest. One side leads to the kitchen and office, the other to a perfect dining/breakfast room with fine ornate *chinoiserie* wallpaper framed by soft green panelling and well-polished wood floors. A stone staircase leads to the bedrooms which are a real treat. All have wooden floors, but you may find rich orange walls with contrasting cool bedding or soft cream, either set off by fresh green-patterned cotton or enhanced by lace and rugs. Children will be happy with the pool and huge grounds. Colette will cook you a five-course dinner while Olivier knows all about wine and golf.

Rooms: 7: 5 doubles/twins, 2 suites for 3.
Price: Doubles/twins €95-€125, suites €155-€180.
Meals: Breakfast €11; hosted dinner €40 including wine, by arrangement.
Closed: Never.

Rocade for Bordeaux/Merignac (airport). Exit 7 N215 to Lesparre/Lacanau. After 1km take D2 for Blanquefort/Pauillac.
After 2.5km, left at lights to N33 for Le Taillan 1km. Signposted.

Map No: 11

Château Julie

Naudonnet
33240 Virsac
Gironde

Tel: (0)5 57 94 08 21
Fax: (0)5 57 94 08 23
E-mail: josvandereijk@wanadoo.fr

Jos & Wim van der Eijk

Interested in wine? Even if Bordeaux is not your favourite, this will be an interesting stay. Making wine is the main business here and if you come at the right time you will have a grandstand view. Château Julie is Dutch-owned and run by Jos and Wim. Rebuilt in the 18th century to typical, charming proportions, the house is surrounded by 80 hectares of land, 40 of them planted with vines. Bordeaux is at hand - and the coast - while at the château you can play tennis, fish or explore the grounds on foot or by mountain bike. You can either stay in the château - rooms are simple and uncluttered, with large bathrooms and plenty of towels - or in a cottage opposite which sleeps six comfortably and has two shower rooms. Breakfast is on the terrace or in a slightly sombre hall, beside an impressive wooden staircase. Jos and Wim can also arrange for you to visit a sister château near St. Emilion. Unless you are in the cottage, which has a large kitchen, you will have to pop into Bordeaux for dinner: your only problem will be choosing where.

Rooms: 9 + 1: 9 doubles;
1 cottage for 6.
Price: €69-€76; cottage €305-€381 per week.
Meals: Breakfast included. Fabulous eating nearby.
Closed: Never.

A10 Paris/Bordeaux, past toll Virsac; 2nd exit 39 B for St Antoine-Virsac. Signposted.

Château de Sanse
33350 Sainte Radegonde
Gironde

Tel: (0)5 57 56 41 10
Fax: (0)5 57 56 41 29
E-mail: sanse@château-hotels.com
Web: www.chateau-hotels.com

Mark & Trish Tyler

What do you do while raising three young boys in Aberdeen and running a successful pizza and sandwich business? You dream of your own hotel and end up buying a run-down 12th-century château in the heart of the Bordeaux wine country. Mad, courageous, or maybe just youthful! Trish and Mark have worked miracles since 1997 and done much of it themselves. A stunning entrance hall, white and minimalist, sets the tone for the whole place; a beautiful teak desk, a colonial wickerwork sofa with white on white cushions. Apart from the metal balustrade the only colour comes from the occasional plant and splash of mauve, clearly Trish's theme colour and hugely successful. The off-white and oatmeal theme continues upstairs with sisal in the corridor and coir in some of the bedrooms, a play of texture rather than colour. Lots of thought has been given to families - triples can be arranged and some rooms interconnect. Most have private balconies big enough to sit out on in comfort with lovely views. The boys eat early, so can your children, and child-minding can be organised.

Rooms: 14: 12 doubles, 2 suites.
Price: Doubles €75-€115,
suites €168.
Meals: Breakfast €10; picnic €12;
dinner from €24.
Closed: February.

A10 exit St Andre de Cubec to Libourne; towards Castillon La Bataille; D17 right Pujols; D18 left Gensac; D15e right to Coubeyrac.
Hotel signed on right.

Map No: 12

Hôtel de Charme les Hortensias du Lac

1578 Avenue du Tour du Lac
40150 Hossegor
Landes

Tel: (0)5 58 43 99 00
Fax: (0)5 58 43 42 81

M Frédéric Hubert

Hossegor is such an unusual name: the locals tell us a Royal Horse Guard was stationed among the pine trees before there was a real town. The memory lived on and, *voilà*, Horse Guard has become Hossegor. Second Empire engineers enlarged the basin of the lake, hence the birth of a salt-water lake and, later, this 30's building in "Basco-Landais" style. Mr Hubert has a distinctive style and recently renovated this jewel with an eye to Feng-Shui; soft yellows and oranges, beiges, whites and off-whites, caramels, chocolates and natural fabrics. There are lots of lamps, archways, curves, candles and bunches of long thin sticks that are said to direct energy. The rugs and lamps were designed by him and made by artisans. All this and the proximity of the lake create an atmosphere of harmony and peace. The basic double is not big but impeccable; some rooms have views of the lake. The suites have balconies for in-house meditation. There are 6kms of jogging paths around the lake and tea and coffee are served in the *salon* every afternoon at 4.30pm. *Taxi service provided for airport and train stations.*

Rooms: 24: 12 doubles, 8 duplexes with balconies for 2-4, 2 suites for 2, 2 large suites with living room for 4-6.
Price: Doubles €85-€145, suites/duplexes €100-€300.
Meals: Champagne breakfast until noon, €14.
Closed: November-March.

A63, exit 7 Bennesse Marenne/Cap Breton follow signs for Hossegor. In centre for plage; 1st right after bridge over canal.

Maison Garnier
29 rue Gambetta
64200 Biarritz
Pyrénées-Atlantiques

Tel: (0)5 59 01 60 70
Fax: (0)5 59 01 60 80
E-mail: maison-garnier@hotel-biarritz.com
Web: www.hotel-biarritz.com

Jean-Christophe Garnier

In glamorous Biarritz, playground of royalty and stars, here is a jewel of sophisticated simplicity. Pristine-white bathrooms have huge showerheads. Bedrooms are done in subtle white, eggshell, dark chocolate and soft coffee with the occasional splash of brilliant colour. The bright breakfast room has Basque floorboards setting off pale walls and white linen as a foil for lovely tableware, light pouring in from great windows. Guests are enchanted by hotel and owner: both have real charm and warmth. Monsieur Garnier was in tourism and fashion. Then in 1999, having fallen in love with Biarritz, he decided to turn this old boarding house into a smart and friendly little hotel. So, no hall counter, just a gorgeous wrought-iron stair-rail, a 1930s-feel *salon* with a deep sofa, an old fireplace and a magnificent oriental carpet - the tone is set the moment you come in. And you will soon be at ease with your delightful, engaging host. On a quiet side street, five minutes' walk from that fabulous surfing beach, this is remarkable value.

Rooms: 7 doubles.
Price: €70-€100.
Meals: Breakfast €7.50. Lunch & dinner available locally.
Closed: Telephone ahead.

From A63 exit Biarritz La Négresse for Centre Ville, Place Clémenceau. Straight ahead for large white building Bank Inchauspé; left onto Rue Gambetta. Free parking on street.

Map No: 16

Le Saint Charles

47 avenue Reine Victoria
64200 Biarritz
Pyrénées-Atlantiques

Tel: (0)5 59 24 10 54
Fax: (0)5 59 24 56 74
E-mail: phildawson@aol.com
Web: www.hotelstcharles.com

Philip Dawson

'Two steps', as the guide books say, from the sophisticated centre of Biarritz, you find yourself in this astonishingly secluded and quiet house, surrounded by greenery, set in an imaginatively designed and carefully-planted garden. Once owned by the Prince of Romania, the 1930s building has been a hotel for 60 years - hard to believe when you take in the countrified atmosphere. The bedrooms vary from very small to very big, with lots of old lace at the windows, good antiques and the faintly shabby charm of a well-loved family home. They all overlook the garden, and the creepers curling around the windows are a perfect backdrop to the arrangements of fresh and dried flowers in the rooms. Philip, the friendly new owner, will take every care to make you want to return. Take a book and relax in the garden, try the excitement of the casinos of Biarritz, the fun of the Atlantic rollers on the Grande Plage, or sample the serious French approach to well-being in the *thalassotherapie* centre. You need never use your car.

Rooms: 13: 6 doubles/twins, 4 triples, 3 quadruples.
Price: Doubles €43-€70, triples €59-€70, quadruples €70-€84.
Meals: Breakfast €6-€7. Many fine restaurants in town.
Closed: Never.

A63 exit 4 La Négresse for Biarritz Centre Ville. Av. du Prés Kennedy joins Av. du M'al Foch and ends at Place Clémenceau. Straight across onto Av. Edouard VII; right on Av. de la Marne. Signposted.

Map No: 16

Hôtel Laminak

Route de Saint Pée
64210 Arbonne (Biarritz)
Pyrénées-Atlantiques

Tel: (0)5 59 41 95 40
Fax: (0)5 59 41 87 65
E-mail: hotel.laminak@wanadoo.fr
Web: www.touradour.com/laminak.htm

M & Mme Proux

The style is country cottage, with all the floral designs, stripes and neatly controlled flourishes that one might expect... almost English. The setting is gorgeous, with all the lush greenery of the Basque countryside at your feet and views up to the mountains. The hotel is on a quiet road outside the village of Arbonne, with a few discreetly screened neighbours and a big, handsome garden filled with mature shrubs and trees. In summer it is a delight to eat breakfast on the terrace. Rooms are neat and attractive, carpeted, wallpapered and with antique pine furniture. You will sleep well here, and be looked after with a quiet and warm efficiency by the owners for whom this place has been a long-cherished dream. You can, too, settle round the open fire in the evenings, warmed by the easy comfort of the place and the satisfying sag of the leather furniture. It is but an easy hop to the coast and the throbbing vitality of Biarritz. Those mountains are worth a week's effort in themselves; just below them, the fish await your line.

Rooms: 12 doubles/twins.
Price: Doubles/twins €54-€90.
Children up to 10 free.
Meals: Breakfast €9.15; dinner €8-€15, by arrangement.
Closed: Mid-November-January.

A63 exit 4 La Négresse and follow signs to Arbonne; signposted.

Map No: 16

Irigoian

Avenue de Biarritz
64210 Bidart
Pyrénées-Atlantiques

Tel: (0)5 59 43 83 00
Fax: (0)5 59 43 83 03
E-mail: irigoian@wanadoo.fr
Web: www. irigoian.com

M Phlippe Etcheverry

In this lovely place of contrasts, rustic and refined, old and new march hand in friendly hand: a beautiful Basque farmhouse virtually on a golf course (first hole is by the back door), with 17th-century timbers and heavy old stone door frames outside, minibars and minimalist décor inside - pastel-sponged rooms, each different; rustic headboards softly stained to match; simple, practical furniture on polished floorboards. Philippe is a journalist, constantly on the go; deeply attached to his homeland, he knows every Basque detail, every good eating house and has arranged special deals at the golf and thalassotherapy centres for his guests. He runs a tidy, clean house where rooms have all mod cons and independent entrances - but guests to his grandmother's old house are treated like family with typical, unintrusive Basque hospitality. All this plus rolling green views and the sea just 400m away. *There's a nearby bus service to St Jean de Luz and Biarritz and Biarritz airport is only 4km away.*

Rooms: 5: 3 doubles, 2 twins.
Price: €76-€122.
Meals: Breakfast €7.50. Wide choice of restaurants nearby.
Closed: Never.

On A63 exit Biarritz then N10 for 2km to r'about; right towards Biarritz. House 600m on left.

Château d' Urtubie

64122 Urrugne
Pyrénées-Atlantiques

Tel: (0)5 59 54 31 15
Fax: (0)5 59 54 62 51
E-mail: chateaudurtubie@wanadoo.fr
Web: www.chateaudurtubie.fr

Laurent de Coral

The Château d'Urtubie was built in 1341 with permission from Edward III. The keep is still intact, except for the roof which was changed in 1654 to resemble Versailles, using the expertise of local boat builders. Your host, Laurent, is a direct descendant of the builder of the castle, Martin de Tartas, and opened Urtubie as a hotel in 1995 to make sure he can keep it alive. The castle is classified and also operates as a museum: the *Antique Roadshow* could run an entire series here. You can have a 'prestige' bedroom on the second floor, very grand and imposing: not 'light and airy' which we often praise but a touch sombre and totally in keeping with the age and style. Upstairs, you have the 'charm' bedrooms, which are slightly smaller. Bathrooms are a mix of ancient and modern, with stylish touches such as airy mosquito nets draped over old-fashioned baths. On the outskirts of a pretty little Basque town, only five minutes' drive from the beach, Urturbie is also set in beautiful gardens. Don't be worried it might be stuffy: Laurent couldn't be more friendly and families are most welcome.

Rooms: 9: 1 single, 8 doubles.
Price: €60-€130.
Meals: Breakfast €10. Good restaurants in town.
Closed: Mid-november-mid-March.

A63 Bayonne/St Sebastien, exit St Jean de Luz Sud onto N10 for Urrugne. Right just before roundabout entering Urrugne.

Lehen Tokia

Chemin Achotarreta
64500 Ciboure
Pyrénées-Atlantiques

Tel: (0)5 59 47 18 16
Fax: (0)5 59 47 38 04
E-mail: info@lehen-tokia.com
Web: lehen-tokia.com

Yan Personnaz

The extraordinary name of this house means 'The First Place' in Basque, and the place is as extraordinary as its name implies. Built in the 1920s by the Basque architect Hiriart for a British 'gentleman' and his Mexican-Basque wife, it is a monument to Art Deco. Indeed, Hiriart himself invented the expression to describe the style the house epitomises. With stained glass by Gruber, marble and parquet floors, furnishings, carpets and pictures custom-made, it feels, the owner suggests, as if it has been preserved '*dans son jus*', like *confit* of goose. And here it is now for us to enjoy. The bedrooms, like the rest of the house, make you feel as if you are in a luxurious private house: the panelling, furnishings and fabulous bathrooms have tremendous style. And if the architecture isn't enough, the house has the most stunning views over the bay of St Jean de Luz, a rose garden and sumptuous breakfasts. This is the perfect haven for those who appreciate Art Deco style.

Rooms: 7: 6 doubles, 1 suite.
Price: Doubles €77-€145, suite €183-€213.
Meals: Breakfast €9. Excellent restaurants in the area.
Closed: Mid-November-mid-December.

From A63 exit St Jean de Luz Sud to Ciboure. After sign to 'Kechiloa' turn left; signposted.

Hôtel La Devinière

5 rue Loquin
64500 Saint Jean de Luz
Pyrénées-Atlantiques

Tel: (0)5 59 26 05 51
Fax: (0)5 59 51 26 38

M Bernard Carrère

Louis XIV married the Spanish Infanta here and the church door was walled up for ever! In the middle of this historic border town, Bernard first renovated his fine old mansion as a private home and then decided to "let outsiders in too": become an insider and feel welcome. In the *salon* with its lamps, sumptuous antique books, grand piano and lovely old French armchairs, you will want to curl up with a book, peeking through the richly-draped curtains at the little green haven of a garden, so unexpected in the city centre. You can sit and read there too, in summer, after breakfast among the flowers. Your room has the same atmosphere: fine fabrics and antique furniture, wrought-iron, brass or beautifully-renovated wooden Basque beds, co-ordinated bathrooms, excellent sound insulation, attention to detail. The Carrères are a generous, artistic family; Bernard's daughter's paintings enhance *salon* and staircase, he's passionate about his region, writes about the Basque Country and will entrance you with his tales.

Rooms: 10 doubles/twins.
Price: €100-€130.
Meals: Breakfast €8. Many fine restaurants in town.
Closed: Never.

From A63 exit St Jean de Luz Nord for town centre. Hotel signposted but ask in advance for exact dirctions through pedestrian areas.

Map No: 16

Château d'Agnos
64400 Agnos
Pyrénées-Atlantiques

Tel: (0)5 59 36 12 52
Fax: (0)5 59 36 13 69
E-mail: chateaudagnos@wanadoo.fr

Heather & Desmond Nears-Crouch

Originally an aristocratic hunting lodge, Agnos was a convent for 30 years until this exceptional couple converted it into a fabulous guest house. Heather, warmly communicative, and Desmond, a talented retired architect, both widely travelled and with a great sense of fun, have done wonders with cells and refectory - and still do all the cooking. The black and white bathroom with the antique cast-iron bath and concave ceiling used to be the château's treasure room - it is now attached to the gilt-furnished *Henri IV* suite. The whole house left us agape: high ceilings framing remarkable mirrors, original paintings set into panelling, a cunning mixture of period and modern furniture and a panelled dining room with a superb floor of ancient yellow and stone-coloured tiles and a black marble fountain. Look out for the medieval kitchen, the old prison. Your hosts would be grateful if you could find the secret passage which King François I is said to have used (he stayed here and had regular amorous escapades). A place of great style, much history and refined food.

Rooms: 5: 2 twins, 2 suites for 3, 1 suite for 4.
Price: €58-€100.
Meals: Breakfast included; dinner €15-€18.
Closed: Two weeks in February; two weeks in November.

From Pau N134 to Oloron Ste Marie; through town; South on N134 for Zaragoza for 1km. In Bidos, right for Agnos.

Map No: 16

Château de Méracq

64410 Méracq-Arzacq
Pyrénées-Atlantiques

Tel: (0)5 59 04 53 01
Fax: (0)5 59 04 55 50
E-mail: chateau-meracq@wanadoo.fr
Web: www.chateau-meracq.com

M & Mme Guerin-Recoussine

Madame will give you a warm welcome in excellent English and is always happy to help or just to chat. She is very proud of the château, her dog, her hens and her husband's cooking. Assisted by another chef he has established a menu that combines the south-west's predilection for *foie gras* and duck with exotic sprinklings of spices and rose petals. If you take the half-board option, you can juggle your meals around as you like: even by eating more the next day if you miss one. The pretty château is at the end of a long and inviting driveway through large grounds with chairs under shady trees. One oak, just as you reach the château, is 200 years old, perhaps planted by proud new owners. The eight bedrooms are an unusual mix: some in fresh stripes or flowers, others with bold turquoise or rose walls, with contemporary patterns on the beds. The first-floor rooms are grander, with bath and shower, while those on the second floor are simpler but all have their own shower. Rooms have lace-trimmed sheets, bowls of fruit and flowers and even bathrooms have plants. There are no numbers on the doors. As Madame says: "It wouldn't feel like home".

Rooms: 8: 6 doubles, 2 suites.
Price: Doubles €62-€86, suites €124-€148.
Meals: Country breakfast €8-€11; lunch & dinner from €26.
Closed: Never.

20 min north of Pau. N34 for 12km towards Aire/Mont de Marsan then left on D944 through Thèze. Château on edge of village of Méracq.

Château de la Côte

Biras Bourdeilles
24310 Brantôme
Dordogne

Tel: (0)5 53 03 70 11
Fax: (0)5 53 03 42 84
E-mail: chateau@chateaudelacote.com
Web: www.chateaudelacote.com

Michel & Olivier Guillaume

For four centuries the du Lau family owned the château and the new young owners are equally passionate about the place; they are modern in outlook yet deeply aware of the privilege of history. Not only that, but they have created some of the grandest bathrooms; in the top-floor suite you can, as you soak, star-gaze through the glass ceiling. The panache can be seen everywhere, without the place looking as if an International Designer has got at it. It is thoroughly French, with a huge range of styles and sizes in the bedrooms. Some walls are papered, some show the old stone, some show their age, some are worthy of several stars. The panache carries over to the food - try *magret de canard en croute de fruits secs* - served in a lovely, formal, half-panelled dining room with an open fire. You can play snooker in a panelled sitting room, formal again and very French. It is all utterly quiet, thanks to the six hectares of parkland. There are some very beautiful places to visit nearby so you have a clutch of good reasons for staying here.

Rooms: 16: 8 doubles/triples, 8 suites.
Price: Doubles €68-€88, suites €98-€150.
Meals: Breakfast €10; lunch & dinner €27-€66; children's meals €11.
Closed: 15 November-15 March, except 2 weeks at Christmas.

From Périgueux D939 for Brantôme. Left before Brantôme onto D106E1. Château 3.5km on right. Signposted.

L' Enclos

Pragelier
24390 Tourtoirac/Hautefort
Dordogne

Tel: (0)5 53 51 11 40
Fax: (0)5 53 50 37 21
E-mail: rornsteen@yahoo.com
Web: www.hotellenclos.com

Robert & Dana Ornsteen

Robert will tell the intriguing history of house and village. He and Dana, who live half the year in Mexico, will welcome you enthusiastically. L'Enclos encompasses The Manor (two guest rooms here), a series of converted stone cottages, the former bakery (two bread ovens remain) and the chapel in a skirt-roofed, blond-stone huddle round the courtyard - enormous personality! The sensational cobbled floor in the hall just begs for admiration; the dining room, marble-floored and rustic-walled, dark beamed and Turkish-rugged, conjures up the Ornsteens' natural/sophisticated style. Light bathes the American potted plants in the *salon*. Each room/cottage has its own character, all use bright fabrics that lift and give vibrancy to the bare stone or off-white walls; most have sisal or sea-grass matting in simple unspartan good taste. And those menus? The smaller is served, candlelit, by the pool: possibly *foie gras*, salads and cheese; the other is several courses, candlelit, in the dining room. A lush, quiet place for Dordogne explorers, with space for all in its gorgeous garden.

Rooms: 7 cottages: 6 for 2, 1 for 3. Two cottages have kitchenettes.
Price: €70-€140.
Meals: Breakfast €8.50; dinner €20-€30.
Closed: October-May.

From Limoges N20 for Uzerche 2.5km; right D704 for St Yrieix la Perche. Before Hautefort right on D62 for Tourtoirac; right on D67. Pragelier is signed approx. 1km on left.

Manoir d'Hautegente
24120 Coly
Dordogne

Tel: (0)5 53 51 68 03
Fax: (0)5 53 50 38 52

Edith & Patrick Hamelin

The ancient manor, first a smithy, later a mill, has been in the family for 300 years but is paradoxically just 50 years old: burned down in the Second World War, it was rebuilt. The millstream has become a fabulous waterfall feeding a pond that shimmers beneath the bedroom windows and a riot of colour in the thoroughly kempt garden. Hautegente is rich inside too, like a private house, with two sumptuous dining rooms clothed in silk and hung with well-chosen paintings and prints. There's a cosy drawing room where a large fireplace and a vast array of Cognacs summon the sybarite. Lavishly-decorated bedrooms have fine thick curtains, antiques and pretty lamps; some are small, some enormous and the soft, expensive feel of padded wall fabrics contrasts with the lovely old staircase leading up from the hall. The rooms in the converted miller's house are more modern; four have mezzanines and the ground-floor room is truly vast. Bathrooms are all beautifully tiled and properly equipped. Madame rules this empire with regal authority, and her more relaxed son. A splendid and peaceful place.

Rooms: 15: 11 doubles, 4 triples.
Price: Half-board €85-€153 p.p. obligatory in high season. Doubles €79-€167, triples €219-€307.
Meals: Breakfast €11; dinner €39-€58; picnic hampers available.
Closed: November-April.

From Brive N89 for Périgueux through Terrasson. Left at Le Lardin on D704 for Sarlat then left at Condat on D62 to Coly. Manoir signed on left just before village.

Auberge de Castel Merle

24290 Sergeac
Dordogne

Tel: (0)5 53 50 70 08
Fax: (0)5 53 50 76 25

Anita Castanet & Christopher Millinship

The Auberge has been in Anita's family for five generations. Husband Christopher is English, and also devoted to this atmospheric place. They have renovated the old buildings with consummate care, keeping the traditional look (no short cuts), using wood from their own land to restore walnut bedheads and oak doors. Christopher is an enthusiastic hunter of truffles and head chef, serving up to 100 meals a day in the summer. There's a vast cast-iron cauldron in the banquet room in which he once conjured up a cassoulet for the entire village. This is *sanglier* (wild boar) country and cooking the beast is one of his specialities. Flowery curtains, pelmets and hand-painted flowers on the walls prettify the dining room. Bedrooms have a straightforward country look, with Provençal prints, beamed ceilings and exposed stone walls. Some rooms overlook the courtyard, others the woods. And the views - the glory of the place is its position, high above the valley of the Vézère, with river, forests and castles beyond - best admired from one of the check-clothed tables on the large, leafy terrace.

Rooms: 5: 4 doubles, 1 twin.
Price: €34-€40. Half-board
€39-€40 p.p.
Meals: Breakfast €5; lunch & dinner €11-€30. Restaurant closed Mondays.
Closed: November-February; last week of September.

From Brive to Montignac, then D706 for Les Eyzies. At Thonac left over bridge then right to Sergeac. Signposted.

Hôtel Les Glycines
4 ave de Laugerie
24620 Les Eyzies de Tayac
Dordogne

Tel: (0)5 53 06 97 07
Fax: (0)5 53 06 92 19
E-mail: les-glycines-aux-eyzies@wanadoo.fr
Web: les-glycines-dordogne.com

Pascal & Maud Lombard

Potential for name-dropping here: Prince Charles stayed here in the 60's with his Cambridge tutor. Les Glycines has been lodging people since 1862, when it was a *relais de poste*. It has been enlarged over the years, with the stables being turned into more rooms as they were not needed for horses. The gardens are fabulous: they were planted by the son of a head gardener at Versailles. You meander down to the pool under arches laden with roses and honeysuckle and there is a vegetable garden too. Just past the lobby you enter the dining room which runs the breadth of the building and overlooks the garden. The Lombards took over Les Glycines three years ago and have thrown themselves into decoration. Pascal did plan to do all the cooking himself, but found he had enough on his plate; after finding a great chef (his words), he is hoping for a Michelin star. Don't be put off by the busy road and the station nearby: once in the garden you could be in the country. Though you might ask for a room at the back or in the annex. Families can have interconnecting rooms, which sleep five comfortably.

Rooms: 23: 19 doubles, 4 triples. Some of the doubles interconnect.
Price: €66-€99.
Meals: Buffet breakfast €10; picnic lunch €9-€23; lunch €21-€45; dinner €30-€45. Restaurant closed Monday & Saturday lunchtimes except July & August.
Closed: November-April.

From Perigueux D47 to Sarlat. Cross river and Les Glycines is on left immed. before Les Eyzies station.

Le Domaine de la Barde

Route de Périgueux
24260 Le Bugue
Dordogne

Tel: (0)5 53 07 16 54
Fax: (0)5 53 54 76 19

André Darnaud

A sensational place. Once a weekend cottage for the 14th-century nobility who owned it, the Domaine has now become a luxurious but immensely friendly and easy-going hotel. The owners, unlike most restorers of ancient buildings, began with the grounds which they arranged as a perfect *jardin à la française* saving several centuries-old trees in the process, before they tackled the mill, the forge and the manor house. There is an informal 'family' feel about the place which in no way detracts from the professionalism of the management: the Darnauds' priority is your comfort, and it shows in their staff and in the immaculate, lavish but personal decoration and furnishing of the bedrooms. They also have a flair for the dramatic visual touch - witness the glass floor under which flows the millstream in the old mill, the *oeil de boeuf* window in the forge and the 'menacing Eros' who surveys you as you stroll through the gardens. There's plenty to do; the swimming pool has a jet-stream massage, there's table tennis and, in the *orangerie,* a sauna.

Rooms: 18 doubles/twins.
Price: Doubles/twins €72-€196.
Meals: Breakfast €11; lunch & dinnner €25-€54.
Closed: Mid-October-mid-April.

From Périgueux N89; D710 to Le Bugue. 1km before Le Bugue, Domaine signposted on right.

Map No: 12

Château Les Merles

24520 Mouledier
Dordogne

Tel: (0)5 53 63 13 42
Fax: (0)5 53 63 13 45
E-mail: lesmerles@aol.com
Web: www.golf-lesmerles.com

Jenny Lyon

After running a hotel near Edinburgh, Jennifer came here planning to run a gîte. She soon decided, however, that she would miss the closer contact with guests so runs Les Merles - heaven for golfers - more like a hotel. In the apartments a cleaner comes in daily, and makes the beds as well. On the other hand, although there is no restaurant, guests can use either of two kitchens and in a gesture typical of the generosity of spirit that prevails here, fridges are stocked with water and drinks which guests can replace or 'chalk up'. You arrive at the château up an unmade tree-lined drive alongside the driving range. Neighbouring farm buildings give a pleasantly relaxed feel to a place which could feel rather grand. Jenny lives in a 17th-century house next to the château – the informal 'reception' is here too - and has outbuildings converted into a clubhouse, where you can have breakfast, snack lunches or good espresso coffee all day; it's also a place to store golf bags. Elegant ground-floor rooms face south with views of the course or range, while upstairs rooms are smaller but pretty, in pink or blue with pine floors.

Rooms: 6 + 2 apartments: 5 doubles, 1 suite for 2; 2 apts for 2-4.
Price: Doubles €84, suite €100; apartments €183.
Meals: Buffet breakfast included.
Closed: 5 January-February.

From Bergerac D660 for Sarlat. At Tuimières, left onto D36 for Pressignac. Château approx 200m.

Hôtel Restaurant Le Château

1 rue de la Tour
24150 Lalinde
Dordogne

Tel: (0)5 53 61 01 82
Fax: (0)5 53 24 74 60

Guy Gensou

Overhanging the river Dordogne - a lovely hotel in a spectacular position - the narrow terrace and swimming pool built into the rocks above the river have views of both the rising and setting sun across the water. The entrance is up a one-way street then through an old arched doorway. You are in the town here but insulated from it. The reception area is small and unpretentious; what is sensational is the stone staircase that winds up from the foyer to an understatedly elegant sitting area. Then come the bedrooms: from the smallest attic room to the biggest suite with balcony, they have pastel-painted walls and simple furnishings and are very refined, very calming. Most overlook the river, others have windows on two sides and overlook the pool and entrance cul-de-sac. Bathrooms are impeccable, with either white or champagne tiles or terrazzo marbled walls. The dining room couldn't be more inviting; it's light and airy with stone and soft apricot-coloured walls, beautiful china, linen napkins, fresh flowers and a spectacular river view through the French windows. Monsieur Gensou cooks, very well. A great place.

Rooms: 7: 6 doubles, 1 suite.
Price: €49-€145.
Meals: Breakfast €10; lunch & dinner €21-€34. Restaurant closed Mondays all year & Sundays from Nov-Mar.
Closed: 3rd week in Sept; 15 December-15 February.

From Bergerac D660 to Lalinde; right at post office - hotel at end of street.

La Couleuvrine

1 place de la Bouquerie
24200 Sarlat
Dordogne

Tel: (0)5 53 59 27 80
Fax: (0)5 53 31 26 83

Isabelle Lebon

This is either a haven for grass-snakes or guns, depending on how you translate the name. It is more likely the latter, for the hotel, built right *into* the city walls of the medieval town of Sarlat, once shook under the recoil of the canon on the ramparts above as they defended the town against the perfidious English. If feeling vulnerable, you may sleep at the top of one of the city towers and take your shower in the thickness of the wall itself, or you may have a private balcony overlooking the pedestrianised centre of Sarlat. Each room has its individual character, with few reminders of the 21st century. Mesdames Lebon (mother and daughter) run the place with an enthusiasm and concern for the comfort of their guests which is rare in this much-visited part of France. Their attention to detail extends - of course - to the cuisine, *du terroir* but 'judiciously re-imagined' for modern tastes, and the choice of lovely old prints and drawings on the walls. Better avoided in high summer, this is a good place to be at those moments when you want to escape into history.

Rooms: 23: 20 doubles, 1 triple, 2 quadruples.
Price: Doubles €42-€52, triple & quadruples €63-€73.
Meals: Breakfast €6; lunch & dinner €18-€32. Restaurant closed 2nd half of January & 2nd half of November.
Closed: Never.

From A20/N20 exit Souillac to Sarlat. Hotel signposted in town centre.

Le Relais du Touron

Le Touron
24200 Carsac Aillac
Dordogne

Tel: (0)5 53 28 16 70
Fax: (0)5 53 28 52 51
E-mail: relais.touron@wanadoo.fr

Viala family

Such an attractive approach up the drive lined with neatly-clipped box hedges and spiræa - it is all very elegant-looking, surrounded by broad lawns and handsome, mature trees. Reception is in the main entrance hall, by the high open fireplace, but only the big triple bedroom is actually in the main house: all the other rooms and the dining room are in the converted barn and stable block with the pool just below. The new dining room has one all-glass wall overlooking the pool and garden beyond and is flooded with light. Bedrooms give onto a narrow terrace above the dining area and have the same decoration in straightforward, unfrightening style: plain carpets and walls, bright bedcovers and curtains and adequate lighting. The nearby road is well screened by thick trees and shrubs. Indeed, the three-hectare garden, which also contains a small pond, is a great asset with lots of private corners to be explored. A delightful bicycle and foot path of 6km will take you right into Sarlat. A good base to visit this richly cultural area.

Rooms: 12: 11 doubles, 1 triple.
Price: Doubles €47-€59, triple €69-€75.
Meals: Breakfast €6; lunch & dinner €14-€31.
Closed: Never.

From Sarlat D704 to Gourdon. Hotel signed on right before Carsac.

Map No: 12

Manoir du Soubeyrac

Le Laussou
47150 Monflanquin
Lot-et-Garonne

Tel: (0)5 53 36 51 34
Fax: (0)5 53 36 35 20
Web: www.manoir-du-soubeyrac.com

Claude Rocca

Those high, wrought-iron courtyard gates dignify you as you pass through them and you never know quite what to expect. Here there's white paving, a central statue, climbing and potted plants. Walk into the well-planted garden and there's one of those amazing swimming pools *une piscine à débordement,* that looks as if it spills over the edge of the hill. Most bedrooms have that same beautiful hillside view; their décor is opulently traditional with themed colours, chintzy touches, lots of paintings and prints, some genuine old furniture, and rugs on wooden or tiled floors. Bathrooms have all the cosseting extras; jacuzzi-type massage sprays, hair-dryers, colour co-ordinated dressing gowns and essential oils. The courteous M Rocca has thought it all through with great care and enthusiasm and cooks gastronomic dinners too. Exposed beams, stone and brickwork and an open fireplace in the dining room set the scene for those candlelit meals and there is plenty of space to relax (with books, games and music) in the huge living room above it. Just the place for an up-market country holiday.

Rooms: 4: 3 doubles, 1 suite.
Price: Doubles €104-€119,
suite €145.
Meals: Breakfast €8; dinner €27.
Closed: Mid-October-mid-April.

From Villeneuve sur Lot D676 to Monflanquin, then D272 for Laussou. After bridge, left to Envals for 3km; left for Soubeyrac.

Manoir de Roquegautier

Beaugas
47290 Cancon
Lot-et-Garonne

Tel: (0)5 53 01 60 75
Fax: (0)5 53 40 27 75
E-mail: roquegautier@free.fr
Web: www.roquegautier.free.fr

Christian & Brigitte Vrech

In its beautiful park with long views across the rolling hills of the Lot valley, the old house is wondrously French with masses of drapes, swags and interlinings - all done, but never overdone, by Madame. The rooms in the old tower of the main château are truly memorable with their own entrance and spiral stone staircase. Some are carpeted, some have polished wooden floors with good solid furniture that's not too ornate, there are claw-footed baths and huge old basins and taps, and each top-floor suite has one round tower room. Rooms in the converted outbuildings have character too, and are eminently comfortable. There are fine mature trees to shade your picnic lunches and superb local dinners (home-grown vegetables and lamb from the Vrechs' farm 2km away) are served outside at a convivial trestle table; children can sup early, giving adults the chance to eat and talk in peace. There are swings, a games and telly room, a pool that is hidden from view, gazebos and pergolas around the garden - and such a gentle, friendly welcome from the owners that you will want to relax and stay for ever.

Rooms: 5 + 1 apartment: 3 doubles, 2 suites for 3-4; 1 apt for 6-7.
Price: Doubles €52-€65, suites €94-€101; apartment €127.
Meals: Breakfast included; dinner €19 including wine; children's meals €11.
Closed: October-April.

From Villeneuve sur Lot north on N21 for Cancon for 15.5km. Manoir signed on left 3.5km before Cancon.

Map No: 12

Limousin
Auvergne

He added that a Frenchman in the train had given him a
great sandwich that so stank of garlic that he had been
inclined to throw it at the fellow's head.

Ford Madox Ford, Provence (1935)

CDT Cantal

Domaine des Mouillères

23250 Saint Georges la Pouge
Creuse

Tel: (0)5 55 66 60 64
Fax: (0)5 55 66 68 80

Mme Elizabeth Blanquart-Till

A small backwater of a village, a big clearing in the Limousin forest - here is a walker's paradise. On a South-facing slope with only distantly rolling hillsides, fine trees and a couple of donkeys to disturb the eye, the long stone hotel was built in 1870 as a farmhouse for the Madame's great-great-grandfather and feels as solid as her lineage. Inside, you get that sense of long-gone days of endless country peace: leather-bound tomes, gild-framed sepia photographs of Grandmama or great-aunt Gladys as a baby, palely gentle floral designs on wallpapers and bedcovers. But the warm carpeting, the neat little bathrooms, the stripily plush modern furniture in the lounge betray a thoroughly contemporary care for comfort. And there's a lovely terrace outside. The delightfully friendly owners and their children, the geese and their goslings, the donkeys and their foals (summer population of course), welcome you and your family into their rural world and Madame will serve you dinners of high authenticity: old family recipes made with fresh local produce. After which, peace will decend. *No smoking here.*

Rooms: 7: 4 double/twins with wc and bathroom; 1 double & 2 singles with basin, wc and bidet, sharing bath.
Price: Doubles €38-€61, single €18.
Meals: Breakfast €8; dinner €14-€18; picnic available. 2 restaurants 3 & 7km.
Closed: October-March.

70km from Limoges towards Bourganeuf/Aubusson N141. Left at Charbonnier to St George La Pouge.

Au Pont de l'Hospital

B. P. 38
L'Hospital
19400 Argentat sur Dordogne
Corrèze

Tel: (0)5 55 28 90 35
Fax: (0)5 55 28 20 70
E-mail: au-pont@wanadoo.fr
Web: www.argentat.co.uk

Jim & Fiona Mallows

Beside the little, trout-rich Maronne that rushes over rapids towards its destiny in the great Dordogne stands a house run with a minimum of rules and constraints by people who trust that guests will understand it is a family home. With a relaxed and helpful atmosphere and space for all to spread, it is ideal for fishing buffs and families (young children need supervision by that untamed water). Jovial Jim Mallows advertises snacks for passers-by, knows the area backwards and will tell you exactly where to eat great meals of remarkable value - he and Fiona are the most delightful hosts. Bedrooms are small but adequate, some with bathroom, some without. Fiona's anatomical portraits of fish and Jim's watercolours hang in the attractive breakfast room with its wooden tables and woodburning stove. With warning, they will do a barbecue and salad meal on the wooden pontoon projecting over the river. Come for the fantastic position in great walking country with five fishing rivers within 20 minutes, lots of places to visit and such unspoilt simplicity.

Rooms: 9: 7 doubles, 1 triple, 1 family; 5 doubles have their own bathrooms, others share 2 shower rooms and wcs.
Price: €24-€37.
Meals: Continental breakfast €5; English breakfast €8; picnic €7. Good restaurants in town.
Closed: Mid-November-March.

From Tulle N120 through Argentat; 2nd right opp. garage after bridge; D116 for L'Hospital (or L'Hopital) 2km; hotel on right imm'ly after bridge over Maronne.

Au Rendez-Vous des Pêcheurs

Pont du Chambon
19320 Saint Merd de Lapleau
Corrèze

Tel: (0)5 55 27 88 39
Fax: 05 55 27 83 19
E-mail: fabry@medianet.fr
Web: www.medianet.fr/fabry

Mme Fabry

The proof of the fishing... is in the 15Kg pike hanging in the bar of this delectable place - it isn't called 'Fishermen's Lodge' for nothing. But there's more than fish. The house and its exquisite lakeside setting are intimately linked. Fifty years ago, the Fabrys built a house on the banks of the Dordogne; at the same time, a dam was started just downstream. Madame opened a kitchen for the site workers - and began her life's work; the house became an inn which she now runs with her daughter-in-law; and naturally, this being Perigord, food looms as large as that great fish. The restaurant, a fine room full of light and plants and Limoges china, overlooks the view reaching off the distant wooded hills of the gorge; menus are brilliantly short and to the point. Bedrooms are in a similar vein, all differently decorated in simple, pleasing country style with co-ordinated bathrooms and, for five of them, ...the river. The terrace is generous, the garden pretty, the view a gift to treasure. Remarkable value in one of France's gentlest, loveliest pieces of country.

Rooms: 8 doubles/twins.
Price: €41-€43.
Meals: Breakfast €6; picnic available; lunch & dinner €15-€32.
Closed: November 12-mid February.

45 mins E of Tulle: D978 until St Merd de Lapleau via Marcillac la Croisille, then D13 until 'lieu-dit' Pont du Chambon.

Map No: 13

Hostellerie de la Maronne

Le Theil
15140 Saint Martin Valmeroux/Salers
Cantal

Tel: (0)4 71 69 20 33
Fax: (0)4 71 69 28 22
E-mail: hotelmaronne@cfi15.fr
Web: www.cfi15.fr/hotelmaronne

M & Mme Decock

Silence and rolling green space! In glorious country where the little Maronne hurtles towards its gorge and brown cows echo the russet of autumn, this 1800s manor looks out to wooded hills and dark mountains. You will meet its charming, subtly humorous owner and be well fed by his Madagascan wife in a dining room with soft quiet colours and pretty rugs. The lovely double drawing room has deep sofas, two fireplaces, more rugs, some intriguing Madagascan furniture. Bedrooms, all with excellent bedding, vary in size on different levels in a small warren of buildings, past flowering terraces and an indoor flowerbed. Nearly all have the sweeping valley view (two rooms at the back are up against the hillside); the best are the terrace rooms. Sober décor is enlivened by exotic pieces (a Japanese dressing table, an inlaid coffee table); good-sized bathrooms. The pool is ideal for landscape-gazing, there's fabulous walking, saunas too, and you will be made to feel very welcome in this house of silence: no seminars, no piped music, headphones for telly - bliss.

Rooms: 21: 18 doubles, 3 suites.
Price: Doubles €79-€113, suites €110-€137.
Meals: Breakfast €10; lunch & dinner €23-€43. Restaurant closed evenings from November-end March.
Closed: November-April.

From Aurillac D922 north for 33km to Saint Martin Valmeroux, then D37 towards Fontanges.

Auberge de Concasty

15600 Boisset
Cantal

Tel: (0)4 71 62 21 16
Fax: (0)4 71 62 22 22
E-mail: info@auberge-concasty.com
Web: www.auberge.concasty.com

Martine & Omar Causse-Adllal

Half a mile high stands the river-ploughed plateau, the air is strong, the country wild, the space immense. Here stands a good square family mansion, built 300 years ago and proud beneath its curvy shingle roof. Over the last 40 years, the Causse family have restored it, bringing everything thoroughly up to date: jacuzzi, Turkish bath and organic or local-grown produce to keep you blooming (lots of veg from the sister's farm next door). The dining room, dominated by a great inglenook fireplace where a fine plant collection live in summer, and the covered patio overlooking the pool and valley beyond, are the stage for great shows of of *fois gras* and asparagus, scallops and *confits*, where the supporting cast is an impressive choice of estate wines; a fine breakfast spread, too. Guest rooms, some in the main house, some in a restored barn, are Stylish Rustic with space, good floral fabrics, new mattresses and an evocative name each - no standardisation here, except for the great view. You will love the smiling, attentive staff and the warm family atmosphere they generate.

Rooms: 15: 14 doubles & 1 suite for 2.
Price: Doubles €54-€91 some with private terrace, suite €103-€125.
Meals: Breakfast €13; picnic available; dinner €24-€32.
Closed: Mid-December-mid-March.

From Aurillac towards Figeac N122, left to Manhès on D64; from Figeac N122 then D17 after Maurs.

Map No: 13

Le Pré Bossu
43150 Moudeyres
Haute-Loire

Tel: (0)4 71 05 10 70
Fax: (0)4 71 05 10 21

M & Mme Grootaert

The silence is part and parcel of this fabulous setting in the depths of the countryside. A hotel for the past 30 years, Le Pré Bossu oozes warmth and solidity. Bedrooms are fairly basic but each has at least one piece of fine furniture. Its Belgian owners are passionate about the environment so there's strictly no smoking, and they organise mushroom-hunting weekends in the spring and autumn. Mr. Grootaert handles the cooking, inspired by his own vegetable garden or the fresh produce he brings back from his regular trips to Lyon. Specialities include a vegetable menu (not called 'vegetarian' since he doesn't consider it a philosophy) as well as fish. 'Well-behaved' children are welcome and it's an ideal spot for either a quiet stay or an adventure holiday taking in canoeing, ballooning and lots of country hikes. At an altitude of 1,300m it can get chilly at any time of the year so there's always a huge fire lit every morning in the library/breakfast room where you are treated to freshly-squeezed orange juice and a choice of home-made jams. *No smoking here.*

Rooms: 11: 10 doubles, 1 suite for 4.
Price: Dinner is obligatory,
€160-€180 room and dinner for 2.
Meals: Buffet breakfast €12; picnic lunch on request.
Closed: November-Easter.

From Le Puy en Velay D15 for Valence for 15km. At Les Pandraux D36 towards Laussonne for 6km; left for Moudeyres. Hotel at entrance of village.

Château de Maulmont

Saint Priest Bramefant
63310 Randan
Puy-de-Dôme

Tel: (0)4 70 59 03 45
Fax: (0)4 70 59 11 88
E-mail: hotel.chateau-maulmont@wanadoo.fr

Mary & Théo Bosman

This extraordinary place, built in 1830 by Louis Philippe for his sister Adélaïde, has long views and architecture: medieval crenellations, 16th-century brick patterning, Loire-Valley slate roofs, Neo-Gothic windows, even real Templar ruins - a cornucopia of character. The Dutch owners provide endless activities (golf driving range, riding, swimming, rowing on the pond) and cultivate a certain 'formal informality'. They have preserved original features - carved inside shutters, the old spit, the astounding banqueting hall with its stained-glass portraits of Adélaïde in various moods - and collected some stunning furniture. Bedrooms go from small to very big, from plain honest comfortable with simple shower room (standard) to draped and four-postered château-romantic with marble bathroom (the *luxe* rooms are worth the difference). And do visit the *King's Room*, a round blue and white (original paint!) 'tent' in a tower, for a brilliant whisper-to-shout effect. Dining rooms are tempting, there are evening entertainments - wine-tasting, music, spit-roast dinner - and staff are alert and eager.

Rooms: 19: 15 doubles/twins, 1 suite for 4, 3 apartments for 4-6.
Price: Doubles €70-€165, suite €215, apartments €215-€245.
Meals: Breakfast €9.50; lunch & dinner €17-€44.
Closed: January-mid-February.

From A71 exit 12 A719, N209 for Vichy. Continue for Vichy then Hauterive & St Yorre. Leave Hauterive on D131, D55 to St Priest Bramefant Les Graveyrons (not on map but signposted) right on D59 to château.

Hôtel Relais Sainte Anne

Rue du Pourtanel
46600 Martel
Lot

Tel: (0)5 65 37 40 56
Fax: (0)5 65 37 42 82

Pierre Bettler

Un ange passe is what one says at the table as the conversation flounders, a special kind of sudden silence coming suddenly in the midst of a flow of words. Perhaps the angels in the tiny chapel of Sainte Anne, at the heart of this beautiful cluster of ancient buildings, are a reminder of another, quieter time when the hotel was a girls' convent. The chapel is intact and used occasionally for small concerts and art exhibitions and the whole ensemble has been lovingly and sensitively restored with no jarring architectural mishaps. The large pool is discreetly tucked away and the walled garden, a cunning combination of formal French structure and English informality, manages to retain a strong feeling of the past - young charges playing hide-and-seek in the shrubbery, or gathering in the little courtyards or around the fish pond. Inside is equally atmospheric; warm old stone, fine wallpapers, opulent curtains, heavy rugs and proper attention to lighting. Most of the ground floor bedrooms have their own terraces. Sophisticated surroundings without any self-consciousness. Rare.

Rooms: 15: 11 doubles, 4 suites.
Price: Doubles €67-€135,
suites €116-€190.
Meals: Continental or full breakfast €8-€13.
Closed: Mid-November-mid-March.

From Brive A20 for Cahors exit 54 for Martel. Rue Pourtanel and hotel on right at entrance of town.

Hôtel Beau Site

46500 Rocamadour
Lot

Tel: (0)5 65 33 63 08
Fax: (0)5 65 33 65 23
E-mail: hotel@bw-beausite.com
Web: www.bw-beausite.com

Martial Menot

The perfect way to see Rocamadour: stay in this old hostelry, enjoy the stupendous cliff-hanging view from the restaurant and terrace, visit the historic village in the early morning and leave for the day when it fills with trippers. Rocamadour cracks at the seams between 11am and 7pm so return for dinner and a peaceful evening's stroll along the, by-then, walkable streets. The Beau Site is seriously old with a fairly wild history - stones and timbers could tell many a tale. It has belonged to charming Monsieur Menot's family for five generations and the reception area dazzles with medieval antiquities and shiny brasses on old flagstones worn by endless pilgrims' feet. The *salon* and games room are in the old vaulted kitchens and pantries, but we found fake leather and spindly legs disappointing. Bedrooms vary in size; recently-renovated rooms have pleasant wooden furniture, rich fabrics and good bathrooms. A friendly, welcoming place in an exceptional position. Hotel guests may drive right to the hotel and park in its private car park. *No smoking here.*

Rooms: 41 + 1 apartment: 40 doubles/twins, 1 triple; 1 apt for 4.
Price: Doubles/twins €48-€80, triple €76-€95; apartment €88-€106.
Meals: Buffet breakfast €9: picnic €7.50; lunch from €19; dinner à la carte.
Closed: 2 February-12 November.

In Rocamadour take road to Cité. Through medieval gates into village and park in front of hotel. Only hotel guests may use this lane.

Map No: 12

La Terrasse
46200 Meyronne
Lot

Tel: (0)5 65 32 21 60
Fax: (0)5 65 32 26 93
E-mail: terrasse.liebus@wanadoo.fr
Web: www.hotel-la-terrasse.com

Gilles Liébus

This is a fortress rather than a château and has stood guard over the Dordogne since the 11th century, though with the scars of much violence. A child might build a castle like this: tall and straight, with a mix of round towers, square towers, fat towers and thin towers. Gilles and Françoise have made it an inviting country retreat once again. Entered from the back through magnificent doors off a pretty courtyard, the entrance lobby has an amazing polished flagstone floor. The bedrooms are all different, with the more interesting ones in the oldest part of the building. Most overlook either the river or the pool - set high into the walls with a fantastic view, this is a rare swimming pool with atmosphere. The main dining room is a touch 'interior designed' but you will love the vaulted 'winter' dining room, or eating on the terrace under the vines. Food is real southwest: wonderful concoctions with truffles and top quality ingredients. Save it for dinner or you'll miss seeing Rocamadour, the Lascaux caves or canoeing on the river.

Rooms: 20: 15 doubles, 3 triples, 2 suites.
Price: Doubles & triples €49-€86, suites €122-€228.
Meals: Buffet breakfast €8; lunch & dinner €15-€46. Restaurant closed Tuesday lunchtimes.
Closed: Mid-November-April.

From Limoges A20 at Souillac. D703 for Martel 6km, right at Le Pigeon onto D15 for Figeac 4km. Left after crossing bridge at St Sozy.

Hostellerie La Source Bleue

Moulin de Leygues
46700 Touzac
Lot

Tel: (0)5 65 36 52 01
Fax: (0)5 65 24 65 69
E-mail: sourcebleue@wanadoo.fr
Web: www.sourcebleue.com

M Jean Pierre Bouyou

If you like the unexpected, here it is: a three-acre bamboo forest deep in *la France profonde*. Our inspector didn't explain how this came to be... It isn't just any old bamboo, but ranges from dwarf varieties to the 15-foot-high *Phyllostachis violaescens*. Meandering walkways lead to a lake full of koi carp and waterlilies: a magical place for children. The hotel itself is a fascinating ensemble of three old mills - one built in the 11th, one in the 12th and one in the 17th century - beside a spring that sparkles true blue, on any but the cloudiest day. With cars parked near but out of sight, the effect is peaceful and inviting, the rushing water soothing you to sleep and providing a cheerful, cooling background to meals. Bedrooms are spread out through three buildings, the restaurant being entirely separate, and vary. Those in the tower are 60's-style but due to be done up. Nos. 10 and 14 are generous in size and traditional, while No. 8 has a private terrace. Despite its size, this is very much a family hotel and would be great for children – though perhaps not the smallest sort.

Rooms: 14: 12 doubles, 2 suites.
Price: Doubles €53-€84, suites €84-€114.
Meals: Breakfast €6; picnic €8; lunch & dinner €15-€36.
Closed: 8 December-March.

From Villeneuve sur Lot take D911 for Fumel & Cahors. By-pass Fumel; after Soturac right for Touzac & follow signposts.

Map No: 12

Château La Gineste

46700 Duravel
Lot

Tel: (0)5 65 30 37 00
Fax: (0)5 65 30 37 01

M & Mme André Lamothe

This wine-growing château, brilliantly restored by André Lamothe, breathes restraint without austerity, luxury without ostentation and spans some five or six centuries (Richard the Lionheart hunted here): a courtyard with a line of elegant classical columns, carved stone lintels, a fluted, fan-vaulted ceiling over a spiral staircase - photographs cannot do it justice. With vines as far as the eye can see, the château wines are Monsieur Lamothe's delight - he's happy to show you his restored old-style winery. Dinner is in the old stone-vaulted cellar or the smaller breakfast *salon*: both have fireplaces and an elegantly relaxed feel. Bedrooms are big, the yellow suite especially, and done in faultless taste using generous quantities of rich materials that lend lushness to soft white walls, polished wooden floors and genuine antique furniture and doors. Bathrooms are just as luxurious with double basins, big mirrors, good lighting. Three rooms give onto a covered colonnaded terrace looking across well-kept lawns, ancient plane and chestnut trees and the sea of vines to the hills beyond. Superb.

Rooms: 4: 3 doubles, 1 suite.
Price: €87-€144.
Meals: Breakfast included; dinner €25.
Restaurant closed October-end May.
Closed: December-January.

From Fumel D911 towards Cahors.
Château just before Duravel.

Domaine de Saint Géry

46800 Lascabanes
Lot

Tel: (0)5 65 31 82 51
Fax: (0)5 65 22 92 89
E-mail: duler@saint-gery.com
Web: www.saint-gery.com

Pascale & Patrick Duler

An ancestor unearthed by Patrick's archeologist mother, and the beauty of the old farm buildings were enough to inspire this remarkable young couple to purchase a very run-down property in 1986. Now the grassed and paved areas between the buildings are decorated with loads of large-scale exotica - lemon trees, bays, oleanders, olives... and a fountain. A truffle oak and hazelnut forest spreads out behind the buildings. The Duler's also seem to ably manage two small children, a 60-acre cereal farm, an organic vegetable garden and a restaurant - in addition to making and marketing their own sausages, hams, *confits* and truffle-enhanced *foie gras*. You can sample all of these delectables and more, as Patrick performs superbly in the kitchen and Pascale handles the divine desserts. Bedrooms are traditionally furnished with solid old wooden bedframes, generous curtains, no frilly bits or clutter - and all come with their own terrace or sitting out space. The delightful pleasures of the table and genuine hospitality are united here in such an intimate and peaceful setting that you may find it difficult to leave.

Rooms: 5: 4 doubles, 1 suite for up to 5.
Price: Halfboard only: doubles €104-€120 p.p., suite €160 p.p. for two, extra people €58.
Meals: Farmer's breakfast included. Breakfast charged separately, €14. Mondays & Tuesdays.
Closed: Mid-October-mid-May. (Except by reservation.)

From Cahors N20 for Toulouse; right for Montcuq & Agen for approx 500m. D7 left for Labastide Marnhac. Continue to Lascabanes. Signposted.

Map No: 12

Hôtel Restaurant Le Vert

Le Vert
46700 Mauroux
Lot

Tel: (0)5 65 36 51 36
Fax: (0)5 65 36 56 84
E-mail: hotellevert@aol.com

Bernard & Eva Philippe

The alchemy of family tradition - three generations and 20 years for this young couple - has rubbed off onto the very stone of the walls here. An unpretentious, authentic country inn where Bernard and his brother successfully combine their skills in the kitchen. All is simplicity with fresh flowers, glowing silverware, old flagstones leading you from the small lobby into the dining room - glance at the blackboard for the day's special to get your appetite going. The local food cognoscenti are greeted as friends here. The rooms in the garden annex are big, cool and elegant with beamed ceilings, stone walls and antique furniture lightened by simple white curtains and delicate bedspreads. Three rooms in the main house are to be made into two - they will be roomier still and have bigger bathrooms. The pool is hidden on the far side of the garden. In a country where politicians are authors, cooks are philosophers: Michael, Bernard's brother, is working on his doctorate in philosophy and recently co-authored *Le Cuisinier Alchimiste & le Diamant Noir* (The alchemist cook and the black diamond). His ivory tower is in the kitchen.

Rooms: 6 doubles.
Price: €55-85
Meals: Breakfast €7; lunch & dinner €22-€38. Restaurant closed Thursdays.
Closed: 12 November - 13 February.

From Villeneuve sur Lot D911 for Fumel; south of Fumel D139 for Montayral. Continue past Mauroux towards Puy l'Evêque for approx. 500m. Hotel on right.

Domaine de Cantecor

La Madeleine
82270 Montpezat de Quercy
Tarn-et-Garonne

Tel: (0)5 65 21 87 44
Fax: (0)5 65 21 87 44
E-mail: info@cantecor.com
Web: www.cantecor.com

Lyndi & René Toebak

Whether you are in the main house or one of the three converted Quercy stone outbuildings with their garden-level patios, all the colour co-ordinated rooms are bright and cheerful. Bottled water, tissues and plenty of towels are a generous touch. Some of the rooms are spare and small but the property has masses of character and the new owners make it clear that they want you to feel at home. On summer nights, the floodlit pool is simply enchanting and during the day you may well be unable to resist a game of boules on the lawn or the delights of a never-to-be-forgotten village fête. Comfortable sofas around an open fireplace, bookshelves stacked with paperbacks, a billiard table in the oak-timbered gallery, a country kitchen (the central meeting place) and samples of wine bought from local growers complete this charming picture. This is a good base for exploring the subterranean caves, rafting on the meandering river between Figeac and Cahors or sampling the full bodied wines from this area. Lydi and Rene keep a good supply of information on all the activities in the area. Between them, Lydi and René can hold their own in English, German, Spanish and Dutch.

Rooms: 6: 4 doubles, 1 triple,
1 family room.
Price: €50-€60.
Meals: Breakfast included. Good restaurant 600m, two fine restaurants 2km.
Closed: October-end May

From Cahors N20 towards Montauban for 20km; La Madeleine on left. Signposted.

Map No: 12

L' Arbre d'Or

16 rue Despeyrous
82500 Beaumont de Lomagne
Tarn-et-Garonne

Tel: (0)5 63 65 32 34
Fax: (0)5 63 65 29 85

Peggy & Tony Ellard

The 'golden tree' is Chinese and turn-of-the-century (the last one); it's a Ginkgo Biloba, and probably the finest in France. Tony will tell you its story and will explain why he believes Beaumont de Lomagne is the finest example of a bastide town in south-west France; it's certainly very handsome. He and Peggy came here some 10 years ago, obviously love the place, and take great care of their guests; they've given thought to disabled access, are happy to look after cyclists and walkers and actively host their evening meals. Peggy's a keen cook and has adopted traditional, regional recipes which you can eat outside in the shaded garden or in the dining room with its tiled floor, open fire and exposed beams. There's a comfortably old-fashioned, lived-in, atmosphere in the sitting room - large sofas, books (and TV) - and in the bedrooms too, which are mostly large-windowed; some overlook the garden, some the street, and have marble fireplaces, interesting old furniture and pretty decorative touches. A 17th-century gentleman's residence-turned-hotel with plenty of character.

Rooms: 6 doubles.
Price: €45-€50. Reductions for stays of more than 3 nights.
Meals: Breakfast included; dinner €15-€18, including aperitif, wine and coffee by arrangement.
Closed: 1-15 January.

From A62 exit Castel Sarrasin. From A20 exit Montauban. D928 towards Auch. L'Arbre d'Or is opposite Beaumont post office.

Castelnau des Fieumarcon

32700 Lagarde Fimarcon
Gers

Tel: (0)5 62 68 99 30
Fax: (0)5 62 68 99 30
E-mail: castelnaulagarde.org

Jean Calviac

Getting there is almost an initiation. Pass through a large gothic portal and spot a music stand, a welcome sign and a gong. If a large friendly Alsatian dog is about, you are in the right place. Built in the 18th century by local feudal lords, who for a time during the 100 Year War had pledged allegiance to the English crown, this village was left to crumble until discovered by a tribe of gypsies who used it to store their copper treasures. Six years ago the Calviac family moved in but have left much of the creeper-clad old stone and ramparts untouched. It's not 'interior decorated', but simple, clever touches lend sophistication: framed dried herbs on the painted walls, mosquito-net baldaquins, terracotta tiles, a massive Louis XV armoire. Jean is a renowned gourmet and uses his home-grown organic produce in the kitchen. On high ground so the views from every window are astounding - a timeless hazy glow from the low lying hills and surrounding fields. Stendhal called it the French Tuscany. He would be at home here: no cars, no TV's, no telephones.

Rooms: 14 houses for 2-6. Each room has own bathroom. Most houses have kitchens. Ask for room breakdown.
Price: Rooms €107-€200, weekly €550-€900. Houses €200-€305, weekly €900-€1,372.
Meals: Breakfast €8; picnic available; dinner €38-€76, by arrangement.
Closed: Never.

A61 exit Agen/Auch for Auch on N2. From Lectoure D7 for Condom 6km; right on D166 to Nerac. Lagarde signed on left after 4km; village 3km on. Look for large portal & ring gong.

Map No: 12

Hotel Mycelium

Place de Shiitake
Champignon

Tel: (0)8 16 00 00 00
E-mail: buttonup@notmushroom.ici
Web: www.motmushroom.ici

Designed by the architect who designed the canopy over the Abbesses metro station entrance in Paris – this bizarre but stunning construction was built as a centre-piece for the Tuileries and then moved here just recently. It has become the first hotel in France to provide all-round views of the ground, from that under-lit glass floor. It is a parody of the defensive mediaeval towers with all-round views of attackers below. The one entrance is visible in the photograph. Rather charmingly, the one lavatory is in the little wooden outhouse that you see in the small photograph, providing a view of passers-by from the sitting position. Many a friendship has been struck up here. The hut is, of course, modelled on the traditional custodian's hut. Your hosts are better known in the breach than in the observation – as it were. They are rarely here. But you have the freedom to indulge in your fantasies. The place is ideal for circle dancing, Scottish reels and skate-boarding; there is little furniture and precious little to do, but the park is handsome and you can just do your own thing. Altogether a fine and unusual addition to our glittering and eclectic collection of the unusual and the improbable.

Rooms: Chanterelle suite.
Price: 16 billion spores.
Meals: Nightcaps available.
Closed: Every 17-25 days when picked. Check when booking, or you may end up in an exquisite omelette.

Just follow the peat moss trail. Arrive early in the morning and watch the hotel grow before your eyes.

Le Relais de Saux

Route de Tarbes
Le Hameau de Saux
65100 Lourdes
Hautes-Pyrénées

Tel: (0)5 62 94 29 61
Fax: (0)5 62 42 12 64
E-mail: relais.de.saux@sudfr.com
Web: www.sudfr.com/relais.de.saux

Bernard & Madelaine Hères

A dream of a place. 300 to 500 years old, high on a hill facing Lourdes and some dazzling Pyrenean peaks, the house still has a few unregenerate arrow slits from sterner days. You come in through the leafy multi-coloured garden that spreads across lawns and terraces, a splendid first impression, and enter a house where you feel instantly at home. Bernard Hères inherited Saux from his parents and, with the help of his wife's flair and energy (regularly stoked with cigarettes!), has recently opened it to guests. They are an enthusiastic and interesting couple who can guide you to fabulous walks, climbs or visits before welcoming you back to deep armchairs in the dark old timbered *salon* with its peaceful garden view, or a refined meal in the elegant dining room. Bedrooms are in the same traditional, elegant mood with draped bedheads and darkish carpetted or flock-papered walls. One has no fewer than four tall windows, another has a gorgeous old fireplace, the two second floor rooms are big yet cosy with their lower ceilings. And carpetted, well-fitted bathrooms for all.

Rooms: 6 doubles.
Price: €75-€90. Half-board
€131-€143 p.p.
Meals: Breakfast €8; picnic available;
lunch €27-€47.
Closed: Never.

Left 3 km north of Lourdes. Signposted but difficult to spot. 1st property 100m from main road.

Grand Hôtel Vignemale

Chemin du Cirque
65120 Gavarnie
Hautes-Pyrénées

Tel: (0)5 62 92 40 00
Fax: (0)5 62 92 40 08
E-mail: hotel.vignemale@wanadoo.fr
Web: hotel-vignemale.com

Danielle & Christian

The site is outstanding, smack bang in the middle of the glacial Cirque de Gavarnie. It is the Mont Blanc of the Pyrenees. Surrounded by horse pastures, granite, snow and ice; not even a souvenir shop to spoil the view. Danielle and Christian chanced upon the place a decade ago, when the building was on its last legs - an eccentric edifice built by an Anglo-Irish count in 1903. For the local pair it was love at first sight; not only were they overwhelmed by the surroundings, they loved all the place has to offer: horses, wild animals, hiking. The residence, in spite of its grand name, has not quite recovered its former glory; more Vegas motel than four-star hotel. But rooms are perfectly adequate and the bedrooms carpeted and comfortable, with modern floral bedcovers, drapes and beige-flocked walls. A few have balconies. Your hosts are relaxed and easy, forever running after horses and resident dogs and cats. It's a great spot for a young family. Lots of horseback riding round the Cirque on the famous Meres horses - a species that thrives at high altitude - and truly wonderful walks.

Rooms: 24: 18 doubles, 4 triples, 2 family.
Price: €106-€136.
Meals: Breakfast included; picnic on request.
Closed: October-May.

From A64 exit Soumoulou or Tarbes Ouest for Lourdes; N21 for Argelès Gazost; D921 for Luz. 49km from Lourdes.

Hôtel du Taur

2 rue du Taur
31000 Toulouse
Haute-Garonne

Tel: (0)5 61 21 17 54
Fax: (0)5 61 13 78 41
E-mail: contact@hotel-du-taur.com
Web: www.hotel-du-taur.com

M & Mme Catherine Garcia-Beliando

Labyrinthine, simple and welcoming, the Taur is as close as you would want to be to the great Place du Capitole (pictured) the pink city's throbbing heart. Coming up the stairs from the student-filled pedestrian street, you enter a soft quiet space of crimson carpet and cleancut 1970s furniture. Prints and paintings are bull - but not bull-fight - based, some of them by Toutain, a renowned local artist whose monumental sculptures stand in the city squares. The rooms? A good size for their two stars, simply done with white walls and bright contemporary fabrics, new mattresses, bedding and carpets and decent, plain bathrooms; all on the first floor, all giving onto courtyards. One of these is grandly arcaded, others are less decorative, all are blessedly quiet. The pale parquet floor of the breakfast room glows in the light from the three low arched windows that look over the 17th-century street. The name? *Taur* means bull. In about 250 AD, early Christian Saturnin (i.e. St Sernin), refusing to join a pagan bull-worship ritual, was tied to the animal's neck and chased down this very street till he died, thus gaining fame and sainthood. Toulouse is a richly fascinating old city.

Rooms: 38: 6 singles,
28 doubles, 4 twins/triples.
Price: Singles €33-€36, doubles
€41-€48, triples €55.
Meals: Breakfast €6. Lunch & dinner
available locally.
Closed: Never.

From ring road follow Centre Ville to Place du Capitole. Rue du Taur leads off the Place. Underground car park Place du Capitole. Metro: Capitole.

Map No: 12

Park Hotel

2 rue Porte Sardane/
13 rue d'Austerlitz
31000 Toulouse
Haute-Garonne

Tel: (0)5 61 21 25 97
Fax: (0)5 61 23 96 27
E-mail: contact@au-park-hotel.com
Web: www.au-park-hotel.com

Ann Beliando

In the heart of old Toulouse, the Park Hôtel is two old red-brick town houses joined in a charming warren of corridors and rooms with two staircases inside and three little streets outside (all rooms are double-glazed and most are air-conditioned). In contrast to the old brickwork, which can be met again in the very attractive basement fitness and jacuzzi area, and the delicious little antique shop opposite, the rooms are cleancut and modern with smart grey corridors and pinstripe bathrooms. The owner is the dynamic young soul of her hotel - she and her smiling staff create an atmosphere of warm, relaxed helpfulness - and she has introduced dabs of personality to the renovation with interesting lamps, strong decorative paper flowers, old mirrors, prints and engravings. The smallish, city-hotel rooms are based on lavender or pink tints with functional modern furniture and soft fabrics. You can rely on everything to be perfectly maintained and the welcome to be marvellous. And the hotel has an illustrious, listed neighbour in the form of... a car park, designed by a student of Le Corbusier, one of the masters of modern architecture.

Rooms: 44: 41 doubles, 3 triples.
Price: Doubles/triples €44-€57.
Meals: Breakfast €6. Wide choice of restaurants nearby.

From ring road towards Centre Ville/Place du Capitole; Place Wilson; Place Victor Hugo. Right into Rue Porte Sardane: 5 mins. to unload then move to Parking Victor Hugo. Metro: Jaurès.

Map No: 12

Hôtel Cuq en Terrasses

Cuq le Château
81470 Cuq Toulza
Tarn

Tel: (0)5 63 82 54 00
Fax: (0)5 63 82 54 11
E-mail: cuq-en-terrasses@wanadoo.fr
Web: www. cuqenterrasses.com

M Philippe Gallice & M Andonis Vassalos

Even the name is appealing. Come to the Pays de Cocagne, their brochure says. Where is that exactly, you may wonder, have I drunk that wine? It is in fact an imaginary land of pleasure, from the old French 'land of cakes'. Brochures often stretch the truth, but this place is magical. Philippe and Andonis, who is Greek, gave up good jobs in Paris two years ago to buy this 18th-century presbytery after coming here on holiday. You might want to do the same. Perched in a beautiful garden on the side of a hill, between Toulouse and Castres, the tall, mellow stone house with white shutters looks so inviting. All the rooms, including a two-floor apartment by the salt water pool, are full of character, all different, with old terracotta floors, hand-finished plaster and some antique beds. But it is worth staying here just for the bathrooms! These are all different too, in wood and white or terracotta and with hand-painted tiles. You can have breakfast on a long narrow terrace blending into the garden. If you manage to drag yourself away to do some sightseeing, come back for some real Mediterranean food, bought earlier at the local market.

Rooms: 8: 7 doubles, 1 suite.
Price: Doubles €85-€115, suite €145.
Meals: Breakfast €10; snacks available; dinner €28, by arrangement. Half-board for minimum 4-day stay.
Closed: January-March.

N126 to Cadix/Cuq Toulza. Then D45 towards Revel. After 2km on left at top of hill in old village.

Château de Garrevaques

81700 Garrevaques
Tarn

Tel: (0)5 63 75 04 54
Fax: (0)5 63 70 26 44
E-mail: m.c.combes@wanadoo.fr
Web: www.garrevaques.com

Marie-Christine & Claude Combes

"The walls were breached under fire of bombards and culverins". Then came the Revolution, and more fire, then the German occupation; but the family is adept at rising from the ashes and the 15th generation of Ginestes is now in charge. Marie-Christine has all the charm and passion to make a go of such a splendid place - slightly faded in parts, stuffed with interest. There are huge reception rooms, magnificent antiques, some original 18th-century wallpaper by Zuber, wood-block floors, a dining room with wood-panelled ceiling. Up the spiral stone stairs there is a games room, with billiards, cards, easy chairs and antiques pieces. The Blue Room next door is blue throughout; in such a vast room the effect is stunning. Bathrooms are modern if not luxurious, perhaps a necessary afterthought. All the bedrooms on this floor are charming, one with a four-poster. Upstairs again the rooms are smaller, but equally colourful and stylish. The pool is less remarkable, and the orangerie is for group receptions. But the garden is a good place to be, studded with old trees as grand as the château.

Rooms: 8: 7 doubles, 1 suite for 4-5.
Price: Doubles €121, suites €198.
Half board from €84 p.p.
Meals: Breakfast included; buffet lunch
€12; dinner €30 inc. aperitif, local
wine & coffee, by arrangement.
Excellent restaurants nearby.
Closed: Never.

*From Revel D1 for Caraman. Opposite
gendarmerie in Revel, D79F to
Garrevaques, 5km. Château at end of
village on right.*

Midi-Pyrénées

It is not really an exaggeration to say that
peace and happiness begin, geographically,
where garlic is used in cooking.

X. Marcel Boulestin (1878-1943)

CDTL-32

Château de Gandels

81700 Garrevaques
Tarn

Tel: (0)5 63 70 27 67
Fax: (0)5 63 70 27 67
E-mail: dupressoir@chateau-de-gandels.com
Web: www.chateau-de-gandels.com

Martine & Philippe Dupressoir

Roles are clearly divided here: Philippe devotes his time to the grounds – designed by Le Nôtre in the 17th century – while Martine, who is as friendly as she is elegant, spent five years doing up the château and now, their five children grown and gone, looks after her guests. An accomplished horsewoman, she is happy to take competent guests out for a ride, but her first love is cooking. She devises the evening menu in the local farmers' market each day. Antique dealers in Paris before settling here, Philippe and Martine still dabble in the trade as they love it and their eye has really come into its own in the château. The bedrooms are all named, all huge, all look onto the gardens and are all different. Floors are polished wood or tiled with rugs, but while *Baldaquin* has *toile de Jouy* and an ornate four-poster, another is painted in soft blue with simple, though unusual wooden beds and blue and white covers. Dinner will be a treat and Martine loves entertaining guests. If you fancy something more romantic, however, she is happy to lay a candlelit dinner for two in a quiet room. *The attractive pool is 20 metres long.*

Rooms: 8: 5 doubles, 3 suites for 4-6.
Price: Doubles €107, suites €183.
Meals: Breakfast included; snacks available on request; dinner €30, including wine, by arrangement.
Closed: Never.

From D622 Revel/Castres road 2kms outside of Revel take D45 to Garrevaques. After 2.5km Chateau is signposted on right.

Map No: 13

Logis des Pères

Le Pavillon des Hôtes
6 rue Lacordaire
81540 Sorèze
Tarn

Didier Petit

Tel: (0)5 63 74 44 80
Fax: (0)5 63 74 44 89
E-mail: contact @hotelfp-sorèze.com
Web: www.hotelfp-oreze.com

Just outside the quaint village of Sorreze on the pilgrims' route to Santiago de Campostela, you turn into an avenue lined with huge plane trees. Founded by the Benedictines in 754, Notre Dame de la Sagne Abbey was pillaged and destroyed several times in the Middle Ages, before the order set up a school there in 1682: you can still see the pond where pupils took an icy dip. In 1776, Louis XVI named it a Royal Military College. Saved from closure after the revolution, La Sagne reopened as a school under a Dominican in 1854 and closed only in 1991. It is now a peaceful retreat for exploring the Black Mountains: on foot, mountain bike or by horse. The 18 bedrooms manage to look spartan while really being very comfortable: with white walls, crisp white sheets and simple desks and chairs. In spring 2002 another 57 rooms will open, but don't worry. They will be just as stylish and the grounds are so huge that there is no fear of any overcrowding. The new rooms, ranging from large to enormous, will be up a sweeping stone staircase from a central terrace, all very in keeping with the feel of the place. Meals are in the pink and green restaurant or in a shaded courtyard.

Rooms: 70: 18 standard doubles, 52 luxury doubles.
Price: €39-€130.
Meals: Breakfast €10; lunch & dinner €14-€27.
Closed: One month in winter.

From Toulouse, A61 exit Castelnaudary, then towards Revel and Sorèze.

Map No: 13

Domaine de Rasigous
81290 Saint Affrique les
Montagnes
Tarn

Tel: (0)5 63 73 30 50
Fax: (0)5 63 73 30 51

Fons Pessers & Ben Wilke

The drawing room is the magnet of this exceptional house: gentle colours, fabulous furnishings and, in winter, log fire in marble fireplace. The soft yellow and white dining room is full of modern art collected in Fons and Ben's native Holland. Never twee, the tables are beautifully decorated for good-looking, varied food and local wines (especially the delicious Gaillac). Natural light, bare floorboards with fine rugs or luxurious plain carpets give that country-house feel to the large, heavenly bedrooms, sensitively decorated with rich colours and interesting furniture. The three suites are elegantly unfrilly. Luxurious bathrooms have been ingeniously fitted into odd spaces - the free-standing bath is most handsome. Even the single room, with its *lit bateau*, lovely linen and bathroom in a walk-in cupboard, is on the 'noble' floor, not under the eaves. The courtyard is ideal for summer breakfasts and the park keeps the house safe from outside intrusions. A dream! The owners' artistic flair and hospitality make this a wonderful place to stay - try to give it at least two nights.

Rooms: 8: 1 single, 4 doubles/twins, 3 suites.
Price: Singles €38-€53, doubles €69-€84, suites €99-€114.
Meals: Breakfast €8; 3-course dinner €23. Restaurant closed Wednesdays.
Closed: Mid-November-mid-March.

From Mazamet D621 for Soual for 16km; left on D85 to St Affrique les Montagnes. 2km further on D85. Green sign on left.

Château de Montlédier

Pont-de-L'Arn
81660 Mazamet
Tarn

Tel: (0)5 63 61 20 54
Fax: (0)5 63 98 22 51
E-mail: hotel-montledier@wanadoo.fr
Web: www.montledier.com

Marc Bodenez & Christelle Batard

Montlédier has seen change and upheaval of all sorts in its 900 years, from feudal fights in the 12th century to major alterations in 1999. Planted majestically on a cliff above a thickly wooded valley, its two solid stone courtyards now shelter a haven for weary humans. The glazed veranda restaurant and the radically-refitted rooms that now speak in highly contemporary tones are clearly bows to modernity; rooms awaiting their refit have been freshly decorated and their good, antique-value bathrooms are pieces of poetry in deep khaki, rich ginger, lime green. Towels are smartly monogrammed. The new rooms on the red and yellow corridor, smaller and great fun: with stripped wood doors, brave colour schemes and neat little quarry-tiled two-tone bathrooms; *Africaine* has hot red sponged walls that pale towards the ceiling, ranch-style doors and properly tropical furnishings. The older, larger *Héloïse* wears deep orange and beige, with a Florentine-pattern bed hanging, a royally rich quilt and a soft velours convertible sofa. Old or new, regal or rustic, they have character and comfort; the sitting and dining rooms are splendid, the grounds disappear into the woods and you will be most warmly received.

Rooms: 20 doubles.
Price: €92-€228.
Meals: Breakfast €13; lunch & dinner €25-€50.
Closed: First three weeks January.

*From Mazamet N112 towards Béziers.
On edge of Mazamet, at car wash, left
Pont de l'Arn; over two bridges; 200m
then right towards 'Lacs' & Montlédier;
up hill 2km, entrance after green barn on right.*

L'Oustal del Barry

Place du Faubourg
12270 Najac
Aveyron

Tel: (0)5 65 29 74 32
Fax: (0)5 65 29 75 32
E-mail: oustal@caramail.com
Web: www.oustaldelbarry.com

Catherine Miquel

Madame Miquel takes food and wine seriously. The kitchen and cellar are the first priority in her 18th-century townhouse in the centre of one of France's loveliest villages. At the top of the hill, surrounded by shaded gardens, the 'quiet, agreeable rooms' have deep views of the château and the surrounding dramatic countryside. Madame is the fifth generation of her family to live in this house and her first source of inspiration is *la tradition*. Her chef makes all his own jams and patisserie; he grows his own vegetables and fruit and buys locally what he does not grow. The cuisine, therefore, is seasonal and regional but he adds that *petit grain de folie* which gives menus their originality. The wine is treated with the respect it deserves. As one of their guests has said, Madame Miquel and her staff epitomise the saying of Brillat Savarin: 'True hospitality takes complete responsibility for a guest's happiness throughout the time he is under your roof'. It sounds better in French... so go and find out.

Rooms: 20: 17 doubles, 3 triples.
Price: Doubles €32-€52, triples €64.
Meals: Breakfast €8; picnic €8; lunch & dinner €19-€46; children's meals €10. Restaurant closed Monday & Tuesday lunchtimes April-June & October.
Closed: Mid-November-April.

20km south of Villefranche de Rouergue on D922. Right to Najac on D39 for 5km.

Hostellerie du Levézou

Rue du Château
12410 Salles Curan
Aveyron

Tel: (0)5 65 46 34 16
Fax: (0)5 65 46 01 19
E-mail: info@hostellerieduvezou.com
Web: www.hostellerieduvezou.com

Christine Michel

A sturdy, Virginia creeper-clad 14th-century château - a marvellous old place that's been in the family for four generations. Christine is engaging and loves looking after her guests. Her father, David, is the chef, and specialises in country cooking with a modern twist. Step back in time as you enter the reception area with its high vaulted ceiling, oak panelling and stone walls lined with settles. The dining room is equally grand, all upholstered chairs, crisp linen, candles and gleaming silver - but again, there's a charmingly old-fashioned feel to it. The courtyard is reached through yet another fine stone archway, this one dominated by a carved oak door. Shaded by an enormous vine, the *cour* is a delightful, sunlight-dappled arbour in which to enjoy breakfast or lunch - very French, all bright geraniums in pots and graceful, white, metalwork chairs. Bedrooms, reached by a wide, spiral, wooden stairway, are plain but spotlessly clean; bathrooms well-mirrored and well-lit. Ask for a room with a view because the views are special - the château stands at the top of the village.

Rooms: 18 doubles.
Price: €35-€69.
Meals: Breakfast €7-€14; dinner €15-€46; children's meals €11. Restaurant closed Sunday nights and Mondays.
Closed: November-Easter.

From Rodez N88 & D911 direction Millau for 26km; 2.5km after Pont Salars, right on D993 to Salles Curan. Signposted.

Map No: 13

Hôtel la Musardière

34 avenue de la République
12100 Millau
Aveyron

Tel: (0)5 65 60 20 63
Fax: (0)5 65 59 78 13
E-mail: hôtel-lamusardiere@wanadoo.fr
Web: www.millau-clic.com/musardière

Anne & Emmanuel Roux

Between the flowing Tarn and the daredevils launching off the clifftops on silk wings stands this haven of civilised grandeur. The elegant mansion, built by a wealthy 19th-century glove-maker, attentively renovated by charming young Mathilde Cabiron, is now a classy yet welcoming hotel. High moulded ceilings and arches, fine parquets, a sweeping stone staircase and cool, sober cream tones invite you to relax in the salon's leather armchairs where aperitifs await on the mantelpiece, read in the little conservatory, eat superbly in the restaurant (Michelin-starred chef) and sleep in a different bedroom each night. *Empire* has space to waltz in, two flash-red 1930s leather armchairs beneath Empire mouldings and its own panelled, double jacuzzi bathroom; *Domino* is a gentle symphony of ivory, beige and brown looking out of two great windows to the park over the road; *Perroquet* is perky in its parrot curtains and yellow leather sofa. There are fascinating emblems in carved armoires (Masonic and Templar messages), lower ceilings on the second floor, super bathrooms and an unbelievably round, white wedding room of huge flair and originality. Dazzling.

Rooms: 14: 12 doubles, 2 suites.
Price: €60-€191.
Meals: Breakfast €10; lunch €15-€46;
dinner €23-€46.
Closed: Never.

In Millau follow Centre Ville to Place du
Mandarous then turn towards Cahors into Rue de la
République - hotel 300m on right; ask reception for
car park.

Map No: 13

Languedoc-Roussillon

Another article of cuisine that offends the bowels of
unused Britons is garlic. Not uncommonly in southern
climes an egg with a shell on is the only procurable
animal food without garlic in it. Flatulence and
looseness are the frequent results.

Dr. T.K. Chambers, A Manual of Diet in Health and Disease (1875)

JL. Seille, CDT Vaucluse

Manoir de Montesquiou

48210 Malène
Lozère

Tel: (0)4 66 48 51 12
Fax: (0)4 66 48 50 47
E-mail: montesquiou@demeures-de-lozere.com
Web: www.manoir-montesquiou.com

Evelyne & Bernard Guillenet

Malène is a beautiful little town in the heart of the spectacular Tarn Gorge, and the Manoir is right in the heart of the town, beneath towering limestone cliffs. When Louis XIII quelled a rebellion in 1652 and ordered all local castles razed, the 15th century fortress escaped being destroyed when a royal letter ordered it spared as the Montesquiou family had helped him. You enter the hotel through the original stone gate, into a courtyard dotted with wrought iron tables and chairs; the greenery creeping halfway up the towers gives a fairytale feel. Several terraces are built on to the castle. You can eat out on one, leading off a cheerful yellow and blue dining room. The more formal dining room is in the old vaulted guardroom, with a huge fireplace. Bedrooms are up a spiral stone staircase. Rooms are traditional and a touch sombre; some with a separate sitting room area which can be curtained off. Evelyne and Bernard run the Manoir with their daughters and use local produce whenever possible. The restaurant has something of a reputation in the area and locals often pop into the bar for a drink and a chat.

Rooms: 12 doubles/twins.
Price: €64-€125.
Meals: Breakfast €10; lunch & dinner €21-€40.
Closed: November-end March.

A75 towards Millau. Exit 42 at Severac for Les Gorges de Tarn. At Les Vignes D907 12km to La Malène. Hotel in middle of town.

La Lozerette

Cocurès
48400 Florac
Lozère

Tel: (0)4 66 45 06 04
Fax: (0)4 66 45 12 93
E-mail: lalozerette@wanadoo.fr

Pierrette Agulhon

In September 1878, Robert Louis Stevenson set off from Le Monastier with his donkey, Modestine, to walk the 220km to St. Jean du Gard. Towards the end of his journey he stopped in the Cevennes village of Cocurès, on the river Tarn, just above the National Park. Here Pierrette runs the country inn started by her grandmother and passed on to her by her parents. Her father is still around to advise on the best walks. The staff are especially warm and friendly and cope smilingly with all-comers to this busy hotel. Pierrette is very much a hands-on owner, running the reception, taking orders in the restaurant and managing the wine cellar: she is a trained sommelier and will pick you out just the right bottle. Bedrooms are fairly large, with wood floors and headboards and are done in stripes, checks or flowers: colour co-ordinated but not twee. All have balconies with flower boxes. The whole hotel is spotless without looking clinical. You can play boules in the garden, walk in the National Park or follow Stevenson's trail, either on foot, on a donkey or on horseback. *The chestnut in all its forms is the speciality here.*

Rooms: 21 doubles/twins.
Price: Doubles/twins €43-€69. Half-board for two €44-€57 p.p.
Meals: Breakfast €7; lunch & dinner €14-€38. Restaurant closed Tuesdays & Wednesday lunchtimes during low season.
Closed: November-Easter.

From Florac on N106 for Mende. Right on D998 for Le Pont de Montvert. After 4km Cocurès village. La Lozerette is on left. Well signposted.

Map No: 13

Auberge L'Atalaya
66800 Llo
Pyrénées-Orientales

Tel: (0)4 68 04 70 04
Fax: (0)4 68 04 01 29
E-mail: atalaya@francimel.com
Web: www.chez-com/atalaya

Ghilaine Toussaint

A place of majestic beauty and wild poetry; a timeless Catalan farmhouse clinging to a rocky hillside; an owner of rare taste and talent - poet, philosopher, musician and lover of beauty. Such is l'Atalaya: a house that captures the imagination and promises riches earthly and spiritual. Family antiques are in all rooms, fine fabrics dress lovely old beds, bathrooms are de luxe, stained-glass windows illuminate corridors, fresh figs may grace the tables in the intimate little breakfast room and in the big, light-filled dining room, mouth-watering meals are served before that boggling view, while the grand piano awaits its pianist. Your hostess has put her heart into renovating the house she bought as a ruin and it has a quiet, cosy, hideaway atmosphere that is also very elegant: the architecture and décor are in harmony and people of sensitive taste feel utterly at home here. The wonderful little village has hot springs, the river gorges are home to rare butterflies, the hills have sheep and Romanesque churches, there are innumerable activities. What a place!

Rooms: 13: 11 doubles/twins, 1 triple, 1 suite for 2/4.
Price: Doubles/triple €78-€120, suite €290.
Meals: Breakfast €10; lunch & dinner €26-€41.
Closed: November; 20 January-Easter.

From Perpignan N116 west through Prades to Saillagouse. Left for Llo; left for Eyne. Hotel 1km on right.

Map No: 18

La Terrasse au Soleil
Route de Fontfrède
66400 Céret
Pyrénées-Orientales

Tel: (0)4 68 87 01 94
Fax: (0)4 68 87 39 24
E-mail: terrasse-au-soleil.hotel@wanadoo.f
Web: www.la-terrasse-au-soleil.com

M Leveillé Nizerolle

Take at least a weekend, for a splurge of activity and delicious indulgence. It has space: a four-hectare garden, a terrace with olive and mimosa trees, a vineyard; and sports: a big pool and a tiny golf course, a tennis court and three jogging circuits, and deep green views over the hills to Mont Canigou. It's a self-contained retreat of "luxurious simplicity" (the owner's expression) in four connecting villas where the yellow, blue and green colour schemes bring a fresh, casual atmosphere - what one might call Southern California in French Catalonia. Rooms are big and airy, done in excellent fabrics with custom-made wooden furniture, but not overfilled; suites have terraces and two bathrooms. Food counts a lot and delicious meals are served on china made to order in Italy; there's a warm, inviting bar between the indoor and outdoor dining rooms, the sitting area is pleasantly cool - all designed for guests to feel pampered but not softened. A path has even been cut to Céret so that you don't have to walk along the road. Monsieur Leveillé is very present and very attentive - you will like him.

Rooms: 21: 14 doubles, 7 suites.
Price: Doubles €128-€229, suites €189-€295.
Meals: Breakfast included; picnic available; dinner from €43.
Closed: Never.

From Perpignan A9 S to Le Boulou; D115 southwest to Céret. Hotel is 4km beyond Céret on road to Fontfrède.

Map No: 18

La Belle Demeure

Auberge du Roua
Chemin du Roua
66700 Argelès sur Mer
Pyrénées-Orientales
Ricardo Danesi

Tel: (0)4 68 95 85 85
Fax: (0)4 68 95 83 50
E-mail: belle.demeure@little-france.com
Web: www.belle-demeure.com

Hard to guess that this small hotel was once an 18th-century mill: only the old stone walls and the odd beam remain. But this is the south, where life is lived *en plein air*. And outdoors at the Auberge is special: you could happily spend all day on the elegant terrace by the pool, surrounded by tropical plants. Tables and chairs are modern, wooden-slatted; parasols stylish. There is ample opportunity to escape the sun's dazzle without retreating indoors, and the views of the Pyrenees are splendid. Inside, all is spick-and-span. Bedrooms are anonymous but comfortable; bathrooms are attractive, some of marble, all a good size. This is a family-run hotel, a labour of love for the young Italian who first set eyes on it six years ago. The atmosphere is relaxed but the dining room, with its white napery and crystal, is formal and rightly so: Ricardo and his young chef have brought new life to the restaurant which has a terrific reputation. Impossible to stay here without sampling the mushroom ravioli with white truffles and similar delights. People travel from miles around to enjoy them.

Rooms: 14: 13 doubles, 1 triple.
Price: €50-€91.
Meals: Breakfast €9; dinner €27-€53.
Restaurant closed Sunday evenings & Mondays.
Closed: November-February.

From Perpignan N114 south for 20km, exit 10 for Argelès sur Mer. In town, right at lights and follow signs.

La Bastide de Cabezac

Hameau de Cabezac
11120 Bize en Minervois
Aude

Tel: (0)4 68 46 66 10
Fax: (0)4 68 46 66 29
E-mail: bastidecabezac@aol.com
Web: www.labastidecabezac.com

Sabine & Hervé dos Santos

The hotel and restaurant - brand new - are becoming as popular as the Minervois wines that come from next door Château de Cabezac. The exterior of this old coaching inn - sunflower yellow walls with ocean blue trim - is intense like the sun that beats down on this land that produces deep purple powerful wines. Hervé directs two restaurants in Paris; he has built himself a magnificent kitchen here and already planted a kitchen garden next to the pool. The Bastide de Cabezac is still feeling its way - the fresh paint is hardly dry but everything is in place. There are good-sized bedrooms, each in different pastel shades with plenty of air and natural light, king size beds and minimalist accessories. The public areas and the interior *cour* on the first floor are warm yellow and, as is proper in hot lands, terracotta tiles are ubiquitous. The restaurant is named *l'Olivier* in homage to the working olive orchard nearby; they also transplanted a 300-year-old tree as a symbol of their new endeavour and to add a bit of gravitas.

Rooms: 12: 8 doubles, 2 triples, 2 suites for 4-5.
Price: Doubles €69-€107, triples & suites €107-€198. Special prices for min. 3-night stay.
Meals: Breakfast €9.50; lunch and dinner from €15-€55. Restaurant closed Mondays and Tuesdays.
Closed: Mid-December-mid-January.

From Narbonne D607 to intersection of D5, D11 &
'Route de Vins' 18km.

Map No: 13

Château de Floure

1 allée Gaston Bonheur
11800 Floure
Aude

Tel: (0)4 68 79 11 29
Fax: (0)4 68 79 04 61
E-mail: contact@chateau-de-floure.com
Web: www.chateau-de-floure.com

Mme Dominique Assous

Floure started life as a Roman villa, the Villa Flora, on the Via Aquitania between Narbonne and Toulouse: a peaceful refuge from the military post just a couple of leagues away. In the Middle Ages it became a monastery, until in the reign of Henri IV a local official made it his country retreat. Hidden away behind the austere stone walls, an ivy-draped 18th-century château stands in the centre of matching mellow-tiled cottages and outbuildings, in interesting grounds where you can wander from a formal French garden, through a tree-shaded meadow to the vineyard or the swimming pool. The vaulted bar, complete with grand piano, is in the 12th-century keep. Bedrooms are vast, with beds to match, antique desks and deep comfortable chairs. Some rooms are in the château itself, others gathered around the courtyard. Bathrooms are for luxuriating, with deep baths and attractive tiles. After dinner you can settle in the Bergère drawing room, where one wall was painted by the Vicomte de Laguepie in 1762. Ancient Carcassonne is only ten minutes' drive away, but it may be hard to drag yourself away from these peaceful gardens.

Rooms: 13 + 5 apartments: 10 doubles, 3 suites for 4-5; 5 apts for 2-3
Price: Doubles €100-€120, suites €230; apartments €150-€170.
Meals: Breakfast €12-15; dinner €35-€55. Restaurant closed Monday & Wednesday lunchtimes.
Closed: Mid-January-mid-March; mid-November-mid-December.

A61 exit 24 then take N113 towards Narbonne. Go past Trébes then follow sign to Floure. Hotel in village. Signposted.

Le Relais du Val d'Orbieu

Route D24
11200 Ornaisons
Aude

Tel: (0)4 68 27 10 27
Fax: (0)4 68 27 52 44
E-mail: relais.du.val.dorbieu@wanadoo.fr
Web: http://perso.wanadoo.fr/relais.du.val.dorbieu

Agnès & Jean-Pierre Gonzalvez

This looks like a Spanish hacienda deep in the vineyards of Corbières: perhaps not too surprising since the border is only a short drive away. Agnès and Jean-Pierre have spent almost 20 years making the Relais their special place. The rooms and apartments all open onto the flower-filled gardens and terraces. Many have their own terrace and are a mix of old and new - one even has a four-poster. It is the sort of place where you will find your bed turned down at night and plenty of fresh towels. Jean-Pierre loves running his hotel and has a southern charm that makes you feel really welcome. He is also very knowledgeable about the local vineyards. The food is colourful and Mediterranean with vegetables from the garden and plenty of fish: red mullet with artichokes, baby squid with asparagus or fresh anchovies being regulars on the menu. Hidden among the trees are a fair-sized pool, a tennis court, table tennis and a place to play pétanque. The sea is a short drive away and there is plenty to explore, with the Cathar castles and the abbeys of Fontefroide and Lagrasse within easy reach, as well as Carcassonne and all the vineyards.

Rooms: 19: 14 doubles/twins, 5 family rooms and suites for 2-4.
Price: Doubles/twins €70-€105, family rooms & suites €105-€227.
Meals: Breakfast €12; lunch & dinner €30-€60.
Closed: December-January.

From Narbonne N113 towards Carcassonne then D24 to Ornaisons. 3kms to the hotel. Clearly signposted.

Le Relais de Saint Dominique

Prouilhe
11270 Fanjeaux
Aude

Tel: (0)4 68 24 68 17
Fax: (0)4 68 24 68 18
E-mail: relaisstdominique@libertysurf.fr

Nadine Micouleau

In the 1800s, this coaching-inn was the last stop for a quick mug of ale and change of horse before heading up into the Pyrenees. Today, you won't want to go on. Nadine's cheerful greeting is as genuine as her wanting you to feel utterly pampered while free to come and go as you please. No expense or energy (hers seems endless) has been spared: crisp linens and thick towels in gleaming bathrooms, good beds, sponge-painted walls with a good mix of antique and modern furniture. Unique touches here and there will have you silently wondering why *you'd* never thought of using Grandma's embroidered tablecloth as a simple cushion cover. American buffet breakfasts in the shaded courtyard in summer are a feast, and the 13th-century former monastery next door ideal for a memorable evening meal. Nothing's too much trouble for Nadine, and coming 'home' to sit by the pool is the perfect way to end a busy day. From Roman times onwards, Fanjeaux has survived war and peace in one of France's strategic historical spots. Some of the regional wines, by the way, are an absolute 'must'.

Rooms: 6: 4 doubles/twins, 2 suites.
Price: Doubles €43-€69, suites €76-€107.
Meals: Buffet breakfast included; dinner €11, by arrangement in the monastery.
Closed: Never.

From A61 exit Bram D4 for Fanjeaux. After 5km left at r'bout onto D119 for Montréal - entrance immed. on left.

Map No: 13

237

L'Auberge du Cèdre

Domaine de Cazeneuve
34270 Lauret
Hérault

Tel: (0)4 67 59 02 02
Fax: (0)4 67 59 03 44
E-mail: welcome@auberge-du-cedre.com
Web: www.auberge-du-cedre.com

Françoise Antonin & Lutz Engelmann

No wonder guests return to this big, bustling house. The robust and charming Françoise and her multi-lingual husband Lutz love welcoming walkers, climbers, cyclists and families. Workshop groups are welcome too, there's a special space, separate from the big and comfy sitting room. The mellow-stoned auberge, adorned by green shutters, iron balustrades and *orangerie* windows at the rear, has been carefully restored. Bedrooms are plain, beamy, white, with the odd splash of ethnic colour and terracotta floors that gleam. Bathrooms are shared; this is not the place for those looking for luxury en suite rooms. But sharing keeps the prices down and there have been no complaints. On the contrary, the atmosphere is one of good humour and laughter. Meals, chosen from a blackboard menu, are served in the *orangerie* or on the terrace. A great place for a family to stay: a swimming pool, with toddler pool, at the back, lots of space to run around in, and boules under the chestnut trees before you turn in for the night. Lutz's *cave* makes it a special place for wine lovers.

Rooms: 19: 7 doubles/twins, 9 triples, 3 quadruples.
Price: €18-€24. Half board €29-€34 p.p.
Meals: Breakfast included; light lunch €7. On weekends full choice meals €21-€30.
Closed: January-mid-March.

D17 from Montpellier north for Quissac.
6km north of St Mathieu de Tréviers, left to Lauret-1km.
Through village follow signs for
Cazeneuve & Auberge du Cèdre.

Map No: 13

La Calade

Place de l'Eglise
34800 Octon
Hérault

Tel: (0)4 67 96 19 21
Fax: (0)4 67 96 19 21
E-mail: gille.schmitt@wanadoo.fr
Web: www.lacalade.com

Gilles & Sophie Schmitt

Octon is an unspoilt little village, typical of the flavour and architecture so informed by the Languedoc sun. Right under the old church, Sophie and Gilles Schmitt have created a colourful atmosphere within the white stone walls of the former presbytery. Don't expect great luxury: the setting is perfectly simple and the rooms and bathrooms perfectly adequate. New parquet floors add to the freshness of the place when it's hot, and the beds are comfortable. The terrace, shaded by acacia trees, is very appealing both at breakfast time and in the evenings - it also serves as the sitting area. The overall feel is bright and clean and the owners couldn't be more friendly and helpful. They, like their young son, particularly enjoy welcoming families with children. The La Calade restaurant is becoming quite popular, and there are plenty of places to visit, good paths for hikers, excellent local wines and the fabulous Lake Salagou for swimming and sailing. In short, a great base for daily excursions, where the warm welcome and the authentic atmosphere easily make up for somewhat basic comforts.

Rooms: 7: 3 doubles, 1 triple &
3 family rooms.
Price: Doubles €38, triples €53, family
rooms €69.
Meals: Breakfast €5.50; lunch &
dinner €12-€29.
Closed: December-March.

Leave A75 exit 54 or 55 (Lake Salagou) for Octon on D148. Hotel in village centre next to church. Stone steps lead up to entrance.

Le Sanglier

Domaine de Cambourras
34700 Saint Jean de la Blaquière
Hérault

Tel: (0)4 67 44 70 51
Fax: (0)4 67 44 72 33
E-mail: hotreslesanglier@aol.com
Web: www.logassist.fr/sanglier

Monique Lormier

"One of France's most secret places". Madame, a *Maître Rotisseur*, cares for her menus (including wild pig and local fish), while Monsieur cares for his very good wine cellar in their deeply renovated sheepfold (just one stone wall survives from before). In the setting of vineyards and evergreen-clad hills, white outcrops, bright red earth and dense Mediterranean vegetation - strongly beautiful, even starkly wild - the Sanglier's rambling garden is welcoming with its terraces and masses of shade for eating and sitting outside. You can follow a generous breakfast of fresh cheese, cake and *fougace* with a delicious summer lunch and finish with dinner centred on Madame's wild boar speciality or steak grilled on vine stems. But there's lots to do here: exhibitions in Lodève, medieval St Guilhem, watery delights on Lake Salagou. Bedrooms are comfortable, unremarkably decorated, with mottled beige carpets and pastel bathroom suites. There are some lovely black and white photographs of local people, but come not for décor - the scenery is sublime and food is king.

Rooms: 10: 7 doubles, 3 triples.
Price: Doubles €64-€67, triples €76.
Meals: Breakfast €8; picnic from €6; lunch & dinner €15-€35. Restaurant closed Wednesday lunchtimes in low season.
Closed: November-March.

From Montpellier N109 through St. Félix de Lodez for Rabieux, then D144 for St Jean de la Blaquière.

Domaine de Rieumégé

Route de Saint Pons
34390 Olargues
Hérault

Tel: (0)4 67 97 73 99
Fax: (0)4 67 97 78 52
E-mail: rieumege@wanadoo.fr
Web: www.tbsfrance.com/rieumege

Hubert Henrotte

The truly beautiful dining room - giant beam, old mangers, lovely terraces - is the centre of Rieumégé, honoured by gourmet cooking and very good wines. The owner fell in love with this fascinating group of old, many-levelled stone buildings, left Paris and is aiming to improve an already delightful place, renovating rooms and employing professional and charming staff. There is space for all to find privacy and peace in the luscious garden under the palms, oaks or pines, and the round pool and the tennis court are set properly apart. Big, traditional bedrooms and pretty suites in various buildings have good rugs on the floors and antiques - but not too many. Two suites even share a terrace and a private pool. People like the real but unlavish comfort - some stay three weeks for the fabulous Orb country hiking and climbing, all come back in the evening for the excellent meat, fish and real vegetarian dishes. Monsieur Henriotte loves giving guests the warm welcome, comfortable rooms, good food and, above all, the simplicity he knows they want. And it's a magnificent part of the Languedoc.

Rooms: 12: 10 doubles/twins, 2 suites for 4-6.
Price: Doubles/twins €86-€122, suites €141-€183.
Meals: Breakfast €11; lunch €20; dinner €33. Restaurant closed for lunch except weekends and July-August.
Closed: January-April.

On D908 2.5km after Olargues towards Saint Pons. Signposted on big blue panel. About 55km north of Béziers.

Les Bergeries de Ponderach
Route de Narbonne
34220 Saint Pons de Thomières
Hérault

Tel: (0)4 67 97 02 57
Fax: (0)4 67 97 29 75
E-mail: bergeries.ponderach@wanadoo.fr
Web: www.bergeries-ponderach.com

Gilles Lentin

Monsieur Lentin remembers this *bergerie* when it was full of sheep; he now fills it with contented guests. The whole place is an expression of his cultivated tastes in music, painting (he used to run a well-known art gallery in Montpellier), food and wine. You enter your room through its own little lobby, from the freize-painted corridor. Notice the attention to detail in the choice of fabrics and furnishings, take in the luxury of the bathroom, make your way to your own private balcony and take a deep breath; you've arrived in a sort of earthly paradise. M. Lentin provides music - sometimes live, with quartets in the courtyard on summer evenings - and also the most intriguing and carefully chosen regional cooking. Sculpting your own perfect holiday here is not difficult, given all that's here - maybe one third exercise in the Parc Regional with its wonderful walks, one third culture visiting the Cathedral and its pink marble choir and one third gastro-hedonism with your feet under M. Lentin's beautifully laden table.

Rooms: 7: 6 doubles, 1 suite.
Price: €69-€110. Half-board €125-€150 for two.
Meals: Breakfast €10; picnic available; dinner €18-€43.
Closed: December-February.

From Béziers N112 to St Pons de Thomières. There, left for Narbonne D907. Hotel is 1km out, just after the local swimming pool on left.

Hostellerie de Saint Alban

31 route d'Agde
Nézignan l'Evêque
34120 Pézenas
Hérault

Tel: (0)4 67 98 11 38
Fax: (0)4 67 98 91 63
E-mail: info@saintalban.com
Web: www.saintalban.com

Hansruedi Keiser & Niklaus
Hürlimann

In an enchanting Languedocian village with alleys and archways to be explored, this is a beautifully proportioned, honey-coloured old mansion. The monumental pine tree must have been here before the house; its great twisting branches now hang over the gate. The superbly lush garden surrounds an attractive pool where you can have lunch in summer - fresh local melon, delicious salads - and the lovely old barn is being restored to house all proper pool-side comforts. Indoors, the charming young Swiss owners have gone for less luxuriance: the décor is relaxingly plain, the feel elegant, airy and well-kept. The biggish, light bedrooms have good pastel carpeting, white bedcovers, translucent curtains and sober colour schemes in beiges, greys and soft pinks. Furniture is modern minimal with moulded chairs and laminated headboards - no drowning in flounces here. There are always fresh flowers on the dining room tables in the and food is good. The Saint Alban is ideal for seaside and inland visits and many guests cycle out through the vines to the Canal du Midi.

Rooms: 14: 13 doubles, 1 triple.
Price: Doubles €67-€105, triples €92-€103.
Meals: Breakfast €9; lunch €9-€30; dinner €21. Restaurant closed Wednesdays off-season.
Closed: December-mid-February.

A9 exit 34 for Pézenas/Millau. D13 for 16km to Nézignan l'Evêque. Hotel on right as you enter village.

Hôtel d'Entraigues

Place de l'Evêché
30700 Uzès
Gard

Tel: (0)4 66 22 32 68
Fax: (0)4 66 22 57 01
E-mail: hôtels.entraigues.agoult@wanadoo.fr
Web: www.Icm.fr/savry

Vincent Savry

When you sit on the wide terrace or swim in the mosaic-lined pool you feel some glorious monument might fall into your lap: Uzès is a perfect little Provençal town and Entraigues, in the shadow of Bishop's and Duke's Palaces, is at the heart of it. The hotel is in fact five cleverly connected 15th- and 17th-century houses: an old building with a fascinating history and lots of stairs and corridors leading off the very French lobby where chairs invite you to rest and breathe in the old soul of stones and antiques. Each bedroom is an individual discovery: here a private terrace, there an eminently paintable rooftop view, and wonderful furniture with personality and interest. The décor is exposed stone and white render, good fabrics and no clutter. We thought the family rooms were terrific, there's outdoor space and a simple buffet/family restaurant as well as the splendid 'Jardins de Castille' for gourmets. Vincent Savry, the younger generation of this great hotelier family, is quite delightful: cheerful and efficient, unflappable and proud of his hotel.

Rooms: 34 doubles.
Price: €60-€144.
Meals: Buffet breakfast €9; lunch €12; dinner €22-€43
Closed: Never.

A9 exit Pont du Gard on D981 to Uzès. Follow one-way system round towards cathedral. Park in car park in front of cathedral. Hotel opposite.

Map No: 14

Château d'Arpaillargues/Hôtel Marie d'Agoult

30700 Arpaillargues
Gard

Tel: (0)4 66 22 14 48
Fax: (0)4 66 22 56 10
E-mail: savrychateau30@aol.com
Web: www.lcm.fr/savry

Isabelle & Gérard Savry

This noble house, its 15th-century sternness transformed with gracious 18th-century windows, balconies and décor, is now a hotel that pampers but does not intimidate. Thick stone walls keep summer scorch at bay, balmy evenings are spent at table in the tree-studded courtyard; refined *salons*, vaulted dining rooms and a superb staircase are reminders of a more elegant age. History, aristocratic and literary, hangs in the air: the heroine of *Les Liaisons Dangeureuses* was an Agoult; so was Liszt's mistress, mother of Cosima Wagner, who left her husband here for the composer and Paris. Rooms are big (slightly smaller in the outbuilding), very comfortable, with fascinating antiques and features (double doors, fireplaces and mouldings), interesting smallish but mosaic-decorated bathrooms and occasional private terraces. Back through those great iron gates and across the little road are the secluded garden and swimming pool. This is a deeply serene place of ancient atmosphere and modern, not over-luxurious, comfort where the welcome is relaxed yet efficient.

Rooms: 29: 27 doubles/twins,
2 suites.
Price: €76-€183.
Meals: Breakfast €11; lunch & dinner
€24-€38.
Closed: 4 November-March.

Uzès D982 to Arpaillargues, 4km.
Château on left entering village. Well
signposted.

Le Mas Parasol

Rue Damon
30190 Garrigues Sainte Eulalie
Gard

Tel: (0)4 66 81 90 47
Fax: (0)4 66 81 93 30
E-mail: vieljeux@masparasol.com
Web: www.masparasol.com

Geoffroy Vieljeux

How about a gypsy caravan in the garden with your own quiet terrace looking out onto a field? It sleeps two in roomy quarters painted in clear bright colours and don't worry: there is a shower and loo. The Parasol is a traditional Languedoc farm which Geoffroy Vieljeux opened as a Maison d'Hôte in 1997. He chose the strong colours – some fantastic mellow oranges and darkest green stained wood – from a watercolour sampler used for Sèvres porcelain. Other rooms are in coolest cream with some clever stencilling. The rooms are gathered round a courtyard, while the dining room opens onto a second secluded garden with a large pool and a tennis court. Between Ales and Uzès, within reach of Avignon, the Camargue and Orange: Garrigues Ste Eulalie is quiet and peaceful but by no means the back of beyond. Geoffroy has put together a brilliant mix of outings for anyone interested: guided tours round the old houses of Nîmes or Montpellier, music nights in Orange or trips to the Avignon festival. You can go for wonderful walks, bike rides or riding in the Camargue. You can't eat in every night, but twice a week a delicious local meal is served either inside or at little tables in the garden. *No smoking here.*

Rooms: 7: 6 doubles, 1 suite.
Price: €85-€150.
Meals: Breakfast included; dinner €25 by arrangement (2 nights a week only).
Closed: 7 November-5 March.

From Uzès D982 towards Anduze. At the beginning of village right on Avenue Pigeonnier then right again on rue Damon. Mas is last house after the church.

Le Château de Saint Maximin

Rue du Château
30700 Saint Maximin
Gard

Tel: (0)4 66 03 44 16
Fax: (0)4 66 03 42 98
E-mail: info@chatostmaximin.com
Web: www.chatomaximin.com

Jean-Marc Perry

The light of centuries shines from the simple classical façade and the 12th-century tower, the arches and statue-dotted gallery, the vaulted staircase and great fireplace of this noble house. Currents of European civilisation flow through its several levels - white-stoned Italian pool and delightful French fountain, great Anduze jars on the terrace and silver olive trees in the garden, old tapestries and modern art skilfully placed to catch your attention. Jean-Marc Perry collects glass and has a sure eye for interior design, blending aesthetic refinement and creature comfort to perfection. The great classical tragedian Racine stayed and wrote here: generous bedrooms (the suites are vast), subtly elegant in their châteauesque garments and luxurious bathrooms, are called *Phèdre, Bérénice...* in his honour. One drawing room has a piano, the other, the only (big) television set in the place; tea is served in Sèvres cups, mouth-watering Provençal specialities finish the day. And from the second floor you look straight from exquisite civilisation out to the wild Cevennes landscape.

Rooms: 5: 2 doubles, 3 suites.
Price: Doubles €95-€160, suites €125-€265.
Meals: Breakfast included; dinner €38.
Closed: February.

A9 exit Remoulins/Pt Gard then D981 for Uzès. Right to Saint Maximin 4km before Uzès. Château in centre of village.

L' Hacienda

Mas de Brignon
30320 Marguerittes
Gard

Tel: (0)4 66 75 02 25
Fax: (0)4 66 75 45 58
E-mail: hacienda@altavista.net

Jean-Jacques & Dominique Chauvin

A wonderfully warm welcome from your gentle hosts, so proud of their Spanish-style hotel-restaurant, so pleased to be able to share its comforts with you. Russet-shuttered and terracotta-tiled, this two-storey farmhouse has been transformed into a handsomely decorated five-bedroom hotel in stylish grounds with restaurant, sauna and pool. Relax under a pink parasol; breathe in the sweet scent of lavender - there are fields of it, as far as the eye can see; take a dip in the heavenly pool. The bedrooms are furnished country-style, charming, with white walls, polished beams and delicate Provençal prints; most open onto a private terrace. The sitting room too is flounce-free - tiled floors, white walls, floral sofas and chairs. But if you like good food and wine you'll linger in the stylish, candlelit dining room seduced by the flavours of Provence: turbot and mullet, vegetables and herbs from the local markets and mouth-watering sweet creams flavoured with lavender and thyme. *No smoking here.*

Rooms: 12: 7 doubles, 5 triples.
Price: Half-board only €70-€110 p.p.
June-September. Rooms off season
€75-€136
Meals: Buffet breakfast €11-13; dinner
€30-€54.
Closed: November-mid-December;
7 January-mid-March.

A9 exit Nîmes Est/Uzès for
Marguerittes. In Marguerittes follow red signs.

Atelier de Calvisson

48 Grand'Rue
30420 Calvisson
Gard

Tel: (0)4 66 01 23 91
Fax: (0)4 66 01 42 19
E-mail: corinne.burckeldetel@free.fr
Web: www.bed-and-art.com

Régis & Corrine Burckel de Tell

There's a secret to this old townhouse in the little market town: from the narrow street it looks rather dull, but enter their private courtyard - and it's another world. The courtyard, a wonderful source of light and greenery, is used for art exhibitions and Monsieur gives art lessons: drawing, painting and the *Gobelins* tapestry techniques. There's a biggish living area for guests and a wonderful vaulted dining room for candlelit dinners in a womb-like atmosphere of warm colours and stone walls. Summer breakfast is in the courtyard. Up a spiral staircase, the tempting rooms fan off at different levels - there's a lovely smell of wax-polished stone floors. Most beautifully restored with old doors and good windows that seem to frame pictures, it is all in honest good taste, with simple, solid antique furniture that's genuinely part of the house, and your charming young hostess is eager to help her guests. Nîmes, Montpellier and the Camargue are close by and in summer the house is blessedly cool after the scorching sun. *Weekly rentals only mid-July to mid-September. Three nights minimum in July & August.*

Rooms: 6: 1 single, 3 doubles, 2 suites for 3 (1 with small terrace).
Price: Single €38, doubles €46-€48, suites €58.
Meals: Breakfast included; dinner €15 including wine, by arrangement.
Closed: December-February.

A9 exit Gallargues. Then N113 for Nîmes. Just after bas Rhône canal, D1 to Calvisson. In village, up main street, two doors from Town Hall.

Rhône Valley - Alps

And, most dear actors, eat no onions nor garlic,
for we are to utter sweet breath.
William Shakespeare, A Midsummer Night's Dream

CDT Dauphine

Château Lambert

69840 Chénas
Rhône

Tel: (0)4 77 06 77 74
E-mail: contact@chateau-lambert.com
Web: www.chateau-lambert.com

Marty Freriksen

Marty's passion for textiles, his talent as an upholsterer and his eye for detail make this small 17th-century château an especially warm and pleasant place to be. It sits smack in the middle of Beaujolais country set on a hill overlooking the village of Chénas. Vines and more vines stretch over the Soâne plain and sometimes the snow-topped Alps are visible in the distance. The front opens on to a trellised terrace below which a vegetable garden is slowly coming back to life (the château was purchased just a year ago). A wonderful setting for a slow breakfast or an evening aperitif - try their own *Moulin à Vent*. A fine library takes up one wall in the huge apartment on the ground floor where the neutral walls set off the red plaid low chairs on either side of the fireplace and a pair of *vieux rose* antique armchairs render a curvy touch of elegance. All is light green and pale prune with touches of a darker red in the upstairs suite. A magnificent canopied bed in the alcove has matching *toile de Jouy* drapes and bedspread. The high ceilings, good light and muted tones give all the rooms a feeling of airiness and space. Marty is young and enthusiastic - a fine host who will make you feel at home.

Rooms: 4: 2 doubles, 2 suites for 2.
Price: €75-€115.
Meals: Breakfast included; hosted dinner €23 by arrangement.
Closed: Never.

A6 exit Macon Sud or A40 exit Replonges. N6 towards Lyon. After 12km at La Chapelle de Guinchay, right towards Chénas. At church, take street going up on the right. Château is signposted.

Map No: 9

Château de Pramenoux

69870 Lamure/Azergues
Rhône

Tel: (0)4 74 03 16 43
Fax: (0)4 74 03 16 28
E-mail: pramenoux@aol.com
Web: www.chateau-de-pramenoux.com

Emmanuel Baudoin & Jean-Luc Plasse

Climb into the Mont du Beaujolais hills above Lyon. Rivers pulse down on either side and a great pine forest cleans the air. As you round a curve, Gothic pepperpot turrets pop into view. The château sits in a natural clearing and views from the terrace and bedrooms sweep splendidly down the valley; a small pond in front anchors the eye. Emmanuel, a charming young escapee from the corporate world, will point out the bits that date from the 10th century to the Rennaissance, including the mullioned windows along the gallery that links the towers. He has lovingly patched and painted a great deal of it himself. Rooms are big and comfortable with simply elegant bathrooms. You can choose the cherry-wood panelled room; a gold and white striped bed and Louis XVI chairs dressed in *eau-de-nil*. Or be King and Queen and slumber under a canopied bed in a room lined with royal blue and golden fleur de lys; a textile re-created by Emmanual and the Lyon weavers. These are most discreet and winsome hosts who light the candelabra in the evening and prepare to end your day in a most romantic manner. A very, very peaceful place. *Cash or cheque only.*

Rooms: 4 doubles.
Price: €100-€115.
Meals: Breakfast included; dinner €25 including aperitif, wine & coffee, by arrangement.
Closed: Never.

A6 exit Belleville; D37 Beaujeu , at St Vincent left for Quincié en Beaujolais/Marchampt D9 for Lamure. Almost through village of Lamure, take lane in front of 'terrin de sport' marked Pramenoux and climb.

Le Mont Joyeux

Grand Large
Rue Victor Hugo
69330 Meyzieu
Rhône

Jean Bernard Mollard

Tel: (0)4 78 04 21 32
Fax: (0)4 72 02 85 72
E-mail: monjoyeu@club-internet.fr
Web: www.lemontjoyeux.fr

Just a hop, skip and a jump from the hustle and bustle of Lyon - only 12 minutes - through a bit of suburbia, and suddenly peace reigns. You can tell this is an important feature of the hotel from the speed bumps as you drive in. A glimpse of the wide terrace overlooking the blue-grey lake as you enter the reception area and you know you can really slow down. Sailing or paddleboats can be arranged or you can just relax and watch others enjoying themselves on the water as the sun goes down. The larger rooms in the pavillion have their own private terraces in the garden setting, while the smaller, more functional rooms on the top floor of the hotel have a blue and yellow colour scheme and small balconies with parasols. The food and the view from the terrace are the important things here; many come to relax after doing the rounds of the exhibitions in Lyon. There is a friendly welcome from M Mollard and all of the staff - a very good address if you need a break from that motorway and don't want to brave the centre of Lyon.

Rooms: 20: 16 doubles, 4 family in pavillion.
Price: Doubles €77-87, family €100.
Meals: Breakfast €9; lunch & dinner €20-€43.
Closed: Never.

A46 (Rocade Est), exit the Grand Large. Follow the Grand Large then take a left at the fifth light. Signposted.

Map No: 9

Auberge des Chasseurs

Naz Dessus
01170 Echenevex
Ain

Tel: (0)4 50 41 54 07
Fax: (0)4 50 41 90 61
Web: www.guidesdecharme.com

Dominique Lamy

Dominique is a jolly man who is very proud of the Auberge, which his grandparents built as a farm in 1860, and its fantastic sweeping view of the Jura Mountains and Mont Blanc. You might be a bit surprised by the African theme in the reception area, but don't let it put you off. Most of the hotel looks more Swedish and this does have an explanation. A Swedish woman who lives nearby was employed to decorate the hotel. She spent two years meticulously painting the panelled walls and decorating the ceilings and beams in a typically Swedish style which blends in well here, with the mountain views. The bedrooms are all individually decorated: many once again with panelled and painted ceilings and colour-washed walls, some pale, some in fairly strong colours. The big dining room is panelled in yellow with intricately patterned beams, matching country-style yellow chairs and crisp white cloths. The food is a big reason for staying here and Dominique is an expert on Burgundy wines. In 1964 he won a prestigious prize which was presented in Paris and - rare find - his list is both knowledgeable and suited to any budget.

Rooms: 15: 10 doubles, 5 twins.
Price: €69-€130. Half-board for 3 days or more, €99-€225 p.p.
Meals: Breakfast €9; lunch €19-€30; dinner €30-€50. Restaurant closed on certain days, please check.
Closed: Mid-November-mid-March.

Exit A40 at Bellegarde towards Gex. 2km before Gex follow signs to Echenevex. Hotel signposted.

Château de Candie

Rue du Bois de Candie
73000 Chambéry le Vieux
Savoie

Tel: (0)4 79 96 63 00
Fax: (0)4 79 96 63 10
E-mail: candie@icor.fr

Didier Lhostis

When Didier Lhostis came upon his castle it was love at first sight. Built as a fortress in the 14th century by Knights Templar returning from the crusades, Candie was crying out for attention and, after success as a designer, Didier was looking for a new channel for his energy and passion for antiques. The first owner, awarded the title Lord of Candie after an old name for Crete, chose this spot dominating Chambery, looking across to the mountains. Largely rebuilt in the 17th century, it remained a family home until recently. Didier set about assembling a dedicated team of artisans, cutting no corners in his determination to "restore its soul" to Candie. He has succeeded! Bedrooms are vast and magnificent, each with a different feel. Mellow old pink and brown tiled floors lead around the castle, where each piece has been chosen for itself. You can choose where to dine according to your mood: in the Panelled Room, the Garden Room or the Arcade. The chef, Gilles Hérard, who trained with Ducasse and Bocuse, has been here from the start, sharing Didier's vision for Candie. In case this all sounds a touch intimidating: don't worry, Didier welcomes each guest "as a friend".

Rooms: 20: 15 doubles, 5 suites.
Price: Doubles €99-€191, suites from €206.
Meals: Breakfast €12; lunch & dinner €20-€59.
Closed: Never.

A43/A41 exit 15 to Chambéry Le Haut then Chambéry Le Vieux. Signposted.

Cour des Loges

6 rue du Boeuf
69005 Lyon
Rhône

Tel: (0)4 72 77 44 44
Fax: (0)4 72 40 93 61
E-mail: contact@courdesloges.com
Web: www.courdesloges.com

Georges-Eric Tischker

Once upon a time, when Lyon was a rumbling, prosperous trade centre, there were four Renaissance houses built for the bankers, printers and spice merchants. Even the King came with his court for lengthy visits and decreed Lyon's quarterly trade fairs to be tax free. He and the rest of the nobility were entranced by all things Italian. Old Lyon (listed now by UNESCO) with its tiny meandering streets and arched passageways - weather protection for the porters of bolts of cloth - looks like Siena, all brick, ochre and yellow walls. Cour des Loges *is* those four houses, encapsulated under a 20th-century glass roof that links galleries, porticoes, arches and corkscrew staircases; you are inside but feel as if you are outside in a huge piazza. Jocelyne Sibuet, the owner and decorator, has enhanced that feeling by adding large terracotta pots of sculpted bushes and elegant benches. The bedrooms are sensuous with carefully chosen textiles (still a Lyon speciality) - red velvets, grey taffetas, mauve linens and silks, each with an eye-catching Renaissance or Baroque antique cupboard or trunk. Then there are the hanging gardens overlooking the brick-red roofs - a magical spot for lunch or dinner. The chef already has a reputation for one of the best tables in Lyon, no mean achievement.

Rooms: 59 + 4 apartments: 51 doubles/twins, 8 suites for 2-3; 4 apts for 3-4.
Price: Doubles €200-€320, suites & apartments €380-€520.
Meals: Buffet breakfast €20; lunch & dinner à la carte approximately €40-€80. Restaurant closed Sundays & Mondays & 5-20 August.
Closed: Never.

From A42/43 towards
'centre ville' for Place Bellecour. Cross
Rhône and Saône right on Quai Romain
Rolland and left on rue Louis Carrand.
Garage is at end of street; valet will park your car
and bring your bags.

Map No: 9

Chalet-Hôtel les Skieurs

Hirmentaz
74470 Bellevaux
Haute-Savoie

Tel: (0)4 50 73 70 46
Fax: (0)4 50 73 70 46

Bernaz Family

This guide might not be your first thought when contemplating a skiing holiday – but now you have spotted Les Skieurs give it some thought. The skiing here would not suit the experienced, but in a good season you will put your skis on at the front door and enjoy the atmosphere of a small French village – so different from the big international resorts. The Bernaz family originally farmed in the village. Now, after hotel school in Thonon, Claude is the chef and manager, his wife Céline runs the reception, his father looks after the bar and his mother is housekeeper. This would be a great place for families with young children, as long as you aren't desperate for an English ski school. Everyone in the hotel will make you feel at home, it won't break the bank and if you ski enough you won't have to worry about getting fat on Claude's excellent regional food. There's plenty to do in the summer too: walking, mountain biking and trips to Annecy or Geneva; and swimming, riding and tennis nearby – or paragliding, gliding for the more adventurous.

Rooms: 21: 9 doubles & 12 family rooms.
Price: Full-board only in winter €40-€49 p.p., half-board €34-€41 p.p. Rooms €37 for 2, add €8 per additional person.
Meals: Breakfast €5; lunch & dinner €8-€14.
Closed: Mid-April-20 June; September-mid-December.

A40 exit 15; follow signs for Boëge Vallée Verte; at Habère-Poche head for Bellevaux; then Hirmentaz.

Hôtel Auberge Camelia

74570 Aviernoz
Haute-Savoie

Tel: (0)4 50 22 44 24
Fax: (0)4 50 22 43 25
E-mail: info@hotelcamelia.com
Web: www.hotelcamelia.com

Suzanne & Roger Farrell-Cook

Roger loves to talk about local history, including stories about the Resistance: the woman who owned the Camelia during the war had strong connections with the clandestines. But the inn was thoroughly modernised by Roger and Sue ten years ago and now the breakfast buffet is laid out in the old dining room; there's a small, intimate restaurant in the old kitchen, and the bedrooms, carpeted and larger than average, are straightforwardly comfortable with white walls, unfussy furnishings and good big bathrooms. The delicious, open garden has a spring-fed fountain and a sunny terrace where meals are served whenever possible in the sight of impressive hills. Your happy hosts have apparently boundless energy and will take you in their red minibus to the start of some glorious walks. See the spectacular flower meadows, taste wine, ski at all levels - you can even watch the Alpine cattle stroll past your window, their great bells ringing nostalgically. A very welcoming inn with delightful owners and friendly staff who make sure your every need is met, including the need for good food.

Rooms: 12: 5 doubles, 6 triples, 1 quadruple.
Price: €60-€78.
Meals: Breakfast €5; picnic on request €7; lunch & dinner from €15.
Closed: Never.

From Annecy for Chamonix/Mt Blanc/LaRoche to N203. Right at mini r'bout at Pont de Brogny then under railway bridge. After 4km right for Villaz on D175. In village keep left then turn left for Aviernoz. Auberge on left.

L'Ancolie

Lac des Dronières
74350 Cruseilles
Haute-Savoie

Tel: (0)4 50 44 28 98
Fax: (0)4 50 44 09 73
E-mail: ancolie.hotel@wanadoo.fr

Yves Lefebvre

L'Ancolie is exceptionally welcoming and staff are eager to please, reflecting the owner's cheerful efficiency. In a well-kept garden with woods at its back and a lake lapping at its feet, it was custom-designed in 1993 to replace the family's original hotel; they wanted modern comfort in traditional style. So there are wooden balconies and fitted carpets, great log fires in the stone fireplace and a picture window for guests to watch the chefs preparing rich, traditional Savoyard specialities in the kitchen. In summer, the big restaurant opens onto a terrace where you are served before the supremely tranquil lake view. Big bedrooms have lots of wood, of course, and clean cut modern furniture; some have balconies; luxury bed linen adds a touch of class and bathrooms are as up-to-date as you could wish. As well as fishing in the lake and great walks from the door, there's a good golf course nearby plus delightful little Annecy and cosmopolitan Geneva to be visited (each 20km away). L'Ancolie is ideal for families although small children need supervising near the lake, and excellent value.

Rooms: 10 doubles.
Price: €63-€91.
Meals: Breakfast €10; lunch & dinner €22-€41.
Closed: Two weeks in February (French school holidays).

From Annecy RN 201 to Cruseilles. In village take D15 - hotel immediately after Institut Aéronautique.

Hôtel Le Cottage Fernand Bise

Au Bord du Lac
74290 Talloires
Haute-Savoie

Tel: (0)4 50 60 71 10
Fax: (0)4 50 60 77 51
E-mail: cottagebise@wanadoo.fr
Web: www.cottagebise.com

Jean-Claude & Christine Bise

Not many cottages have 35 bedrooms; not many have this fabulous setting, either - you might be in a Wagner opera as you gaze at the sun setting over the 'Roc de Chère' across the Lac d'Annecy from the terrace. The three buildings which make up the hotel look, unsurprisingly, like Alpine chalets and are set in pretty, well-planted gardens in which you can wander on your way to meet one of the local millionaires or perhaps Wotan himself. M and Mme Bise run this welcoming, relaxed establishment with a quiet Savoyard efficiency, which, at its heart, has a proper concern for the comfort of guests. *Douillette* - that lovely word which is the French equivalent of 'cosy', perfectly describes the atmosphere in the bedrooms, with their floral chintz fabrics and comfortable furniture; they all have views of the lake or the mountains. Well away from the bustle of Annecy itself, but close enough to everything it offers, this is a wonderfully adult holiday centre, offering multifarious activities for the sporty and inspiration for the arty who wish to follow in the footsteps of Cezanne or Lamartine. Comfort *and* culture - what more could you want?

Rooms: 35 doubles.
Price: €76-€198.
Meals: Breakfast €12; lunch & dinner €30-€45.
Closed: 10 October-20 April.

In Annecy follow signs Bord du Lac for Thônes D909. At Veyrier du Lac follow D909A to Talloires. Well signposted in Talloires.

Au Coin du Feu

252 Route de Rochebrune
74120 Megève
Haute-Savoie

Tel: (0)4 50 21 04 94
Fax: (0)4 50 21 20 15
E-mail: contact@coindufeu.com
Web: www.coindufeu.com

Mireille Baud

Outside the bustle of 'central Megève', here is another house converted by Jocelyne and Jean-Louis Sibuet into a delicious and intimate place to stay; just a short walk from the village and the ski-lift. It feels more like sharing a big chalet with friends than being in a normal hotel and the décor makes the whole place hum warmly. In the sitting room, a log fire burns in the sculpted fireplace, a chessboard awaits its players by the tartan-covered sofa, the floor glows with burnished old tiles and most things are made of wood. There are thick curtains, mountain antiques and dried flowers, naive paintings and hunting memorabilia, and 'tastings' by the fire with a huge choice of teas and comforting blueberry tart, has become a ritual. Bedrooms are cosy chalet style, beds are in alcoves or under little canopies, their duvets are fluffy, their fabrics flowery, their pictures interesting. The Restaurant Saint Nicolas is one of Megève's favourite eating houses where tradition and invention join hands with all the local tastes and specialities.

Rooms: 23: 19 doubles/twins, 4 suites.
Price: €86-€163; suites €145-€191. Half-board available in winter.
Meals: Breakfast included; dinner €27. Restaurant closed during summer season.
Closed: April-22 July; Late August-mid-September.

Exit A40 Sallanches then N212 towards Albertville. 13km to Megève. Follow hotel signs to center of village and 'Rochebrune Téléphérique'.

Les Roches Fleuries

74700 Cordon
Haute-Savoie

Tel: (0)4 50 58 06 71
Fax: (0)4 50 47 82 30
E-mail: info@rochesfleuries.com
Web: www.hct.net

Jocelyne & Gérard Picot

Brigitte Bardot tried to keep this winter retreat a secret but word got out and countless others have fallen under the spell of the panoramic vision of Mont Blanc and its sister peaks from these balconies. It's hard to find the old farmhouse-turned-hotel buried beneath a grandiose chalet but search and you will find parts of it in the bedrooms and other parts in the snug restaurant downstairs. Warm honey-coloured wood is used everywhere: in ceilings, doors, panelling and huge beams over the fireplaces. The Picot's have also gathered an impressive collection of antiques: carved dressers, farmhouse tables, children's chairs, intricate butter prints, cooking utensils - even an amazing collection of cow bells - contribute to a comfy and homely atmosphere. Guests don't come to be seen anymore but to enjoy sleeping in the cosy beamed bedrooms with matching quilted coverlets and curtains. Carved panels - usually heart patterns - are used to hide radiators or as details on the balconies. Depending upon your mood, dine on Savoyard specialities in the casual restaurant or on more international fare in the larger restaurant.

Rooms: 25: 20 doubles, 5 suites for 4.
Price: Doubles €87-€137, suites €152-€213. Half-board only at some periods €190-€381 for 2.
Meals: Breakfast €12; lunch & dinner €24-€52 by reservation.
Closed: Mid-April-10 May;
25 September-mid-December.

A40 exit Sollarches then D113 for Cordon for 6km. Hotel 400m after church.

Map No: 10

Hôtel Chavant

2 rue Emile Chavant
Bresson
38320 Grenoble
Isère

Danièle Chavant

Tel: (0)4 76 25 25 38
Fax: (0)4 76 62 06 55
E-mail: chavant@chateauxhotels.com

The street is named after their father and the Chavant was founded by their grandfather. So it is no wonder that Danièle and her brother Jean-Pierre continue to hone the family traditions of fine food and hospitality. Some of the warmth comes from Danièle's passion for wood - cherry, oak and walnut. There is the glow of the blond panelling in the dining room, the burnished antiques in the sitting room, the golden bottles of *digestifs* in the 'open' wine cellar displayed in their handsome wooden and glass cases. There is even a kitchen table featured in the lovely still life above the Provençal fireplace where a fire lights up chilly days. The *salon* with large swagged French windows leads to a terrace where one can dine among the islands of flowers in warmer weather. Fine taste, too, upstairs - brass beds, crisp white coverlets, soft red and green textiles, tiny flower-patterned wall paper, a glassed-in veranda in one room and views over the hills. What a pleasure to find such kindness and comfort tucked away in a tiny village only 7 km from Grenoble.

Rooms: 7: 5 doubles, 2 suites.
Price: Doubles €104-€113,
suites €160.
Meals: Breakfast €11; lunch & dinner
€39-€43. Restaurant closed Mondays,
Saturday lunch and Tuesday evenings.
Closed: 25-30 December.

*4km east of Grenoble exit 6 Rocade
Sud/Genève, towards Bresson (Route
Napoléon).*

Château de la Commanderie

17 avenue d'Echirolles
38230 Eybens
Isère

Tel: (0)4 76 25 34 58
Fax: (0)4 76 24 07 31
E-mail: resa@commanderie.fr
Web: www.commanderie.fr

M de Beaumont

Grand it is, and some of the makers of that grandeur - Knights Templar and Maltese, princes and prime ministers, presidents and financiers - look down upon you as you eat in the magnificent dining room, a favourite restaurant for the discerning palates of Grenoble. But the atmosphere is of an intimate family-run hotel. The whole place is awash with family antiques and heirlooms, good taste prevails in every room and fresh flowers add that touch of life and genuine attention. Bedrooms are divided among four separate buildings, adding to the sense of intimacy. Rooms in *Château* and *Chalet* are the more traditional with carved wooden beds and gilt-framed mirrors, though some of them give onto a small road. The *Orangerie* has rooms that, once you have negotiated the rather plain corridors, look out over fine parkland and are deliciously peaceful. The least expensive rooms are in the *Petit Pavilion*, on the road side. But whichever you choose, you will feel thoroughly welcome and pampered, and it's excellent value for families. *Signs for 'La Commanderie' indicate the local police, not the Château.*

Rooms: 25 doubles/twins.
Price: €74-€110.
Meals: Breakfast buffet €9; lunch & dinner €26-€47. Restaurant closed Mondays, Saturday lunchtimes & Sunday nights.
Closed: 20 December-3 January.

From Grenoble exit 5 Rocade Sud for Eybens; right after Esso garage. Entrance to hotel is 300m on left at turning in road.

Map No: 14

Le Clair de la Plume

Place de Mail
26230 Grignan
Drôme

Tel: (0)4 75 91 81 30
Fax: (0)4 75 91 81 31
E-mail: plume2@wanadoo.fr

Jean-Luc Valadeau

Famous for its old-fashioned and English roses spilling into winding streets, Grignan is a paradise for rose-lovers in the summer. Yet pushing open the courtyard gate of this pink-façaded guest house brings you to something new. Jean-Luc Valadeau has created such a feeling of warmth and hospitality - as he puts it, "a home with all the comforts of a hotel". His bustling staff are equally welcoming, leading you through elegant, cosy rooms, antique pieces catching your eye on the way. The small terraced garden adds to the feeling of privacy and light floods in over the original staircase. The bedrooms are very quiet; beautifully decorated - Louis Philippe wardrobes in some, country-style wicker chairs in others - and all have luxurious bathrooms. Stencilled walls, ragged walls, original floor tiles or shining oak planks - a great combination of good taste and authenticity. After an excellent breakfast, the *Salon de Thé* is open from 10am to 10pm for exotic selections of tea, sandwiches, mouth-watering pâtisseries and locally-made traditional ice-cream. There are also lots of restaurants nearby. *No smoking here.*

Rooms: 10 doubles.
Price: Doubles €85-€150.
Meals: Breakfast included. Dinner available locally.
Closed: Never.

A7 exit Montélimar Sud for Bollène/Nyons/Gap then Grignan. Signposted in town.

Provence - Alps - Riviera

I have read in one of the Marseille newspapers that if certain people find aïoli indigestible, it is simply because too little garlic has been included in its confection, a minimum of four cloves per person being necessary.

Richard Olney, Simple French Food.

D. LeFranc, CDT Vaucluse

Auberge de Reillanne

04110 Reillanne
Alpes-de-Haute-Provence

Tel: (0)4 92 76 45 95
Fax: (0)4 92 76 45 95

Monique Balmand

The solid squareness of this lovely old 18th-century house, so typical of the area, reassures you, invites you in. And you will not be disappointed: you'll feel good here, even if you can't quite define the source of the positive energy. Madame Balmand clearly has a connection to the spirit of the place and has used all her flair and good taste, making all the curtains and bedcovers herself, to transform the old inn into a very special place to stay. Bedrooms are large and airy, done in cool, restful colours with big cupboards and rattan furniture. There are beams, properly whitewashed walls and books. Bathrooms are big and simple too. Downstairs, the sitting and dining areas are decorated in warm, embracing colours with terracotta tiles, white tablecloths and flame-coloured curtains. This would be a place for a quiet holiday with long meditative walks in the hills, a place to come and write that novel or simply to get to know the gentle, delicate, smiling owner who loves nothing better than to receive people in her magical house. She organises painting exhibitions, three times a year.

Rooms: 6: 1 single, 2 doubles,
3 triples.
Price: €44-€69, half-board €61 p.p.
Meals: Breakfast €7.50; dinner €21.
Closed: November-April.

From Avignon N100 through Apt and Céreste. About 8km after Céreste left on D214 to Reillanne. Hotel on right (80km from Avignon).

Map No: 14

265

La Bouscatière

Chemin Marcel Provence
04360 Moustiers Sainte Mairie
Alpes-de-Haute-Provence

Tel: (0)4 92 74 67 67
Fax: (0)4 92 74 6572
E-mail: tonia@labouscatiere.com
Web: www.labouscatiere.com

Tonia Peyrot

If you ever had a dream of dramatic Provence, this must be it. The cliffs rise indomitably, the water tumles down, the odd village looks as if it grew here. This enchanting vertical house, fixed firmly to the rock since 1765, was originally an oil mill. It's lowest level, in the village centre houses the oil press; its highest, seventh level, opens through the lush secluded garden with its tiny, ancient chapel (now a delicious bedroom with heavily-carved Spanish bed and a little terrace) to the top of the village and its perfect Romanesque church. Inside, all is country elegance, antiques and supreme comfort against a backdrop of exposed rock, white limewashed walls, Provençal tiles and original beams. A family home turned guest house, it is decorated in exquisite taste by designer Tonia Peyrot; her son sells his china in the old oil press; her staff are utterly delightful; deep sofas call from the vast sitting-room fireplace; *Maïa*, the biggest bedroom, is pretty grand, *Antoinette* has a tracery alcove, all are softly attractive with big, new, Victorian-style fitted bathrooms *No smoking here*.

Rooms: 5 doubles.
Price: €114-€117.
Meals: Breakfast €11.50. Wide variety of restaurants in village.
Closed: Mid-November-20 December; 4 Jan-mid-March.

A8 from Nice exit 36 to N555 for Draguignan; D557 to Aups. D957 to Moustiers St Marie. Follow road to highest point of village to parking area. Do not drive into village.

Les Méans
04340 Méolans Revel
Alpes-de-Haute-Provence

Tel: (0)4 92 81 03 91
Fax: (0)4 92 81 03 91
E-mail: lesmeans@chez.com
Web: www.chez.com/lesmeans

Elizabeth & Fréderic Millet

Beds are just for sleeping here as the beauty of the place and its surrounding area will have you up early, climbing mountains - Fréderic is a qualified mountain guide - rafting or canoeing down the Ubaye river or just taking a slow trek on one of the many nearby trails. The Millets (lucky things!) have double lives: ski instructors in the winter and hospitable hosts of this wonderful 16th-century farmhouse in the summer. They have made it a breeze for families by furnishing communal washing machines, a fridge packed with soft drinks, a microwave and a kettle. Elizabeth cooks on the roasting spit three nights a week - pigeon is one of her specialities - in a wonderful open-plan dining room and kitchen filled with baskets, drying herbs and all sorts of colourful odds and ends picked up over the years. If you insist, a day of doing nothing in particular can be arranged - mountain gazing from the garden is not too strenuous; you could stir yourself to visit the small chapel, or to admire the bread oven beautifully restored by Fréderic.

Rooms: 5: 4 doubles, 1 suite for 4.
Price: €56-€60, suite €85-€115.
Meals: Breakfast included; picnic €8;
dinner €20 inc. wine & coffee,
available 3 days a week.
Closed: Mid-October-mid-May.

*From Gap towards Barcelonnette D900.
10km from Lauzet-Ubaye after La
Fresquiere, do not turn right into
Méolans village but continue for 500m;
left. Signed.*

Villa Morélia

Vallée de l'Ubaye
04850 Jausiers
Alpes-de-Haute-Provence

Tel: (0)4 92 84 67 78
Fax: (0)4 92 84 67 78
E-mail: rboudard@aol.com
Web: www.villa-morelia.com

Robert & Christine Boudard

Villa Morélia has a fascinating history: far from isolating themselves in this village deep in the Alps, on the edges of both Switzerland and Italy, the inhabitants, proudly known as the 'Barcelonnettes' exported their textile skills first to Flanders, then to the Caribbean and in the 19th century to Mexico: where some 60,000 descendants still live. Many however, returned and put their money and taste for things foreign to good use, building exotic villas in their valley. With its imposing height, asymmetric façades and coloured chimneys, the villa Morélia, designed by renowned Marselles architect, Eugène Marx, stands out from the rest. Now Robert, a former financial controller for the army, and Marie Christine have opened it as a hotel and you can be among the first to enjoy staying with this charming couple: both lovers of music, dogs and a relaxed style of living. You will love everything inside: high airy ceilings, walnut windows and doors, beautiful tiles and spacious bedrooms which manage the trick of looking both elegant and welcoming. On top of this, you can ski, go rafting or canyoning, the chef comes from the Eden Roc in Antibes and Robert will pick you up if you don't want to drive.

Rooms: 5: 4 doubles/triples,
1 suite for 2.
Price: €53-€91.
Meals: Breakfast €9; picnic lunch available; dinner €29.
Closed: Never.

7km from Barcelonnette on the D900 Gap-Cuneo road. Villa in centre of village.

Map No: 15

Hôtel Arène

Place de Langes
84100 Orange
Vaucluse

Tel: (0)4 90 11 40 40
Fax: (0)4 90 11 40 45

M & Mme Coutel

You can drive here, and park, but you are really in a pedestrian area and it's beautifully quiet in the middle of this ancient town and a stone's throw from the Roman theatre. Monsieur and Madame Contel have run the Arène for some 30 years and have kept all their staff for ages: always a good sign. The entrance hall may be a touch overpowering, but go on in, you won't regret it. Newly-decorated bedrooms are in what our inspector described as "joyful colours"; the older ones are a sort of 'old-fashioned' French but most have been transformed with Provençal blues and yellows, with painted cupboards and beds, or possibly wrought iron and with flowers on the table. The bathrooms are new and white, with coloured tile details and some have big corner baths. Painted furniture, pots and urns and the odd statue add to the Provençal feel, while the stained glass, which looks a bit much in the entrance, is great viewed from the other side and casts a pleasant light into the breakfast room. A special place right in Orange, where your children will be made really welcome.

Rooms: 30: 29 doubles/twins, 1 family room for 3-4.
Price: Doubles/twins €77-€122, family room €122-183.
Meals: Breakfast €10. Good restaurant next door.
Closed: Three weeks in November.

A9-A7 exit Orange to Centre Ville. Left after Office du Tourisme along Cours Aristide Briand, first right on President Daladier, immed. right on Victor Hugo, second left onto Places de Langes. Centre is pedestrian but cars can get to hotel via this route.

Map No: 14

Les Florets

Route des Dentelles
84190 Gigondas
Vaucluse

Tel: (0)4 90 65 85 01
Fax: (0)4 90 65 83 80

M & Mme Bernard

The setting is magical, the food imaginative, the greeting from the Bernard family is warm and the walks are outstanding. Les Florets sits just below the majestic Dentelles de Montmirail - a small range of mountains crested with long, delicate fingers of white stone in the middle of Côtes du Rhône country. Over 40 kms of paths wind through here, so appetites build and are satiated on the splendid terrace under the branches of plane, chestnut, maple, acacia and linden trees; the low stone walls are dressed with impatiens and hydrangeas (and the peonies were blooming in March!). You'll also be sampling some of the wines that this family has been producing since the 1880s. Bright blue and yellow corridors lead to rooms which are simply and florally decorated; all have big, sparkling, tiled bathrooms. We liked the tiny 50's reception desk dressed with a huge bouquet from the garden; a wonderful ceramic *soupière* brightens one corner, a scintillating collection of delicate glass carafes stands in another. They keep a list of the regional markets here. Book ahead, people return year after year.

Rooms: 15 + 3 apartments: 15 doubles; 3 apts for 2-4.
Price: Doubles €80-€115; apartments €107-€137.
Meals: Breakfast €11; lunch & dinner €22-€32. Restaurant closed Monday evenings, Tuesdays & Wednesdays Nov-Dec & March.
Closed: January-mid-March.

From Carpentras D7 for Beaumes de Venise/Vacqueyras. After Vacqueras right on D7 to Gigondas for 2km. Signposted.

270

Map No: 14

Château Talaud

D 107
84870 Loriol du Comtat
Vaucluse

Tel: (0)4 90 65 71 00
Fax: (0)4 90 65 77 93
E-mail: chateautalaud@infonie.fr
Web: www.chateautalaud.com

Conny & Hein Deiters-Kommer

Lavish and elegant - a stunning place and lovely people. Hein has a wine export business, Conny gives her whole self to her house and her guests. Among ancient vineyards, the ineffably gracious 18th-century château speaks of a long-gone southern way of life. Enter, and you will feel it has not all vanished. Restored by the owners to a very high standard, the finely-proportioned rooms have been furnished with antiques, many of them family pieces, and thick, luxurious fabrics. The big bedrooms mix old and new - *Directoire* armchairs and featherweight duvets - with consummate taste and bathrooms are old-style hymns to modernity. But the high point must be the exquisite swimming pool, an adapted 17th-century irrigation tank: through an arch to the first, shallow cistern, leading to a deeper pool beyond - incredibly beautiful. Guests may laze in the lovely gardens but Conny is happy to help you plan visits in this fascinating area. Then return to one of her delicious meals where guests all sit together: An exceptionally fine, well-kept guesthouse - *A cottage, studio and apartment available for weekly rental.*

Rooms: 6 + 3: 5 doubles, 1 suite; studio for 2, cottage for 5, apartment for 2. All have cooking facilities.
Price: Doubles & suite €125-€185; studio, cottage, apartment €925-€1,230 per week.
Meals: Breakfast included; dinner, 4 courses including wine, €38, served twice a week.
Closed: February.

Leave N7 on D950 for Carpentras. Exit D107 at Loriol du Comtat/Monteux Est. On r'bout left for Loriol. After 1km château on left, signposted Propriété Privée.

Hostellerie du Val de Sault

Route de Saint-Trinit
Ancien chemin d'Aurel
84390 Sault
Vaucluse

Tel: (0)4 90 64 01 41
Fax: (0)4 90 64 12 74
E-mail: valdesault@aol.com
Web: www.valdesault.com

Yves Gattechaut & Ildiko de Hanny

Jean Giono, calls this landscape "a sea of corn gold and lavender blue": from your terrace here you can contemplate the poet's waves and the familiar shape of Mont Ventoux, the painter's peak, beyond. The charming, communicative owners - she with an artistic background, he a passionate cook - have gathered all possible information, know everyone there is to know on the Provence scene and are full of good guidance; they also provide imaginative food in the informal atmosphere of their light, airy restaurant. And... children can eat earlier, allowing the adults to savour their meal in peace. Perched just above the woods in a big garden, this is a modern building with lots of space inside and out; wooden floors and pine-slatted walls bring live warmth, colour schemes are vibrant, storage is excellent; baths in the suites have jacuzzi jets. Each room feels like a very private space with its terrace (the suites have room for loungers on theirs): the pool, bar and restaurant are there for conviviality; the fitness room, tennis court and boules pitch for exercise.

Rooms: 16: 11 doubles, 5 suites, all with private terraces.
Price: Half-board May-September: doubles €79-€99 p.p., suites €103-€146 p.p. Rooms: doubles €79, suites €136.
Meals: Breakfast €11 if not half-board. Restaurant closed for lunch certain days April-October.
Closed: November-March.

A7 exit Avignon Nord/Le Pontet for Carpentras (20km). Follow signs Sault/Villes sur Auzon. D1 Col des Abeilles for Sault (30km); towards Saint Trinit/Fourcalquier. After big bend, left between Fire Department and supermarket, 1km to hostellerie in heart of forest.

Auberge de la Fontaine

Place de la Fontaine
84210 Venasque
Vaucluse

Tel: (0)4 90 66 02 96
Fax: (0)4 90 66 13 14
E-mail: fontvenasq@aol.com

M & Mme Soehlke

Line up your taste buds and eye and the ear will join the chorus to sing praises to this place with a difference. It sits discretly behind the central fountain of one of the most beautiful hill towns of Provence. Enter through a small bistro downstairs and then follow a tiny, wonky staircase to the restaurant where you'll find antique cupboards, rush-bottomed chairs and interesting etchings framed and hung with care. It's all very tasteful and traditional - except for a grand piano in the middle of the dining room. If you timed it right you will hear it being played during one of Christian's dinner concerts - about 20 each year - featuring young musicians from all over France and his authentic cuisine. Then up to bed in one of the five suites furnished with modern pieces from young designers of Zen-like sobriety, a black and white theme against terracotta tiles. Some of the small private terraces are up on another level. All rooms have working chimneys, air conditioning, cleverly hidden kitchens (with vegetable peelers and dishwashers!) and sound systems for cassettes and CD's. Outstanding. *30km from Orange and Avignon.*

Rooms: 5 suites, some with individual terraces.
Price: €122.
Meals: Breakfast €8; lunch & dinner from €14 in bistro; dinner from €34 in restaurant; bistro closed Sunday evenings and Mondays; restaurant closed Wednesdays.
Closed: Never.

From Carpentras D4. Hotel is opposite the fountain, a 5 minute walk from parking area. Tiny streets of hill town are pedestrian.

Map No: 14

Le Tonneau

Place de l'Ancienne Mairie
84220 Goult
Vaucluse

Tel: (0)4 90 72 22 35
Fax: (0)4 90 72 22 35
E-mail: famous.provence@wanadoo.fr
Web: leluberon.net/famous-provence.fr

Patrick Payet

Goult is one of those typical hill-top towns in the Luberon - busy, lots of street cafés and entertainment in the summer and relaxed and sleepy in the winter. However there is nothing typical about Patrick. He is a larger-than-life character; very friendly, he seems to find time to talk to everyone. He shines in the market place as he points out the freshest deep purple aubergines or the ripest golden melons of Cavaillon, all from "his" region, of course. Take along your notebook as the tips on food preparation and recipes come quick and fast. If you miss something, don't worry - you can catch up later in the evening when Patrick often demonstrates the finer points of southern French cuisine as you sip a glass or two of Chardonnay. His rooms, all with cooking facilities, are in an 18th-century house across the street from the Baron d'Agoult's castle. They are big, bright and decorated in a simple Provençal style; there is lots of elbow room in the patchwork-tiled bathrooms. Mornings here are easy - fresh croissants, bread, butter and jams will be left outside your door each morning and you can come-to in your own time.

Rooms: 4 doubles/triples all with kitchenettes.
Price: €81-€96. Weekly half-board rates including cooking lessons & cultural visits €1920.
Meals: Breakfast included; dinner €23.
Closed: January-15 March.

After Avignon leave N7 for N100 towards Apt. Turn left up hill into Goult. Restaurant below château. Signposted.

Hôtel Les Romarins

Route de l'Abbaye de Sénanque
84220 Gordes
Vaucluse

Tel: (0)4 90 72 12 13
Fax: (0)4 90 72 13 13
Web: www.luberonnews.com

Anny Charles

Anny Charles has been running this three-star hotel overlooking one of France's most beautiful villages for more than ten years. Forget the buildings on either side: the secluded pool and garden make you feel away from it all and the hotel even has its own private path into town. The fabulous hilltop view of Gordes encourages you to linger over a delicious buffet breakfast, usually taken on the terrace. Inside, the sitting room is comfortable without being over-lavish and the warmth of the open fire is always welcome on days when the chilly mistral wind gets up. The white-walled bedrooms are cool and comfortable, if a little sombre, but quiet. Anny doesn't serve evening meals, but she'll gladly book a restaurant for you or let you explore the local culinary delights (of which there are plenty) on your own. Vivacious, always busy and particularly welcoming, she takes a lot of pleasure in making you feel at home. And her African Grey parrot simply loves hearing all about your day. A happy spot, easy living, great walking.

Rooms: 10 doubles, some with private terraces.
Price: €88-€140.
Meals: Breakfast €10. Restaurants nearby.
Closed: 15 December-15 February.

From Avignon east on N7 then left onto N100 for Apt; left to Gordes. Route de Sénanque is on left on entering Gordes. Hotel 200m on right, well signposted.

Map No: 14

Auberge du Presbytère

Place de la Fontaine
84400 Saignon
Vaucluse

Tel: (0)4 90 74 11 50
Fax: (0)4 90 04 68 51
E-mail: auberge.presbytere@wanadoo.fr
Web: www.provence-luberon.com/auberge1_fr.html

Jean-Pierre de Lutz

"When the wind blows at Saignon, tiles fly off in Avignon," is a local saying about the mistral, the fierce wind that howls down from the mountains to the Mediterranean. This 11th-century village of only 100 inhabitants is in the heart of the Luberon hills and lavender fields; the Auberge du Presbytère is in the heart of Saignon, half hidden behind an old tree near the village's statue-topped fountain. You can have lunch under this tree, or in a pretty terraced garden. The bedrooms are striking, although *Grape* and *Fountain* lack the spartan charm of the others. *Blue* with its stone terrace, looks out onto the hills and the simplest of all the rooms, the little one, *Pink,* has sleigh beds. Jean-Pierre, the owner's quietly charming son, will make you feel at home and, though this is perhaps not an obvious choice with children, provides early supper specially for them. A great place for you to visit the nearby hill towns. Or if you are fit, rent a bike and follow the signs *le Lubéron en vélo.* Lots to explore in the National Park.

Rooms: 12: 11 doubles, 1 suite. 2 third-floor rooms with terrace.
Price: €52-€110.
Meals: Breakfast €8.50; lunch €19; dinner €28. Restaurant closed Wednesday & Thursday lunchtimes.
Closed: Mid-November-mid-December; January-February.

From Apt N100. At r'bout with 1 olive and 3 cyprus trees for Saignon to beginning of village. Left on lane for riverains (residents) to Place de la Fontaine.

Le Mas de Garrigon

Route de Saint-Saturnin d'Apt
Roussillon en Provence
84220 Gordes
Vaucluse

Tel: (0)4 90 05 63 22
Fax: (0)4 90 05 70 01
E-mail: mas.de.garrigon@wanadoo.fr
Web: www.masdegarrigon-provence.com

Christiane Rech-Druart

Christiane, a writer and journalist, settled in the Luberon after years in Africa, bought the plot of land and built the *mas* from scratch in 1979, using local materials and tailoring the house to the hill. The idea was to build a really special place to stay – each room has its own terrace looking out on the wild beauty of the hills. We don't generally recommend piped music… but the classical music Christiane plays does add to the atmosphere. Palest terracotta with lightest blue shutters, the house sits among cypress, olive and almond trees and is perfect in summer, when you can lounge by the pool and perfect in winter too, when you can settle down by a crackling fire, maybe with a book from the well-stocked library. Inside is in complete and striking contrast to the muted, natural tones used outside. Bedrooms are a joyful riot of reds, yellows and blues. Don't worry: Christiane's mix of bold and simple, traditional and daring is never garish, just perfectly at home. Great food too.

Rooms: 10: 9 doubles, 1 family room for 2-3.
Price: Doubles €104-€110, family room €130-€159. Half-board only Easter-October: €234-€272 for 2.
Meals: Breakfast €14. Lunch and dinner €26-€30. Picnic lunch available. Restaurant closed Mondays and Tuesday & Wednesday lunchtimes and from mid-November-end December.
Closed: Never.

*From Cavallion on D2
between Gordes and Saint-Saturnin d'Apt.*

Le Relais du Procureur
Rue Basse
84710 Lacoste
Vaucluse

Tel: (0)4 90 75 82 28
Fax: (0)4 90 75 86 94
E-mail: relaisprocureur@luberon.org
Web: www.luberon.org

Antoine Court de Gebelin

The inner courtyard garden around a pretty pool is a measure of the peace you'll find in this 17th-century dwelling, even when the village streets are thronging with visitors in the summer. Respect for his guests' tranquillity is among the owner's priorities and his professional eye as a photographer ensures more than simple attention to detail in the authentic renovations he embarked on over a decade ago. White stone walls, resplendent with old prints and paintings, reflect both natural light and the soft hues of stylised lamps in an overall tableau dominated by refinement and comfort. The seven bedrooms, some with views over the Luberon hills, are all big (the largest is 39m²) and most enable children and parents to share the same room. The hotel is not really suitable for small children though, partly due to the stone staircases and elegant furniture. But also due to the gentle quietness so appreciated by guests all year round. A far cry from what life might have been like at the enigmatic Marquis de Sade's château overlooking the village!

Rooms: 7: 5 doubles/twins, 1 triple, 1 family.
Price: Doubles/twins /triple €76-€114, family €130.
Meals: Breakfast included; lunch & dinner menus €20-€25. À la carte also available. Restaurant closed November-March.
Closed: Occasionally January-March.

From Avignon N100 east to Lumières; right to Lacoste; in village keep right following signs to Mairie/Poste to one-way main street - hotel next to bakery.

Map No: 14

Mas des Capelans

84580 Oppède
Vaucluse

Tel: (0)4 90 76 99 04
Fax: (0)4 90 76 90 29
E-mail: reservation@masdescapelans-luberon.com
Web: www.masdescapelans-luberon.com

Jacqueline & Philippe Poiri

Why buy a house in Provence and have to do all the work? Here, you will feel at home but be free to lounge by the pool all day, having a leisurely lunch between dips and wandering in to change before an aperitif as you watch the sun go down behind the hills. Jacqueline and Philippe have been running the Mas des Capelans, the 18th-century home of a silkworm breeder set among the vineyards and fields, for more than 13 years now and their personal touch comes through both in the relaxed atmosphere and the house itself. The furniture and bits and pieces in the bedrooms have been collected over the years and not simply bought to give the place the right look. The rooms are largish and simply decorated, with plenty of cushions and flowers. A great place for children; one room has an adjoining room for them and a private terrace while another has children's beds on a split-level. Dinner is under the mulberry trees unless the mistral is blowing. If you feel like a drink later, simply help yourself from the outside bar and settle-up when you leave. *No smoking here.*

Rooms: 9: 5 doubles, 4 family.
Price: Doubles €91-€167, family €145-€229.
Reductions for stays of 3 nights or more.
Meals: Buffet breakfast €10; poolside lunch €17.
Closed: November-February.

*Exit Avignon South towards APT on D22 then
N100. After Coustellet left for Oppède. Signposted.*

La Bastide de Voulonne

84220 Cabrières d'Avignon
Vaucluse

Tel: (0)4 90 76 77 55
Fax: (0)4 90 76 77 56
E-mail: sophie@bastide-voulonne.com
Web: www.bastide-voulonne.com

Sophie & Alain Rebourg

This bastide sits in splendid isolation in the lavender fields stretching beneath the ancient hilltop villages perched on the Luberon Mountains. The heart of this 18th-century farm is an inner courtyard where you can breakfast to the soothing sound of the fountain. The Bastide has been open for guests for some 5 years since Sophie and Alain rescued it from years of neglect. They have done a fantastic job, sticking to natural, local colours, with tiled floors. The bedrooms are huge. The garden - more like a park really - is vast, with a big pool not far from the house. It's a fantastic place for children; Sophie and Alain have young twins. They plan to grow vegetables in the garden and meals already centre round local food. Breakfast is a buffet, in an airy, tiled breakfast room if it's too chilly for the courtyard. Dinner is served at one long table in a big dining hall where the centrepiece is the carefully restored old bread oven. There are loads of places around for lunch, or Sophie will do you a picnic. *Everything you have always wanted to know about truffles; two-day courses in January and February. No smoking here.*

Rooms: 8: 7doubles, 1 suite.
Price: Doubles €107-€213, suite €152-€236.
Meals: Breakfast €9; dinner €25. Restaurant closed Tuesdays and Wednesdays.
Closed: Mid-November-mid December; open by arrangement only January & February.

After Avignon A7 on N100 for Apt. At Coustellet x-roads to Gordes; at r'bout (Collège de Calavon) for Gordes. After 1km right - Bastide 600m on left.

Map No: 14

Hôtel d'Europe

12 place Crillon
84000 Avignon
Vaucluse

Tel: (0)4 90 14 76 76
Fax: (0)4 90 14 76 71
E-mail: reservations@hotel-d-europe.fr
Web: www.hotel-d-europe.fr

M Daudeij

Built in 1580 for the Marquis de Graveson, this mansion, a mitre's throw from the Papal Palace, was taken from its noble owner by the Revolution and turned into a hotel. When you stay here, you will be following in the steps of great writers (Victor Hugo, Tennessee Williams), painters (Dali, Picasso), even Napoleon; in earlier times people arrived by boat but as this is no longer possible, the hotel has a car park. Owner René Daudeij has run the Europe for some 20 years with his impeccable, perfectionist touch - and pretty perfect it is - with the help of his superbly cultivated manager. It is one of our larger hotels but small enough for them to take personal care of each guest. This is traditional French hospitality in all its splendour. Bedrooms vary from large to huge, from simply elegant to sumptuous; many have crisp white cotton bedcovers that give a fresh touch among the moulded, mirrored walls, the antiques and the plush-covered chairs. Meals are served at fine tables in the tapestry-hung dining room or on the terrace where the fountain sings.

Rooms: 45: 38 doubles, 4 triples, 3 suites.
Price: Doubles/triples €120-€385, suites €580-€670.
Meals: Breakfast €19; lunch & dinner €31-84. Restaurant closed 13-18 Jan; 18 August-2 September; 24 November-2 December.
Closed: Never.

Exit Avignon for Centre Ville. From ring road around the ramparts, turn on Porte de L'Oulle for place Crillon. Hotel and place Crillon signposted.

La Barjaquière

84330 Saint Pierre de Vassols
Vaucluse

Tel: (0)4 90 62 48 00
Fax: (0)4 90 62 48 06
E-mail: dponcet@club-internet.fr
Web: www.barjaquiere.com

Guislaine André & Daniel Poncet

There is much more to the Barjaquière than meets the eye. A typical 17th-century town house from the outside; the first surprise in the flowered entrance courtyard, is an outdoor pool. The second is the indoor pool surrounded by trompe l'œil visions of terracotta pots overflowing with greens and reds. Daniel will explain that it was the original structure with its beams, nooks and crannies, mezzanines and terraces that inspired this maze of a Provençal interior. An antique door, stencilled flowers over the staircase, a quiet sitting space with a book of poetry beckoning on the antique table, Guislaine has made it all sing with warmth and colour. The bright, slanted-roofed *Soleillant* has a beaded curtain and a private terrace overlooking the village; apricot floor tiles reflect the pale yellow, waxed walls. The shimmering ochre walls of *Le Parc* seem to hold a hundred layers of light which contrast well with a carmine sofa and quilted bedspreads. Add the engaging hospitality of two inventive hosts; you will find it very hard to leave. *No smoking here.*

Rooms: 5: 3 doubles, 2 suites for 3.
Price: Doubles €100-€150, suites €170 (for 2), €195 (for 3).
Meals: Breakfast included; 4-course dinner €38 inc. aperitif, wine & coffee, by arrangement.
Closed: Mid-January-mid February; 20 November-10 December.

A7 exit 22 for Carpentras; D950 then D13; left at second aqueduct on D974 to Bedoin/Mont Ventoux 7.7km. At Saint Pierre de Vassols left on D85 to village church. La Barjaquière is opposite.

Mas des Comtes de Provence

Petite Route d'Arles
13150 Tarascon
Bouches-du-Rhône

Tel: (0)4 90 91 00 13
Fax: (0)4 90 91 02 85
E-mail: valo@mas-provence.com
Web: www.mas-provence.com

Frédérique & Pierre Valo

Homesick for the south of France and looking for a 'life' change after frenetic professional careers in Paris, Frédérique and Pierre fell for this historic hunting lodge and have just settled in with their four young children. The mas belonged to King René whose château is just up the road; some say the Germans blocked the underground tunnel that connected the two buildings. A massive, sober, elegant stone exterior dating from the 16th century protects the big interior courtyard overlooked by grey-blue shuttered windows. There is lots of space here and the rooms are regal - the suite and the royal suite are 50m² and 100m² respectively. The suite *Roi René* is in tones of ivory, brown and beige; *Garance* in brick and yellow; ironwork chairs and side tables add extra interest. The pool is well hidden from the house in the two-hectare park dominated by 300-year-old plane trees, twisted olive trees, cypress and a profusion of roses. Pierre can direct you to the best canoeing, hiking, cycling, or riding - all just minutes away.

Rooms: 6: 4 doubles, 1 suite, 1 royal suite for 6.
Price: Doubles & suite €122-€145, royal suite €229.
Meals: Breakfast included; dinner €25 inc. aperitif & coffee, by arrangement.
Closed: Never.

Tarascon towards Arles on D35 'Petite Route d'Arles'. 200m after leaving Tarascon, take small road on left. Mas 600m on left.

Hôtel Le Cadran Solaire

5 rue du Cabaret Neuf
13690 Graveson
Bouches-du-Rhône

Tel: (0)4 90 95 71 79
Fax: (0)4 90 90 55 04
E-mail: cadransolaire@wanadoo.fr
Web: www.hotel-en-provence.com

Sophie Guilmet

A soft clear light filters through the house, the light of the South pushing past the smallish windows and stroking Sophie Guilmet's light-handed, rich-pastelled décor where simple Provençal furniture, stencil motifs and natural materials - cotton, linen, organdie and seagrass - give the immediate feel of a well-loved family home. The simplicity of a pastel slip-cover over a chair, a modern wrought-iron bed frame and a white piqué quilt is refreshing and restful - and the house stays deliciously cool in the summer heat. Indeed, the solid old staging post has stood here, with its thick walls, for 400 years, its face as pretty as ever, calmly set in its gentle garden of happy flowers where guests can always find a quiet corner for their deck chairs. You can have breakfast on the shrubby terrace, under a blue and white parasol, or in the attractive dining room where a fine big mirror overlooks the smart red-on-white tables. A wonderful atmosphere, relaxed, smiling staff, an ideal base for visiting Provence and really good value.

Rooms: 12 doubles.
Price: €45-€71.
Meals: Breakfast €5.50.
Closed: Open only by reservation in winter.

A7 exit Avignon Sud for Chateaurenard; D28 to Graveson. Signposted.

Mas de l'Oulivié

Les Arcoules
13520 Les Baux de Provence
Bouches-du-Rhône

Tel: (0)4 90 54 35 78
Fax: (0)4 90 54 44 31
E-mail: contact@masdeloulivie.com
Web: www.masdeloulivie.com

Emmanuel Achard

How refreshing to find a modern hotel that brings together old and new so harmoniously and with such impeccable taste. Having fallen in love with the olive groves, lavender fields and chalky white hillsides of Les Baux de Provence, the family built the hotel of their dreams ten or so years ago: a creamy fronted, almond-green shuttered, Provence-style structure, roofed with reclaimed terracotta tiles, landscaped with cypress and oleander. Every last detail has been carefully crafted, from the locally made oak furniture to the handmade tiles round the pool. And what a pool! Temptingly curvaceous, with a jacuzzi and pebble beach for children. Furnishings are fresh, local, designed for deep comfort. Bedrooms are creamy-coloured, country-style with an elegant twist. The bar/living-room has a rustic fireplace; filled with flowers in the summer. The young Archards love to provide guests with the very best and that includes lunches served by the pool - they also sell their own lavender and oil - Mas de l'Oulivié joins the *crème de la crème* of Provence's small country hotels - a stylish retreat. *Protected parking.*

Rooms: 23: 16 doubles, 6 triples, 1 suite.
Price: Doubles/triples €95-€230, suite €280-€360.
Meals: Breakfast €10; poolside lunches à la carte.
Closed: Mid-November-mid-March.

From North A7 exit 24 for Les Baux. Mas is 2km from village of Les Baux on D78 towards Fontvieille

Map No: 14

Mas de la Brune

13810 Eygalières en Provence
Bouches-du-Rhône

Tel: (0)4 90 90 67 67
Fax: (0)4 90 95 99 21
E-mail: masbrune@francemarket.com
Web: www.francemarket.com/brune/

M & Mme de Larouzière

Built to an alchemist's design in 1572 this jewel of Provençal Renaissance art - whose centre was Les Baux de Provence - is of pure classical style. A watch tower, mullioned windows and a double-tailed mermaid watch over 4 hectares of gardens and lawns while inside one can only guess at the meaning of the combined pagan and Christian icons; snarling gargoyles, carved heads to represent anger and gluttony and the four evangelists who sit alongside a magnificent circular staircase. The entire ground floor is vaulted; a monumental fireplace graces the sitting room and a giant olive press presides over the dining room. The upper half-floor was used for silkworm rearing and now leads to spacious bedrooms; baldaquined-beds, fine-beamed ceilings and large windows, all decorated in sober sophistication. M & Mme de Larouzière are very proud of their alchemist's botanical garden, part of which is dedicated to three mono-colour quadrants; black, white and red. Add a kitchen garden, a show of medicinal plants, giant chestnut trees, lavender, herbs, roses - you can pick your quiet corner in this magical, elegant place.

Rooms: 10: 7 doubles, 2 suites for 2, 1 suite for 3.
Price: Doubles €152-€229, suites €320-€351.
Meals: Breakfast €13. Lunch & dinner available in village.
Closed: December-February.

8km from St Remy de Provence on D99 then D74. Follow signs. Large gates with tree-lined driveway.

Map No: 14

Mas de Cornud

Route de Mas Blanc, D31
13210 Saint Rémy de Provence
Bouches-du-Rhône

Tel: (0)4 90 92 39 32
Fax: (0)4 90 92 55 99
E-mail: mascornud@compuserve.com
Web: www.mascornud.com

David & Nitockrees Tadros Carpita

Guest house and cookery school are combined in a typical farmhouse where two majestic plane trees stand guard and the scents and light of Provence hover. Nito, a nature-lover, cares about how colour creates feeling, how fabrics comfort: she and David, willing American 'exiles', have done a superb restoration where every object is clearly the best (hangings from Kashmir, old French tiles). Bedrooms are big and varied, all beautifully decorated yet warmly simple. The atmosphere is convivial and open: you are a member of a family here, so join the others at the bar, choose a book in the library, have a swim in the big pool then a drink from the honesty bar. The kitchen is the vital centre of Cornud: you eat here if the weather is poor - otherwise the garden has some lovely eating spots - and learn, if you have come for cookery lessons; though many stay without following a course. A traditional country kitchen, with cast-iron range, long wooden table, baskets and dried herbs, it also has a non-slip floor and granite worktops - homely but professional. Come and be part of Provence for a week. *Children over 12 welcome.*

Rooms: 6: 5 doubles, 1 suite.
Price: Doubles €150-€235,
suite €260-€380.
Meals: Breakfast included; picnic available; lunch €21-€25; hosted dinner €46.
Closed: January-February.

3km west of St Rémy de Provence on D99 for Tarascon. Left on D27 towards Les Baux; after 1km left at sign Château des Alpilles D31. Mas is 200m on left.

La Maison

Domaine de Bournissac
Montée d'Eyragues
13550 Paluds de Noves
Bouches-du-Rhône

Tel: (0)4 90 90 25 25
Fax: (0)4 90 90 25 26
E-mail: annie@lamaison-a-bournissac.com
Web: www.lamaison-a-bournissac.com

Alain & Annie Zéau

This huge noble house with its beautiful stone buildings laid out round a courtyard has been converted and decorated with gusto and unfaltering taste - understandably, since the Zéaus are an energetic, artistic couple who also run a restaurant-art gallery; Annie painted lots of the pictures here. There is a wonderful soft beige Provençal finish on the walls, a fine patina on the furniture, a different beautiful bedcover in each room. It feels like a sophisticated private house, with cosy corners - the lovely *salon* with fireplace and books, another sitting area in a wide, sea-grass-floored corridor, pretty objects everywhere, lovely old fireplaces, beams and elegant linens. The big shady terrace outside the dining room is the place to eat in summer, gazing down into the valley and across to the Alpilles (the pool lies discreetly in the lower garden). The owners care about guests' comfort and pleasure: bedrooms are big, bathrooms deluxe, tables most beautifully decorated, meals inventive and refined. Opened in July 1999 it already feels loved and lived-in.

Rooms: 10: 7 doubles, 3 suites (1 suite for 4).
Price: Doubles €104-€176, suites €183-€299. Children under 10 free. Half-board €101-€136 p.p.
Meals: Breakfast €12; lunch & dinner €39-€58.
Closed: 7 January-12 February.

From A7 exit Avignon Sud to Noves; D30 for St Rémy 4km. Right on D29 for Eyragues. Left at top of hill. Signposted.

Map No: 14

La Riboto de Taven

Le Val d'Enfer
13520 Les Baux de Provence
Bouches-du-Rhône

Tel: (0)4 90 54 34 23
Fax: (0)4 90 54 38 88
E-mail: contact@riboto-de-taven.fr
Web: www.riboto-de-taven.fr

Novi-Thème Family

Ever slept in a cave? In a bed with ornate cover and hangings, with a luxurious bathroom next door? Well, here you can. The Novi-Thème family – Christine, Philippe and Jean-Pierre, – have farmed here for four generations and still produce olive oil, fruit and wine. In Val d'Enfer, or Valley of Hell - it would look more like paradise to most people – facing the spectacular cliff-top village of Les Baux de Provence, the property is literally built onto the limestone cliff. The two 'Troglodyte' rooms are separate from the others, and the apartment. Walk up stone steps from the garden to a terrace, where the view is even more amazing than from the rest of the *mas*. There was an olive oil mill here in the 17th century. Now you have *Mireille* or *Vincent* with the canopied bed and beautiful furniture handed down the generations and the overhang of the rockface forming half the ceiling. The family opened an excellent restaurant in 1961 and… yes, it has that view. Now the rooms have just been done, the garden is small but beautiful, with a pool, and the welcome is warm. *Well-behaved children over 10 welcome.*

Rooms: 5 + 1 apartment: 5 doubles; 1 apt for 4.
Price: €168-€229.
Meals: Breakfast €14; poolside lunches €23; dinner €46. Restaurant closed 2 nights a week October-July.
Closed: Mid-January-mid-February.

From St Rémy de Provence D5 to Maussane/Les Baux. Past entrance to village and towards Fontvieille. Hotel on first road to right. Signposted.

Map No: 14

Grand Hôtel Nord Pinus

Place du Forum
13200 Arles
Bouches-du-Rhône

Tel: (0)4 90 93 44 44
Fax: (0)4 90 93 34 00
E-mail: info@nord-pinus.com
Web: www.nord-pinus.com

Mme Igou

There is no other like it. An Arlesian legend, where Spain meets France, ancient Rome meets the 21st century. Built in 1865 on Roman vaults, it came to fame in the 1950s when a clown and a cabaret singer owned it: famous bullfighters dressed here before entering the arena and the arty crowd flocked (Cocteau, Picasso, Hemingway...). Anne Igou keeps the magic alive today with her strong personality and cinema, fashion and photography folk - and bullfighters still have 'their' superb Spanish Rococo room. The style is vibrant and alive at this show of Art Deco furniture and fittings, great corrida posters and toreador costumes, North African carpets and artefacts, fabulous Provençal colours and ironwork. Colour and light are deftly used to create a soft, nostalgic atmosphere where you feel both warm and cool, smart and artistic - where each guest is an individual, each room is differently interesting. And breakfast is a festival of real French tastes - more magic, more nostalgia. As Cocteau said: "An hotel with a soul" - though the tourist invasion may make it noisy during the summer.

Rooms: 25: 20 doubles/twins, 5 suites.
Price: Doubles/twins €128-€166, suites €290.
Meals: Breakfast €13-€18; lunch €17; dinner from €27.
Closed: Never.

From A54 exit Arles Centre for Centre Ancien. Take Blvd des Lices at main post office; right on Rue Jaurès; left on Rue Cloître, right to Place du Forum.

Map No: 14

Le Mas de la Fouque

Route du Petit Rhône
13460 Saintes Maries de la Mer
Bouches-du-Rhône

Tel: (0)4 90 97 81 02
Fax: (0)4 90 97 96 84
E-mail: masdelafouque@francemarket.com
Web: www.masdelafouque.com

M & Mme Rivière

Cowboy boots and brown, weather-beaten faces are as much part of the Camargue as the pink flamingos and the white horses gracing the ponds and grasslands surrounding the Mas de la Fouque. The silver and blue watery surfaces surrounding the hotel are an important detail where everything is luminous, airy and white, with just enough touches of soft blue and yellow. The 11 rooms and three suites all face south and have their own terrace looking out either over the pool or the pond, which the flamingos share with egrets, herons and frogs – the only inhabitants who might break the silence of your siesta. This is no budget break, but you will really enjoy it: you will even have a wonderful view from your bathroom. Breakfast on your terrace or wander along lavender-edged paths to the dining room with its crisp white tablecloths and linger over delicious meals of local produce. If you can bear to leave this peace, the quaint seaside town of Les Saintes-Maries-de-la-Mer is a few minutes drive away, where gypsies from across Europe gather for a spectacular festival at the end of May.

Rooms: 13 + 1 apartment: 10 doubles, 3 suites; 1 apt for 4.
Price: Doubles €259-€305, suites €381; apt €460-€700
Meals: Breakfast included; poolside lunch €12-€38; dinner €38. Restaurant closed mid-November-mid-December.
Closed: January-February.

4km from St Mairies de la Mer. From Arles D570 to St Maries then D38. Hotel is on left 4km before village.

Les Trois Vallons

Hameau de Garandeau
Quartier Le Petit Mousse
13410 Lambesc
Bouches-du-Rhône

Tel: (0)4 42 57 26 31
Fax: (0)4 42 57 25 96
E-mail: infos@3vallons.com
Web: 3vallons.com

Christine de Labouchère & Gérard Bonnaffoux

Christine's passions are paint, old stone and tomatoes. And it shows in this 17th-century hamlet of 51 hectares and four cottages which has been converted with astounding results. Walls and furniture alike have a sophisticated distressed look, achieved by adding egg to the paint, and applying it with a rag. She has managed to match as far as possible the original colours and has left a patch of wall untouched so you can see the layers of different paints used over the years. Despite the sophistication, the houses feel like home with books and fresh flowers everywhere. All have terraces where you can sit and listen to the cicadas and breath in the scent of the pine trees and wild herbs. The tiny *Maison Bleu* has vines over the door and Provençal blue shutters. The larger *Le Bastison*, a former resin store hidden among the trees, is light, space and simplicity. Colour schemes in the bedrooms are deliberately shocking: orange bedcovers against raspberry walls. If you can't be bothered to cook, Christine will order a ready-cooked meal from the delicatessen and you can eat breakfast in the main house if you wish. There may just be a basketful of tomatoes at your door, too. *Minimum stay 2 nights.*

Rooms: 4 cottages for 4-6.
Price: €122-€366; cottages €594-€2439 per week.
Meals: Breakfast €8; dinner from delicatessen €30. Restaurants nearby.
Closed: Never.

Exit Sénas for Aix until St Cannat. There, right at light for Pelissane/Salon D572 for 2.5km; left for Coudoux. 400m after pine forest turn right.

Map No: 14

Hostellerie Bérard

Rue Gabriel-Péri
83740 La Cadière d'Azur
Var

Tel: (0)4 94 90 11 43
Fax: (0)4 94 90 01 94
E-mail: berard@hotel-berard.com
Web: www.hotel-berard.com

M & Mme Bérard

This is a tricky one: should we recommend the food, the cookery and painting classes or the Hostellerie itself, made up of an 11th-century monastery, an old 'bastide' and the 'painters' house. Danièle and Michel Bérard are true belongers: they both grew up in this ancient village, in sight of a mountain called the Grand Bérard. They first opened in 1969 and over the years have lovingly restored the convent. Each bedroom is a surprise: you might find a delicate wrought iron four-poster, with checked counterpane and *toile de Jouy* curtains. You may open green shutters onto the olive and vine-covered hills or blue ones onto the swimming pool. Michel is one of the chosen few: a Maître Cuisinier de France, while Danièle is a highly qualified expert in the local wines. Happy to pursue their own special interests, the couple are gradually leaving management of the hotel to their daughter Sandra, who is smiley, full of enthusiasm and very organised. Michel concentrates on Provençal food, using local produce. If you opt for the cookery course you will go round local producers and markets, not simply cook - pleasure though this is in the special kitchen of the old bastide

Rooms: 40: 36 doubles, 4 suites.
Price: Doubles €79-€148, suites €224-€290.
Meals: Buffet breakfast €15; lunch à la carte; dinner €40-€99.
Closed: January.

A50 towards Toulon exit 11. Hotel is in centre of village.

Map No: 14

293

Le Logis du Guetteur

Place du Château
83460 Les Arcs sur Argens
Var

Tel: (0)4 94 99 51 10
Fax: (0)4 94 99 51 29
E-mail: le.logis.du.guetteur@wanadoo.fr
Web: www.logisduguetteur.com

Max Callegari

We couldn't fault this place: 11th-century décor, 19th-century service, 21st-century comfort. A vertical rabbit warren of brilliantly renovated old stones round a cobbled courtyard at the top of a medieval village beneath the castle keep, the 'Watchman's House' has romance, intimacy, good taste and attractive and welcoming owners. Below the courtyard, the summer dining room is one of the most beautiful, wide, stone-flagged terraces we know - flowers, wonderful food on perfectly-dressed tables and incomparable panoramic view. Along a 'secret' passage, the winter restaurant in the stone-walled, carefully-lit, 'medieval'-furnished vaults is just as cosy as you'd wish in a snowstorm - and the food as delicious as in summer. Bedrooms are not large but are classically chic, extremely comfortable and have perfect little bathrooms. The pool almost makes the cup overflow. Astoundingly, in the 1960s this beautiful little village was a heap of red-grey stones, about to be bulldozed to make way for skyline blocks, when just saved by a group of caring Parisians. Come and give thanks.

Rooms: 10: 8 doubles, 2 suites.
Price: Doubles €99-104, suites €122.
Meals: Breakfast €10; lunch & dinner €26-€41. Restaurant closed 20 January-February.
Closed: Mid-January-5 March.

A8 exit 36 Le Muy. N7 for Le Luc 3km; right into Les Arcs. Le Logis & Vieille Ville signposted at far end of Les Arcs. (Five minutes by taxi from Les Arcs railway station.)

Map No: 15

La Maurette Roquebrune

La Maurette
83520 Roquebrune sur Argens
Var

Tel: (0)4 98 11 43 53
Fax: (0)4 98 11 43 52
E-mail: info@lamaurette.fr
Web: www.lamaurette.fr

Wolfgang Blumberg & Dr. Christine Sckenkelberg

If you wonder about the origins of the seven studio houses around the mas: yes there is a story. The previous owner built the first house for his wife when they divorced. Then the same thing happened again. And again... Apparently he still lives nearby and can be found drowning his sorrows. You enter the gates and drive up a steep private road to the car park, leave your car and then climb some more. Don't look for signs, there are none, Wolfgang doesn't want to "make it look like a hotel". The climb is worth it as La Maurette has spectacular 360° views of the red-brown mountain that gave the village its name. You feel miles from anywhere here, but in fact Roquebrune is only a couple of minutes away. Bedrooms all have quarry tiles and a Provençal style but are otherwise very different: in size, colours and design and some have a fully equipped mini kitchen. They also each have their own terrace with table and chairs, and a bottle of wine waiting for their occupants. More a place for a honeymoon than with the children. If you want dinner, the hotel will ring the local restaurant who will deliver your choice from their menu. Good idea!

Rooms: 11 doubles/twins, 7 with kitchenettes.
Price: €85-€156.
Meals: Breakfast €11. Village restaurants 2km.
Closed: Mid-November-March.

A8 exit 37 for Fréjus/Roquebrune onto N7 then D7
at Le Pont du Prieur for Roquebrune. Right after
crossing Argens River; left, left again, pass tree
in middle of road. Well signposted.

Le Manoir

Ile de Port Cros
83400 Port-Cros
Var

Tel: (0)4 94 05 90 52
Fax: (0)4 94 05 90 89
E-mail: lemanoir.portcros@wanadoo.fr

Pierre Buffet

Circles of bliss: tables beneath fragrant eucalyptus and canvas parasols; the magical dining terrace enfolded in the greenly wooded National Park of Port Cros; the island ringed by a translucent sea whence rises a light breeze. No cars, no mobiles, only one hotel. The lordly family who built the manor in 1835 sold it to the Buffets in 1920. Your aristocratic host runs it as a classy country house bathed in peace and trust: the pool, hidden in a meadow a short walk away, has an honesty bar; you may borrow a motor dinghy to visit the rocky coves - and take a picnic hamper - it is a privilege to experience this attitude from a gentler age. The interior smacks of just that: a large lobby crowded with 'cocktail' tables and old low chairs, a proper, strait-laced dining room - neither used very often - and some gloriously old-fashioned bathrooms (most have been modernised, nostalgics would say unfortunately). Rooms, however, are done in smart fabrics with fine, plain furniture and good lamps. Not just special - unique. *Half-board only.*

Rooms: 19: 15 doubles/twins, 4 duplexes.
Price: Half-board only: €130-€190 p.p.
Meals: Breakfast and dinner included; lunch €45.
Closed: October 4-mid-April.

From Hyères, Le Lavandou or Cavalaire take steamer to Port Cros island. Le Manoir's mini-moke will take your luggage - you may prefer the 5-minute stroll to the hotel.

Le Provençal
Place Saint Pierre
83400 Giens
Var

Tel: (0)4 98 04 54 54
Fax: (0)4 98 04 54 40
E-mail: leprovencal@wanadoo.fr
Web: www.provencalhotel.com

Mme Michel

Perched high up in this peaceful village with a dazzling view of the sea and islands, Le Provençal has large, pine-forested grounds, across the little road below the hotel, which lead down to its sea-water pool on the rocks. On the way down, you notice the well-integrated self-catering complex among the trees. The hotel, whose 1960s façade gives straight onto the village street, is classically, florally comfortable - don't expect luxury at these prices - with fitted carpets and good bathrooms; it's worth paying extra for one of the newer bedrooms which have private balconies overlooking that staggering seascape. But come for remarkable-value food served in a dining room where red-clothed tables flow onto the terrace; choose your lobster or trout from the great tank, relax and enjoy it. Madame Michel keeps a thoroughly professional eye on things. The area is fascinating: from the tiny harbour of La Tour Fondue take a splendid wooden boat to magical Porquerolles or Port Cros, visit Babar's town of Hyères with its palm-lined avenues or walk round pretty Giens itself. Pure Provence.

Rooms: 41 + 23: 31 doubles,
10 triples. 23 self-catering studios &
apartments for 2-7.
Price: Doubles €61-€127, triples €78-
€158; studios & apartments €302-
€1921 per week.
Meals: Breakfast €11; picnic €13;
lunch & dinner €22-€42
Closed: November-early March.

*From Hyères towards Presqu'île de
Giens/Île de Porquerolles. At end of long
straight road and several r'bouts, Giens
signposted right. Hotel on left at beginning
of village.*

Map No: 15

L'Auberge du Choucas

Monêtier les Bains
05220 Serre-Chevalier
Hautes-Alpes

Tel: (0)4 92 24 42 73
Fax: (0)4 92 24 51 60

Nicole Sanchez-Ventura & Eva Gattechaut

In an eternity of pure blue air and pure white glaciers, drenched in sunshine 300 days a year, the Alpine village and its old inn, just behind the Romanesque church, pander to your terrestrial appetites. The lush garden is ideal for summer breakfasts with the birds; the sitting room suggests cosy fireside tea, friendly cat and modern pictures; the stone-vaulted dining room with its great open fire is the place to be bewitched by the young chef's magic - "the art of cookery lifted into the realm of poetry," said one guest. But you are summoned by ski slopes, dramatic ice caves, soul-nourishing walks and natural hot springs. Then return to open one of the beautiful doors, painted by an artist friend of Nicole's, onto a panelled, carpeted, cottagey bedroom with a snug little bathroom. Those with balconies are blissful in the morning sun, duplexes have two (bigger) bathrooms. A brilliant show, led by the amazing whirlwind Nicole who also nurtures a passion for Latin and Greek. Seconded by her charming daughter, Eva, they attend to the minutest details, anxious that it should all be perfect for you.

Rooms: 8: 4 doubles/twins & 4 duplexes for 4-5.
Price: Doubles & duplexes €100-€230. Half-board €85-€130 p.p.
Meals: Breakfast €13. Lunch & dinner €16-€60. Restaurant closed mid-April-June; mid-October-mid-December.
Closed: 3 November-6 December; May.

14km from Briançon on N91. Hotel behind church in centre of village in front of town hall.

Map No: 15

Hôtel Paris-Rome
79 Porte de France
06500 Menton-Garavan
Alpes-Maritimes

Tel: (0)4 93 35 73 45
Fax: (0)4 93 35 29 30
E-mail: paris-rome@wanadoo.fr
Web: www.hotel-paris-rome.com

Gil Castellana

A real find for people who love gardens – or for anyone for that matter. The Paris-Rome was built as a home by Gil's grandfather and has been run as a family hotel for many years. The only garden here is actually a courtyard, where you can have breakfast or afternoon tea among the flowers, but Gil has put together a magnificent programme for visiting the gardens along this bit of coast - from Ellen Willmott's *Hanbury*, to an afternoon with the head gardener at Lawrence Johnston's *Serre de la Madone* and a tour of a rarely-opened botanical garden. Gil also arranges a cooking holiday, taking you to the kitchens of leading restaurants, and fishing holidays where your catch will be cooked to your liking. If you want sun and sand, that's great too: you can have all the comforts of a private beach a short walk away, along the waterfront. As to the hotel itself - rooms are comfortable and traditional and some have a fine view of the sea just across the road. The Castellana family are really friendly and have thought of everything: from a room for rinsing and drying beach things to a little gym.

Rooms: 22: 17 doubles, 2 singles, 3 triples.
Price: Singles €43-€47, doubles €53-€78, triples €81-€93.
Meals: Breakfast €8.50; lunch & dinner €70-€90. Restaurant closed mid-November-mid-December.
Closed: November-January.

A8 exit Menton, proceed to waterfront & towards Italian border. Hotel at traffic lights opposite the Port of Garavan, 100m before Italian border.

Map No: 15

Hôtel Les Deux Frères

Place des Deux Frères
Roquebrune
06190 Cap Martin
Alpes-Maritimes

Tel: (0)4 93 28 99 00
Fax: (0)4 93 28 99 10
E-mail: info@lesdeuxfreres.com
Web: www.lesdeuxfreres.com

Willem Bonestroo

The oriental blue and gold ceiling of *1001 Nuits* will possibly lull you into one of the best night's sleep you've ever dreamed of. Or you may prefer the contrast of a vivid lime green décor, or the nautical hues of *Marine*. Recently renovated, most rooms are fairly small but have great views of the coastline, mountainside or the old village square. You'll get a smiling welcome from the young Dutch owner who has combined Provençal comfort with an exotic flavour, down to the seven languages he speaks and his restaurant's innovative dishes. Long since abandoning suit and tie for less formal wear, Willem is full of ideas for catering to individual tastes, and children simply adore him. After parking in the village, you can either take advantage of the gaily-coloured 'taxi-train' which takes guests and luggage up and down the hill, or opt for the short, fairly steep path leading up to the hotel. Excellent value for money for the area, the place definitely has a lively air to it while remaining practical and professionally-run. Ideal for the young at heart.

Rooms: 10 doubles.
Price: €65-€91.
Meals: Breakfast €9; lunch & dinner €9-€37. Restaurant closed Sunday evenings & Mondays.
Closed: Never.

A10 exit 57 for Menton then Roquebrune. Left at Roquebrune/Vieux Village. Stop at municipal car park and walk 50m.

Map No: 15

Hôtel Windsor

11 rue Dalpozzo
06000 Nice
Alpes-Maritimes

Tel: (0)4 93 88 59 35
Fax: (0)4 93 88 94 57
E-mail: contact@hotelwindsornice.com
Web: www.hotelwindsornice.com

Bernard Redolfi-Strizzot

A 1930s Riviera hotel with pool in palm grove and exotic birds in cages? All that... and much more. Bernard Redolfi-Strizzot brought the '30s into the '90s by asking 20 contemporary artists to do a room each. 20 gifts of wit, provocation, flight of fancy, minimalist sobriety and artistic creation: Joan Mas's *Cage à Mouches*, Jean le Gac's blue figures, cosmopolitan Ben's writing on the walls. The other rooms are far from plain, with Antoine Beaudoin's superb frescoes of Venice, Egypt, India - all our travel myths - and Tintin. Plain white beds have contrasting cushions or quilts; furniture is minimal and interesting; delightful little bathrooms, some directly off the room, are all individually treated. All clear, pale colours, except in the richly exotic public areas: the much-travelled owners chose their exquisitely elaborate Chinese mandarin's bed for the bar, panelling and colourful plasterwork for the restaurant, a fine wire sculpture, stone and bamboo for the hall. Light filters gently through onto warmly smiling staff. And there's a stunning Turkish bath centre. Unbeatable.

Rooms: 57 doubles/twins.
Price: Doubles/twins €87-€120.
Meals: Breakfast €8; lunch & dinner à la carte €23-38. Restaurant closed Saturday lunchtimes & Sundays.
Closed: Never.

In centre of Nice. A10 exit Promenade des Anglais. Left at museum on Rue Meyerbeer. Right on Rue de France and first left Rue Dalpozzo.

Val des Roses

6 Chemin du Laurier
06160 Cap d'Antibes
Alpes-Maritimes

Tel: (0)4 92 93 97 30
Fax: (0)4 92 93 97 24
E-mail: val_des_roses@yahoo.com
Web: www.val-des-roses.com

Frederick & Filip Vanderhoeven

You could drive here, park the car and not use it until you leave: a sandy beach with a view to old Antibes is a minute away, the old town and market 10 and the shops five. Frederik and Filip are Flemish, in their twenties and found the Val des Roses after searching for some time. Filip has all the necessary diplomas; both brothers are charming and sure to make this venture a happy one. They do everything themselves, with the help of one girl, and put on an excellent breakfast, which you can have in your room, on the terrace or by the pool. They will also do a picnic and plan to do light lunches. For dinner, they will recommend, phone ahead and make sure you get a good table. What a find around here. Not cheap: but well worth it. The gracious white house, with white shutters, is enclosed with its garden by high walls, in a quiet little road. Inside, fabrics and walls are mostly white, cool and tranquil. Interestingly, the bedrooms are open plan, with a large oval bath giving a sybaritic touch. Loos are separate! *Convenient for Nice airport. Cash or French cheque only.*

Rooms: 4: 3 suites for 2/3,
1 suite for 4.
Price: €91-€167.
Meals: Breakfast €11; poolside snacks & picnic lunch available.
Closed: November-February.

From Antibes towards Cap d'Antibes/Plages to Salis Plage. Keep shops on right, drive south. At old stone archway, Chemin du Laurier on right.

Map No: 15

Centre International Marie Eugénie Milleret (CIMEM)

37 avenue du Commandant Bret
06400 Cannes
Alpes-Maritimes
Reservation service

Tel: (0)4 97 06 66 70
Fax: (0)4 97 06 66 76
E-mail: cimem.assomption-resa@wanadoo.fr
Web: perso.wanadoo.fr/cimem/

A convent near Cannes! This unlikely establishment offers the best of two totally different worlds: the peace and quiet of a secluded *maison d'accueil* and, 20 minutes away, the worldly sophistication of the film festival town of Cannes. It is run with the dedication and warmth one would expect from 'the best kind of nuns' who, without promoting their faith, simply allow it to inform everything they do. The rooms, once the cells of the 60-odd nuns who lived here before France became a secular state, are plain but perfectly comfortable, many with views over to the sea; breakfast, which you can have in the somewhat austere dining room or take out to the rather more *sympathique* terrace, is both copious and delicious. Lunch (which can be a picnic if you order in advance) and dinner are unfussy, homely affairs, but at this price you could treat yourself with an occasional blow-out in Cannes. This is a place for refreshment of the soul, whether you find it lying in the sun on the beach, under the trees in the garden, or in the chapel.

Rooms: 65 doubles.
Price: Half-board for 2 €55-€76. Full-board for 2 €70-€91.
Meals: Buffet breakfast included.
Closed: Never.

A8 exit Cannes Centre Ville. At top of Bd Carnot left (after lycée & opp. Hôtel Amarante) into Bd des Anglais. At bottom right into Bd de la République. Second T left Av du Commandant Bret. CIMEM 500m up hill on left.

La Grande Bastide

Route de la Colle
06570 Saint Paul de Vence
Alpes-Maritimes

Tel: (0)4 93 32 50 30
Fax: (0)4 93 32 50 59
E-mail: stpaullgb@lemel.fr
Web: www.la-grande-bastide.com

Heinz Johner

This 18th-century *bastide* has been turned into a country-house hotel which provides immense luxury, plus the most fantastic views of one of the jewels of Provence: St Paul de Vence. This is not simply an enchantingly 'typical' village, it is also an important artistic centre, still frequented by musicians, writers and painters following in the footsteps of Matisse, Daudet and Pagnol. From the welcoming entrance ("here, you feel good in the space," said one visitor), along the 'outside corridors' which look out over the gardens, to the rooms, decorated in Provençal style - painted furniture, pretty cotton prints, pastel painted walls - you feel the personal touch of the owners. Cascades are a promised addition to the already luxurious pool which is set in beautifully-planted gardens and overlooked by the terrace where you can eat a breakfast worthy of the setting. You may just want yogurt and honey, or perhaps the full English with a sophisticated French spin appeals? Whatever you choose, peace and quiet, a warm welcome and a truly painstaking attention to your comfort, is guaranteed.

Rooms: 11: 8 doubles, 3 suites.
Price: Doubles €130-€183, suites €152-€274.
Meals: Breakfast €13; informal lunch at poolside.
Closed: 22 November-26 December; January 10-mid-February.

From A8 exit 47 for St Paul de Vence. After La Colle sur Loup, hotel signposted on left.

Map No: 15

French words & expressions

French words and expressions used in this book

l'amuse-bouche - literally to tease the mouth - a little something which is served before the meal.

l'armoire à glace - a wardrobe with more or less elaborate regional-style carving and often a mirrored front. Armoire à glace is also used to describe a beefy rugby player.

la bastide - a stronghold, a small fortified village or, in Provence, it can simply be another word for farmhouse or mas (see below).

la Belle Epoque - 1901-1910.

la bergerie - a barn for sheep.

la chambre d'hôtes - a bed & breakfast.

les Champs - Les Champs Elysées.

le château - a mansion or stately home built for aristocrats between the 16th and 19th centuries.

château fort - a castle with defences and fortifications.

cognicenti - those in the know.

la compôte - stewed fruit.

le confit - parts of goose or duck preserved in their own fat, then fried.

la cour d'honneur - a grand courtyard.

le cuir de Cordoue - tooled leather wallpaper from Cordoba, Spain.

déguster - to taste, sample or savour.

la dégustation - a tasting of wine, oysters, cheese NOT necessarily free.

la demi-lune - a decorative half or full-moon shaped canopy over a bed.

une deux chevaux - A type of car (2CV) with 2 fiscal horses in its engine.

Directoire (armchairs) - 1795-1799, Greek and Roman influences.

en plein air - outside.

l'Exposition Universelle - Universal Exhibition in Paris in 1890.

extra-muros - outside the walls (of a town or city).

la fougace - a flat plait-shaped bread sometimes studded with pieces of bacon, olives or nuts.

gîte - house or cottage to rent on a weekly or monthly basis.

le grand hôtel de campagne - large country hotel.

le magret de canard en croute - duck breast in a pastry shell.

la Mairie and *l'Hôtel de Ville* - town and city hall respectively. They are useful landmarks, easy to find in town centres.

maison close - brothel.

French words & expressions

la maison de maître (country) and *la maison bourgoise* (town) - both big, comfortable houses standing in quite, large grounds and built for well-to-do members of the liberal professions, captains of industry, trade, etc.

la maison Musée - house museum.

le manoir - manor house.

le Marais - marsh or marshland. *Marais Poitevin* near La Rochelle, with its miles of little waterways to be explored by boat. The 4th arrondissement of Paris, *Le Marais*, once a miserable, unhealthy low-lying slum and now entirely gentrified.

le mas Provençal - country house, usually long and low with old stone walls, a pan-tiled roof and painted shutters.

le métier - job or trade (also means loom).

le Midi - synonym of South; by extension, southern France.

la mille-feuille - anything baked in layers of flaky pastry.

le Mistral - the nerve-jangling wind that blows down the Rhône Valley.

le nid d'abeille - honeycomb.

l'œil de bœuf - round window.

le petit grain de folie - light touch of madness.

les petit salons feutrés - small cosy rooms.

piqué - textured cotton.

le pochoir - a method of decorative painting using stencils.

le potager - kitchen garden, whence the French word for everyday vegetable soup *le potage*.

pré salé - adjective used for lamb grazed on salted marshes.

le prix fixe - a two, three or four course meal at a set price.

Soléidado - Provençal patterned textiles.

le sommelier - the waiter in charge of your wine order.

son et lumière - an after dark, outdoor spectacle with lights and music.

la table d'hôtes - a three-course dinner with the owners of the house or château usually served at a long communal table.

du terroir - fashionabe term meaning rural, local, authentic; as coming from the untainted soil in a specific area, e.g. wines (vin du terroir), cheeses, foodstuffs, even people and political movements.

la thalassothérapie - a much in vogue health spa technique using sea water as the main ingredient.

la toile de Jouy - classic French fabrics and wallpapers depicting romantic scenes.

soigné - understated elegance.

le zinc - traditional surface for bar counter-tops.

Avoiding cultural confusion

En suite

'En suite' is not used in France to describe bathrooms off the bedroom and to do so can lead to confusion. To be clear, simply ask for a room *'avec salle de bains et wc'.*

Greetings and forms of address

We drop far more easily into first-name terms than the French. This reluctance on their part is not a sign of coldness, it's simply an Old National Habit, to be respected, we feel, like any other tribal ritual. So it's advisable to wait for the signal from them as to when you have achieved more intimate status.

The French do not say "Bonjour Monsieur Dupont" or "Bonjour Madame Jones" - this is considered rather familiar. They just say "Bonjour Monsieur" or "Bonjour Madame" - which makes it easy to be lazy about remembering people's names.

À table

Breakfast

There may be only a bowl/large cup and a teaspoon per person on the table. If so, you are expected to butter your bread on your hand or on the tablecloth (often the kitchen oilcloth) using the knife in the butter dish, then spread the jam with the jam spoon.

A well-bred English lady would never dream of 'dunking' her croissant, toast or teacake in her cup - it is perfectly acceptable behaviour in French society.

Lunch/dinner

Cutlery is laid concave face upwards in 'Anglo-Saxon' countries; in France it is proper to lay forks and spoons convex face upwards (crests are engraved accordingly). Do try and hold back your instinctive need to turn them over!

To the right of your plate, at the tip of the knife, you may find a knife-rest. This serves two purposes: to lay your knife on when you are not using it, rather than leaving it in your plate; to lay your knife *and* fork on (points downwards) if you are asked to *'garder vos couverts'* (keep your knife and fork) while the plates are changed - e.g. between starter and main dish.

Cheese comes *before* pudding in France - that's the way they do it! Cut a round cheese as you would cut a round cake - in triangular segments. When a ready-cut segment such as a piece of Brie is presented, the rule is to 'preserve the point', i.e. do not cut it straight across but take an angle which removes the existing point but makes another one.

Quick reference indices

WHEELCHAIR FRIENDLY
These owners have told us that they have facilities for people in wheelchairs.

Picardy
8 • 10

Champagne-Ardenne
11

Lorraine
15

Alsace
21 • 24

Burgundy
32 • 36

Paris - Ile de France
63

Normandy
69 • 76 • 77 • 83 • 84 • 85 • 88 • 89 • 91

Brittany
96 • 97 • 98 • 99 • 101 • 102 • 103 • 104 • 112

Western Loire
118 • 120 • 123 • 126 • 130

Loire Valley
136 • 137 • 144 • 146 • 148 • 149 • 154 • 158

Poitou - Charentes
159 • 160 • 161 • 162 • 163 • 171

Aquitaine
175 • 176 • 179 • 187 • 188 • 189 • 191 • 192

Auvergne
202

Midi - Pyrénées
205 • 208 • 213 • 214 • 224 • 225

Languedoc - Roussillon
233 • 234 • 236 • 242 • 243 • 246

Rhône Valley - Alps
252 • 254 • 258

Provence - Alps - Riviera
271 • 275 • 284 • 285 • 288 • 289 • 291 • 303

LIMITED MOBILITY
These houses have bedrooms and bathrooms that are accessible for people of limited mobility. Please check details.

The North
2 • 4

Picardy
6 • 9

Lorraine
16

Alsace
19 • 20

Burgundy
30 • 31 • 33 • 35

Paris - Ile de France
39 • 44 • 47 • 48 • 52 • 60

Normandy
67 • 79 • 80 • 81 • 86

Brittany
100 • 106 • 107

Western Loire
115 • 119 • 128 • 129

Quick reference indices

Quick reference indices

Quick reference indices

COOKERY
Lessons available on premises or nearby.

Quick reference indices

CULTURAL TOURS
Historical walking tours nearby. Some places can provide English speaking guides.

Quick reference indices

WALKING
Good walking trails nearby. Some places can provide maps and guides.

The North
1 • 3 • 4 • 5

Picardy
6 • 7 • 8 • 9 • 10

Champagne-Ardenne
11 • 12 • 13 • 14

Lorraine
15 • 17 • 18

Alsace
19 • 20 • 21 • 22 • 24

Franche Comté
25

Burgundy
27 • 28 • 32 • 33 • 34 • 35 • 36

Paris - Ile de France
41 • 42 • 47 • 62 • 63 • 64 • 65

Normandy
70 • 71 • 72 • 73 • 75 • 76 • 77 • 78 • 79 • 81 • 82 • 83 • 85 • 87 • 88 • 89 • 90 • 92

Brittany
93 • 94 • 95 • 96 • 97 • 98 • 99 • 100 • 101 • 102 • 103 • 104 • 105 • 106 • 107 • 108 • 109 • 110 • 112

Western Loire
114 • 115 • 116 • 117 • 119 • 120 • 121 • 123 • 124 • 125 • 126 • 128 • 129 • 130

Loire Valley
131 • 133 • 134 • 136 • 137 • 138 • 139 • 140 • 141 •

143 • 144 • 145 • 146 • 147 • 148 • 149 • 150 • 151 • 152 • 153 • 154 • 155 • 156 • 157 • 158

Poitou - Charentes
159 • 160 • 162 • 163 • 166 • 167 • 168 • 171

Aquitaine
173 • 174 • 175 • 176 • 178 • 179 • 180 • 182 • 183 • 184 • 186 • 187 • 188 • 189 • 191 • 192 • 194 • 195 • 196 • 197

Limousin
199 • 200

Auvergne
201 • 202 • 203 • 204

Midi - Pyrénées
205 • 206 • 207 • 208 • 209 • 210 • 211 • 216 • 217 • 220 • 221 • 222 • 223 • 224 • 226 • 228

Languedoc - Roussillon
230 • 231 • 235 • 236 • 237 • 238 • 239 • 240 • 241 • 242 • 243 • 245 • 246 • 247 • 248 • 249

Rhône Valley - Alps
250 • 251 • 252 • 253 • 254 • 255 • 256 v 257 • 258 • 259 • 260 • 261 • 262 • 263 • 264

Provence - Alps - Riviera
265 v 266 • 267 • 268 • 269 • 270 • 271 • 272 • 273 • 274 • 275 • 276 • 277 • 279 • 280 • 282 • 283 • 284 • 285 • 286 • 287 • 288 • 289 • 290 • 291 • 293 • 294 • 295 • 297 • 302 • 304

Quick reference indices

What is Alastair Sawday Publishing?

A dozen or more of us work in two converted barns on a farm near Bristol, close enough to the city for a bicycle ride and far enough for a silence broken only by horses and the occasional passage of a tractor. Some editors work in the countries they write about, e.g. France and Spain, others work from the UK but are based outside the office. We enjoy each other's company, celebrate every event possible, and work in an easy-going but committed environment.

These books owe their style and mood to Alastair's miscellaneous career and his interest in the community and the environment. He has taught overseas, worked with refugees, run development projects abroad, founded a travel company and several environmental organisations - many of which have flourished. There has been a slightly mad streak evident throughout, not least in his driving of a waste-paper-collection lorry for a year, the manning of stalls at impoverished jumble sales and the pursuit of causes long before they were considered sane.

Back to the travel company: trying to take his clients to eat and sleep in places that were not owned by corporations and assorted bandits he found dozens of very special places in France - farms, châteaux etc - a list that grew into the first book, *French Bed and Breakfast*. It was a celebration of 'real' places to stay and the remarkable people who run them.

The publishing company is based on the unexpected success of that first and rather whimsical French book. It started as a mild crusade, and there it stays - full of 'attitude', and the more appealing for it. For we still celebrate the unusual, the beautiful, the individual. We are passionate about rejecting the banal, the ugly, the pompous and the indifferent and we are passionate too about promoting the use of 'real' food. Alastair is a trustee of the Soil Association and keen to promote organic growing and consuming by owners and visitors.

It is a source of deep pleasure to us to have learned that there are many thousands of people who share our views. We are by no means alone in trumpeting the virtues of standing up to the destructive uniformity of so much of our culture.

We are building a company in which people and values matter. We love to hear of new friendships between those in the book and those using it, and to know that there are many people - among them farmers - who have been enabled to pursue their lives thanks to the extra income our books bring them.

Alastair Sawday's
Special Places to Stay series

www.specialplacestostay.com

The Little Earth Book - 2nd Edition

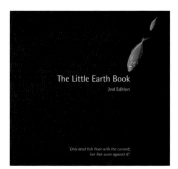

The Little Earth Book
2nd Edition

'Only dead fish float with the current;
live fish swim against it'.

A fascinating read. The earth is now desperately vulnerable; so are we. Original, stimulating mini-essays about what is going wrong with our planet, and about the greatest challenge of our century: how to save the Earth for us all. It is pithy, yet intellectually credible, well-referenced, wry yet deadly serious.

Alastair Sawday, the publisher, is also an environmentalist. For over 25 years he has campaigned, not only against the worst excesses of modern tourism and its hotels, but against environmental 'looniness' of other kinds. He has fought for systems and policies that might enable our beautiful planet - simply - to survive. He founded and ran Avon Friends of the Earth, has run for Parliament, and has led numerous local campaigns. He is now a trustee of the Soil Association, experience upon which he draws in this remarkable book.

Researched and written by an eminent Bristol architect, James Bruges, *The Little Earth Book* is a clarion call to action, a mind-boggling collection of mini-essays on today's most important environmental concerns, from global warming and poisoned food to economic growth, Third World debt, genes and 'superbugs'. Undogmatic but sure-footed, the style is light, explaining complex issues with easy language, illustrations and cartoons. Ideas are developed chapter by chapter, yet each one stands alone. It is an easy browse.

The Little Earth Book provides hope, with new ideas and examples of people swimming against the current, of bold ideas that work in practice. It is a book as important as it is original. Learn about the issues and join the most important debate of this century.

Did you know.....

- If everyone adopted the Western lifestyle we would need five earths to support us

- In 50 years the US has - with intensive pesticide use - doubled the amount of crops lost to pests

- Environmental disasters have created more than 80 MILLION refugees

www.specialplacestostay.com

Adrift on the unfathomable and often unnavigable sea of accommodation pages on the Internet, those who have discovered www.specialplacestostay.com have found it to be an island of reliability. Not only will you find a database full of honest, trustworthy, up-to-date information about over a thousand *Special Places to Stay* across Europe, but also:

- **Direct links to the web sites of hundreds of places from the series.**
- **Colourful, clickable, interactive maps.**
- **The facility to make most bookings by email -**
  even if you don't have email yourself.
- **Online purchasing of our books, securely and cheaply.**
- **Regular, exclusive special offers on books from the whole series.**
- **The latest news about future editions, new titles and new places.**
- **The chance to participate in the evolution of both the guides**
  and the site.

The site is constantly evolving and is frequently updated. By the time you read this we will have introduced an online notice board for owners to use, where they can display special offers or forthcoming local events that might tempt you. We're expanding our European maps, adding more useful and interesting links, providing news, updates and special features that won't appear anywhere else but in our window on the world wide web.

Just as with our printed guides, your feedback counts, so when you've surfed all this and you still want more, let us know - this site has been planted with room to grow!

Russell Wilkinson, Web Editor
editor@specialplacestostay.com

Order Form UK

All these books are available in major bookshops or you may order them
direct. Post and packaging are FREE.

	Price	No. copies
Special Places to Stay: Portugal		
Edition 1	£8.95	
Special Places to Stay: Spain		
Edition 4	£11.95	
Special Places to Stay: Ireland		
Edition 3	£10.95	
Special Places to Stay: Paris Hotels		
Edition 3	£8.95	
Special Places to Stay: Garden Bed & Breakfast		
Edition 1	£10.95	
Special Places to Stay: French Bed & Breakfast		
Edition 7	£14.99	
Special Places to Stay: British Hotels, Inns and other places		
Edition 3	£11.99	
Special Places to Stay: British Bed & Breakfast		
Edition 6	£13.95	
Special Places to Stay: French Hotels, Inns and other places		
Edition 2	£11.99	
Special Places to Stay: Italy		
Edition 2	£11.95	
Special Places to Stay: French Holiday Homes		
Edition 1 (available January 2002)	£10.99	
The Little Earth Book	£5.99	

Please make cheques payable to: **Alastair Sawday Publishing**   Total

Please send cheques to: Alastair Sawday Publishing, The Home Farm Stables,
Barrow Gurney, Bristol BS48 3RW. **For credit card orders call 01275
464891 or order directly from our website www.specialplacestostay.com**

Name:

Address:

Postcode:

Tel: Fax: FH2

If you do not wish to receive mail from other companies, please tick the box ❏

Order Form USA

All these books are available at your local bookstore, or you may order direct. Allow two to three weeks for delivery.

	Price	No. copies
Special Places to Stay: Portugal		
Edition 1	$14.95	
Special Places to Stay: Ireland		
Edition 3	$17.95	
Special Places to Stay: Spain		
Edition 4	$19.95	
Special Places to Stay: Paris Hotels		
Edition 3	$14.95	
Special Places to Stay: French Bed & Breakfast		
Edition 7	$19.95	
Special Places to Stay: British Bed & Breakfast		
Edition 6	$19.95	
Special Places to Stay: Garden Bed & Breakfast		
Edition 1	$17.95	
Special Places to Stay: Italy		
Edition 2	$17.95	
Special Places to Stay: British Hotels, Inns and other places		
Edition 3	$17.95	

Shipping in the continental USA: $3.95 for one book, $4.95 for two books, $5.95 for three or more books. Outside continental USA, call (800) 243-0495 for prices. For delivery to AK, CA, CO, CT, FL, GA, IL, IN, KS, MI, MN, MO, NE, NM, NC, OK, SC, TN, TX, VA, and WA, please add appropriate sales tax.

Please make checks payable to: The Globe Pequot Press   Total

To order by phone with MasterCard or Visa: (800) 243-0495. 9a.m. to 5p.m. EST; by fax: (800) 820-2329, 24 hours; through our web site: www.globe-pequot.com; or by mail: The Globe Pequot Press, P.O. Box 480, Guilford, CT 06437.

Name: _____ Date: _____

Address: _____

Town: _____

State: _____ Zip code: _____

Tel: _____ Fax: _____

FH2

Report Form

Comments on existing entries and new discoveries.

If you have any comments on entries in this guide, please let us have them. If you have a favourite house, hotel, inn or other new discovery, not just in Britain, please let us know about it.

Book title: ______________________ Entry no: __________ Edition: __________

New recommendation ☐ Country: ______________________

Name of property: ______________________

Address: ______________________

____

______________________ Postcode: ______________________

Tel: ______________________

Date of stay: ______________________

Comments: ______________________

____

____

____

____

____

From: ______________________

Address: ______________________

____

______________________ Postcode: ______________________

Tel: ______________________

Please send the completed form to: **Alastair Sawday Publishing, The Home Farm Stables, Barrow Gurney, Bristol BS48 3RW** or go to www.specialplacestostay.com and click on contact.

Thank you.

FH2

Reservation form

À l'attention de:
To:

Date:

Madame, Monsieur

Veuillez faire la réservation suivante au nom de:
Please make the following booking for (name):

Pour	*nuit(s)*	*Arrivant le jour:*	*mois*	*année*
For	night(s)	Arriving: day	month	year
		Départ le jour:	*mois*	*année*
		Leaving: day	month	year

Si possible, nous aimerions   *chambres, disposées comme suit:*
We would like   rooms, arranged as follows:

À grand lit	*À lits jumeaux*	
Double bed	Twin beds	
Pour trois	*À un lit simple*	
Triple	Single	
Suite	*Appartment*	*ou autre*
Suite	Apartment	or other

Nous sommes accompagnés de   *enfant(s) âgé(s) de*   *ans.*
Avez-vous un/des lit(s) supplémentaire(s), un lit bébé; si oui, à quel prix?
Our child is/children are   years old. Please let us know if you
have an extra bed/extra beds/a cot and if so, at what price.

Notre chien/chat sera-t-il le bienvenu dans votre maison? Si oui, y a-t-il un
supplément à payer?
We are travelling with our dog/cat. Will it be welcome in your house?
If so, is there a supplement to pay?

Nous aimerions également réserver le dîner pour   *personnes.*
We would also like to book dinner for   people

Veuillez nous envoyer la confirmation à l'adresse ci-dessous:
Please send confirmation to the following address:

Nom: Name:

Adresse: Address:

Tel No: Fax No:

E-mail:

Index by property name

Index by property name

Index by property name

Index by place name

Index by place name

Index by place name

Exchange rate table

Euro €	Franc F	US $	£ Sterling
5	33	4.60	3.16
10	66	9.19	6.31
50	328	45.97	31.56
60	394	55.17	37.87
70	459	64.38	44.18
80	525	73.58	50.49
90	590	82.77	56.80
100	656	92.02	63.07
150	984	138.08	94.67
200	1312	184.04	126.23
500	3279	460.00	315.00
1000	6560	921.00	631.00

Rates correct at time of going to press October 2001

COMPETITION

All our books have the odd spoof hidden away within their pages. Sunken boats, telephone boxes and ruined castles have all featured. Some of you have written in with your own ideas. So, we have decided to hold a competition for spoof writing every year.

The rules are simple: send us your own spoofs, include the photos, and let us know for which book it is intended. We will publish the winning entries in the following edition of each book. We will also send a complete set of our guides to each winner.

Please send your entries to:

Alastair Sawday Publishing, Spoofs Competition,
The Home Farm Stables, Barrow Gurney,
Bristol BS48 3RW.

Explanation of symbols

Treat each one as a guide rather than a statement of fact and check important points when booking:

 Pets are welcome but may have to sleep in an outbuilding or your car. Check when booking.

 Vegetarians catered for with advance warning. All hosts can cater for vegetarians at breakfast.

 Most, but not necessarily all, ingredients are organic, organically grown, home-grown or locally grown.

 Full and approved wheelchair facilities for at least one bedroom and bathroom and access to all ground-floor common areas.

 Basic ground-floor access for people of limited mobility and at least one bedroom and bathroom accessible without steps, but not full facilities for wheelchair-users.

 This house has pets of its own that live in the house: dog, cat, duck, parrot...

 Credit cards accepted; most commonly Visa and MasterCard.

 Swimming pool on the premises.

 Smoking restrictions exist usually, but not always, in the dining room and some bedrooms. For full restrictions, check when booking.

 You can either borrow or hire bikes here.

 Your hosts speak English, whether perfect or not.

 Good hiking from house or village.

 Restaurant. The hotel has its own restaurant or a separately-managed restaurant next door.

Modem connections available.